READINGS FOR WRITING

Humber College Institute of Technology and Advanced Learning

COMM 200: College Writing Skills

CANADIAN MERCURY WRITER

Custom Publishing

New York   Boston   San Francisco
London   Toronto   Sydney   Tokyo   Singapore   Madrid
Mexico City   Munich   Paris   Cape Town   Hong Kong   Montreal

Senior Vice President, Editorial and Marketing: Patrick F. Boles
Senior Sponsoring Editor: Natalie Danner
Development Editor: Mary Kate Paris
Editorial Assistant: Jill Johnson
Marketing Manager: Brian T. Berkeley
Operations Manager: Eric M. Kenney
Production Manager: Jennifer Berry
Rights Manager: Jennifer Lerman
Art Director: Renée Sartell
Cover Designer: Chrissy Kurpeski

Cover Art: "Riverdance," by Angela Sciaraffa.

**Pearson
Custom Publishing**
is a division of

www.pearsonhighered.com

ISBN 10: 0-558-28115-X
ISBN 13: 978-0-558-28115-1

General Editors

Janice Neuleib
Illinois State University

Kathleen Shine Cain
Merrimack College

Stephen Ruffus
Salt Lake Community College

Contents

Education

Fairy Tales and Modern Stories
Bruno Bettelheim

Bruno Bettelheim (1903–90), a noted psychotherapist, was born in Vienna, Austria. He graduated from the University of Vienna (1938), where he studied with Sigmund Freud. Bettelheim was imprisoned by the Nazis at Dachau and Buchenwald from 1938 to 1939. After his release from prison, Bettelheim emigrated to the United States, where he went to work at the University of Chicago. In 1944, he became director of the University's Sonia Shankman Orthogenic School, a treatment facility for severely disturbed children. Bettelheim gained international recognition for his work with autistic children, although not without some controversy over his methods. He published many books on psychotherapy, including Love Is Not Enough: The Treatment of Emotionally Disturbed Children *(1950),* The Children of the Dream *(1969),* The Uses of Enchantment *(1976), and* Freud and Man's Soul *(1982). He also wrote articles on rearing normal children for lay audiences. In addition to a well-known article on his experiences in Nazi concentration camps (1943), Bettelheim published two books on the death camps,* The Informed Heart: Autonomy in a Mass Age *(1960) and* Surviving and Other Essays *(1979), reprinted as* Surviving the Holocaust *(1986). In this essay, taken from* The Uses of Enchantment, *Bettelheim argues that fairy tales can provide children more comfort than "sensible" stories.*

The shortcomings of the realistic stories with which many parents have replaced fairy tales is suggested by a comparison of two such stories—"The Little Engine That Could" and "The Swiss Family Robinson"—with the fairy tale of "Rapunzel." "The Little Engine That Could" encourages the child to believe that if he tries hard and does not give up, he will finally succeed. A young adult has recalled how much impressed she was at the age of seven when her mother read her this story. She became convinced that one's attitude indeed affects one's achievements—that if she would now approach a task with the conviction that she could conquer it, she would succeed. A few days later, this child encountered in first grade a challenging situation: she was trying to make a house out of paper, gluing various sheets together. But her house continually collapsed. Frustrated, she began to seriously doubt whether her idea of building such a paper house could be realized. But then the story of "The Little Engine That Could" came to her mind; twenty years later, she recalled how at that moment she began to sing to herself the magic formula "I think I can, I think I can, I think I can . . . " So she continued to work on her paper house, and it continued to collapse. The project ended in complete defeat, with this little girl convinced that she had failed where anybody else could have succeeded, as the Little Engine had. Since "The Little Engine That Could" was a story set in the present, using such common props as engines that pulled trains, this girl had tried to apply its lesson directly in her daily life, without any fantasy elaboration, and had experienced a defeat that still rankled twenty years later.

Very different was the impact of "The Swiss Family Robinson" on another little girl. The story tells how a shipwrecked family manages to live an adventurous, idyllic, constructive, and pleasurable life—a life very different from this child's own existence. Her father had to be away from home a great deal, and her mother was mentally ill and spent protracted periods in institutions. So the girl was shuttled from her home to that of an aunt, then to that of a grandmother, and back home again, as the need arose. During these years, the girl read over and over again the story of this happy family who lived on a desert island, where no member could be away from the rest of the family. Many years later, she recalled what a warm, cozy feeling she had when, propped up by a few large pillows, she forgot all about her present predicament as she read this story. As soon as she had finished it, she started to read it over again. The happy hours she spent with the

Family Robinson in that fantasy land permitted her not to be defeated by the difficulties that reality presented to her. She was able to counteract the impact of harsh reality by imaginary gratifications. But since the story was not a fairy tale, it merely gave her a temporary escape from her problems; it did not hold out any promise to her that her life would take a turn for the better.

Consider the effect that "Rapunzel" had on a third girl. This girl's mother had died in a car accident. The girl's father, deeply upset by what had happened to his wife (he had been driving the car), withdrew entirely into himself and handed the care of his daughter over to a nursemaid, who was little interested in the girl and gave her complete freedom to do as she liked. When the girl was seven, her father remarried, and, as she recalled it, it was around that time that "Rapunzel" became so important to her. Her stepmother was clearly the witch of the story, and she was the girl locked away in the tower. The girl recalled that she felt akin to Rapunzel because the witch had "forcibly" taken possession of her, as her stepmother had forcibly worked her way into the girl's life. The girl felt imprisoned in her new home, in contrast to her life of freedom with the nursemaid. She felt as victimized as Rapunzel, who, in her tower, had so little control over her life. Rapunzel's long hair was the key to the story. The girl wanted her hair to grow long, but her stepmother cut it short; long hair in itself became the symbol of freedom and happiness to her. The story convinced her that a prince (her father) would come someday and rescue her, and this conviction sustained her. If life became too difficult, all she needed was to imagine herself as Rapunzel, her hair grown long, and the prince loving and rescuing her.

"Rapunzel" suggests why fairy tales can offer more to the child than even such a very nice children's story as "The Swiss Family Robinson." In "The Swiss Family Robinson," there is no witch against whom the child can discharge her anger in fantasy and on whom she can blame the father's lack of interest. "The Swiss Family Robinson" offers escape fantasies, and it did help the girl who read it over and over to forget temporarily how difficult life was for her. But it offered no specific hope for the future. "Rapunzel," on the other hand, offered the girl a chance to see the witch of the story as so evil that by comparison even the "witch" stepmother at home was not really so bad. "Rapunzel" also promised the girl that her rescue would be effected by her own body, when her hair grew long. Most important of all, it promised that the "prince" was only temporarily blinded—that he would regain his sight and rescue his princess. This fantasy continued to sustain the girl, though to a less intense degree, until she fell in love and married, and then she no longer needed it. We can understand why at first glance the stepmother, if she had known the meaning of "Rapunzel" to her stepdaughter, would have felt that fairy tales are bad for children. What she would not have known was that unless the stepdaughter had been able to find that fantasy satisfaction through "Rapunzel," she would have tried to break up her father's marriage and that without the hope for the future which the story gave her she might have gone badly astray in life.

5   It seems quite understandable that when children are asked to name their favorite fairy tales, hardly any modern tales are among their choices. Many of the new tales have sad endings, which fail to provide the escape and consolation that the fearsome events in the fairy tale require if the child is to be strengthened for meeting the vagaries of his life. Without such encouraging conclusions, the child, after listening to the story, feels that there is indeed no hope for extricating himself from his despairs. In the traditional fairy tale, the hero is rewarded and the evil person meets his well-deserved fate, thus satisfying the child's deep need for justice to prevail. How else can a child hope that justice will be done to him, who so often feels unfairly treated? And how else can he convince himself that he must act correctly, when he is so sorely tempted to give in to the asocial proddings of his desires?

Questions on Meaning

1. Describe why Bettelheim feels that traditional fairy tales are more comforting to children than more realistic stories.
2. What did long hair in the fairy tale *Rapunzel* symbolize to the third subject described by Bettelheim?
3. What does the fairy tale *Rapunzel* offer a child (because of the witch) that *The Swiss Family Robinson* lacks?

Questions on Rhetorical Strategy and Style

1. Find where Bettelheim uses comparison and contrast to argue what he feels are "shortcomings" of the realistic stories he discusses, *The Little Engine That Could* and *The Swiss Family Robinson*.
2. What rhetorical strategy does Bettelheim use in the final paragraph? Identify the elements of the strategy.

Writing Assignments

1. Name your favorite fairy tale. Write an essay explaining its importance to you as a child. Explain how you adapted the fantasy to your own life. Describe how it affected you as an adolescent and how it affects you now.
2. Losing oneself in fantasy is a common and—as Bettelheim might advise—healthy reaction to some aspects of life. Write an essay in which you describe a current fantasy in your life—such as winning a sports contest, buying a car, or dating a special someone. How did the fantasy develop? Are you able to keep it in check as a fantasy?

The Merits of Meritocracy
David Brooks

David Brooks (1961–) is best known for his sharp and witty conservative commentary on public television's News Hour *with Jim Lehrer. Brooks graduated from the University of Chicago with a degree in history. He turned to writing political and social commentary and is now a leading commentator on PBS, CNN, and National Public Radio. He writes for* Newsweek *where he is a contributing editor, as well as for the* New York Times. *He is also a senior editor at the* Weekly Standard. *An anthology of his essays and commentaries is titled* Backward and Upward: The New Conservative Writing *(1996). His books include* Bobos in Paradise: The New Upper Class and How They Got There *(2000) and* On Paradise Drive: How We Live Now (and Always Have) *(2004).*

Children of the privileged must work very hard for what they have and for what they will get. Brooks uses the example of his daughter to show how busy she is and how she will have to compete to get into a great school and to find a greater job after school.

1 My daughter is a four-helmet kid. She has a regular helmet she wears bike riding, pogo sticking, and when she borrows her older brother's skateboard. She has a pink batting helmet, which she wears during her Little League baseball games. She has a helmet for horseback-riding lessons, on Sundays. And she has a helmet for ice hockey, which she plays on Friday afternoons. (For hockey she also has an equipment bag large enough to hold several corpses.) My

daughter's not even a jock (although she is something of a live wire). Her main interest is art, which she does in an after-school program on Tuesdays and at home on her own.

But it's her helmets that really got me thinking. They're generally scattered around the equipment racks in our garage, along with her brothers' helmet collections and all manner of sleds, mitts, scooters, bicycles, and balls, and they represent a certain sort of childhood— a childhood that has now become typical in middle-class America.

It's a busy childhood, filled with opportunities, activities, teams, coaches, and, inevitably, gear. It's a safety-conscious childhood, with ample adult supervision. And it is, I believe (at least I want to believe), a happy and fulfilling childhood that will prepare my daughter for a happy adult life.

This sort of childhood is different from the childhoods Americans have traditionally had. It's not an independent childhood, like Huck Finn's or the Bowery Boys'. Today's middle-class kids, by and large, don't live apart from adult society, free to explore and experiment and, through adventure and misadventure, teach themselves the important lessons of life. Nor is it a Horatio Alger childhood. Middle-class kids by definition haven't come from poverty and deprivation. Nor do they build self-discipline from having to work on a farm. If they hunger for success, it's not because they started at the bottom.

5 Today's mode of raising kids generates a lot of hand-wringing and anxiety, some of it on my part. We fear that kids are spoiled by the abundance and frenetic activity all around them. We fear that the world of suburban sprawl, Game Boys, Britney Spears CDs, and shopping malls will dull their moral senses. We fear that they are too deferential to authority, or that they are confronted with so many choices that they never have to make real commitments. Or we fear that they are skipping over childhood itself. The toy companies call this phenomenon "age compression": Kids who are ten no longer want toys that used to appeal to ten-year-olds. Now it is three-to-five-year-olds who go for Barbie dolls. By the time a girl is seven she wants to be a mini-adult.

But I've come to believe that our fears are overblown. The problem is that the way kids (and, for that matter, the rest of us) live is estranged from the formulaic ideas we have about building character. We assume that character is forged through hardship—economic deprivation, war, and so on—and that we who have had it easy, who

7

have grown up in this past half century of peace and prosperity, must necessarily have weak or suspect souls.

It's true that we live amid plenty; even in time of war we are told to keep shopping. But today's kids have a way of life that entails its own character-building process, its own ethical system. They live in a world of almost crystalline meritocracy. Starting at birth, middle-class Americans are called on to master skills, do well in school, practice sports, excel in extracurricular activities, get into college, build their résumés, change careers, be good in bed, set up retirement plans, and so on. This is a way of life that emphasizes individual achievement, self-propulsion, perpetual improvement, and permanent exertion.

The prime ethical imperative for the meritocrat is self-fulfillment. The phrase sounds New Agey; it calls to mind a Zen vegan sitting on the beach at dawn contemplating his narcissism. But over the past several years the philosophers Charles Taylor, of McGill University, and Alan Gewirth, of the University of Chicago, have argued that a serious moral force is contained in the idea of self-ful fillment. Meritocrats may not necessarily be able to articulate this morality, but they live by it nonetheless.

It starts with the notion that we have a lifelong mission to realize our capacities. "It is a bringing of oneself to flourishing completion, an unfolding of what is strongest or best in oneself, so that it represents the successful culmination of one's aspirations or potentialities," Gewirth wrote in *Self-Fulfillment* (1998). The way we realize our potential is through our activities. By ceaselessly striving to improve at the things we enjoy, we come to define, enlarge, and attain our best selves. These activities are the bricks of our identities; if we didn't write or play baseball or cook or litigate (or whatever it is we do well), we would cease to be who we are. This is what Karl Marx was describing when he wrote, "Milton produced *Paradise Lost* as a silkworm produces silk, as the activation of his own nature."

10 In this mode of living, character isn't something one forges as a 10 youth and then retains thereafter. Morality doesn't come to one in a single revelation or a grand moment of epiphany. Instead, virtue and character are achieved gradually and must be maintained through a relentless struggle for self-improvement. We are in an ongoing dialogue with our inadequacies, and we are happiest when we are most deeply engaged in overcoming them.

This is not a solitary process. Once ensconced in an activity, we find ourselves surrounded by mentors, coaches, teachers, colleagues, teammates, consultants, readers, and audience members. Society helps us in two ways. First, it gives us opportunities to participate in the things that will allow us to realize our capacities: Parents earnestly cast about for activities their children will love, and then spend their weekends driving them from one to another. Good schools have extracurricular offerings. Good companies and organizations allow their employees and members to explore new skills, and great nations have open, fluid societies—so that individuals can find their best avenues and go as far as their merit allows.

Second, society surrounds the individual with a web of instruction, encouragement, and recognition. The hunger for recognition is a great motivator for the meritocrat. People define themselves in part by the extent to which others praise and appreciate them. In traditional societies recognition was determined by birth, breeding, and social station, but in a purified meritocracy people have to win it through performance. Each person responds to signals from those around him, working hard at activities that win praise and abandoning those that don't. (America no doubt leads the world in trophy production per capita.) An individual's growth, then, is a joint project of the self and society.

In this joint project individuals not only improve their capacities; they also come to realize that they cannot fully succeed unless they make a contribution to the society that helped to shape them. A scientist may be good at science, but she won't feel fulfilled unless she has made important discoveries or innovations that help those around her. Few meritocrats are content to master pointless tasks.

Social contributions—giving back—flow easily and naturally from the meritocrat's life mission. Baseball players enjoy clinics where they share tips with younger players. Parents devote many hours to coaching, or they become teachers, managers, and mentors. In the best relationships what follows is a sort of love affair. Mentor and pupil work hard to help each other and to honor each other's effort. Most find that they glimpse their best selves while working with others on an arduous undertaking, whether it is staging a play, competing for a championship, or arguing a case in court.

15 The great moral contest for the meritocrat is not between good 15
and evil or virtue and vice. Most meritocrats are prudent, so they

9

don't commit terrible crimes or self-destructive follies. The great temptation is triviality. Society recognizes the fulfillment of noble capacities, but it also rewards shallow achievements. A person can be famous simply for being rich or good-looking. Sometimes it's the emptiest but splashiest activities that win the most attention. It can be easy to fall into a comfortable pattern of self-approval. Society seems to be rewarding you for what you are doing. Your salary goes up. You get promoted. You win bonuses. But you haven't tapped your capacities to the fullest.

Meritocrats therefore face a continual struggle to choose worthy opportunities over trivial ones. Charles Taylor argues that each of us has an intuitive ability to make what he calls "strong evaluations" of which aspirations are noblest. We do this, he believes, by tapping into any of a variety of moral frameworks, which have been handed down through time and which have "significance independent of us or our desires." It is necessary, then, to dig deep into what it means to be a Christian or a Jew or an American or a doctor. By this way of thinking, society's rebels had it all wrong when they tried to find self-fulfillment by breaking loose from tradition. Their rebellions created selves without roots or moral reference points. Burrowing down into an inherited tradition allows the meritocrat to strive upward.

For decades social critics have sold Americans short. All those books about the Organization Man, the culture of narcissism, the last man, and the flat, commercial materialism of American life underestimated the struggles and opportunities to build character that are embedded in the meritocratic system. The critics applied bygone codes to today's way of life. Inevitably, they have found kids, and us, wanting, and not in the areas where we truly are wanting (chief among these being that we don't sufficiently educate our children in the substance of the moral traditions they are inheriting—the history of Christianity, the history of Judaism, the history of America).

Today's kids live amid peace and prosperity, true. But theirs is not an easy life. Has there ever been a generation compelled to accomplish so much—to establish an identity, succeed in school, cope with technological change, maneuver through the world of group dating and diverse sexual orientation, and make daily decisions about everything from cell-phone rate plans to brands of sugar substitute? The meritocrat's life is radically open, but its very openness creates a series of choices and challenges that are demanding and subtle because they are never-ending and because they are embedded in the pattern of every-day life—rather than being faced, say, at one crucial, life-determining moment on the battlefield.

There is virtue in trying to articulate the codes we live by, open and diverse and sprawling as those codes may be. Perhaps if we can reach a reasonably accurate understanding of the moral landscape of our lives, we will be better able to achieve our dreams and guide our ethical debates—though we will no doubt still have need of protective headgear.

Questions on Meaning

1. Why does Brooks's daughter have to work so hard to achieve her goals when she is already a rich child, by most of the world's standards? What does it mean to merit the things that we have?

2. People in American culture must continue to prove that they are worthy of their privilege. Why do we have to continue to show that we are good people? Why is building character so difficult in modern America?

3. What must adults, especially celebrities, do to show that they are good people? What kinds of activities must they participate in to demonstrate virtue?

Questions on Rhetorical Strategy and Style

1. Brooks has a humorous way of presenting his ideas, almost a kind of gentleness. Why does beginning with his daughter's helmets for her various activities show that his essay is meant to be taken lightly?

2. How do the examples the Brooks uses throughout his essay show that he approves of the need to give back in this culture? He shows that it is hard to be a good person in America, but that is OK because goodness leads to good works. How does he illustrate this argument?

3. The essay ends on a note of self-congratulation and triumph for the American way. Why does Brooks make it all right to be rich and prosperous as long as we suffer a bit for our prosperity?

Writing Assignments

1. Go look in your closet. Describe what you find, and then write about who you are based on your closet. Is it all right to have what you have? Why?

2. What does a young person have to do to assure admission to a good college or to any college, for that matter? When does the pressure begin? What has caused all this pressure? Is it a good thing?

3. Sit for a while at any coffee shop in your neighborhood. Watch the cars that go by and the clothes people wear. Then write about the level of affluence you observe. What does it say about American values?

Students Have Always Been Violent

David Greenberg

With each new and highly publicized account of school violence, many people ask why students have now become so violent. It seems as if no one is safe anymore—our schools are battlefields and children and teachers are the innocent victims. But is this simply a matter of perception or of reality? In the next piece, writer David Greenberg explains that historically, students have always been violent, they are just better armed today.

David Greenberg is a history columnist for Slate *at MSN. He is a graduate fellow of the Institute for Social and Economic Theory and Research at Columbia University. In addition to publishing many articles, Greenberg is the author of* Nixon's Shadow: The History of an Image *(2003). He wrote this column for the May 6, 1999 issue of* Slate.

Critical Thinking

Think about your experiences in elementary and high school. How much violence did you witness? What was the student reaction when someone shouted "fight"?

1   Judging by the histrionic Columbine massacre coverage you'd think that children are by nature innocent, free of violent or sexual thoughts until corrupted by our culture. That schools have traditionally been safe. That the recent spate of killings is unprecedented.

History says otherwise. In every era, American schoolchildren—especially teen-agers—have been unruly and destructive. As late as the 17th century, those "children" we now call teen-agers were considered adults. And preteens swore, drank, had sex, even dueled with guns. If school violence wasn't a problem back then, it's only because few children went to school.

In colonial America, most young children were taught at home. Those who attended school were just as prone to be disorderly as today's youths. Teachers kept problem children in line with corporal punishments that seem positively

Reprinted from *Slate* , May 6, 1999, United Features Syndicare.

barbaric today: They tied children to whipping posts and beat them or branded students for their crimes—a "T" for thievery, a "B" for blasphemy. Occasionally children were put to death.

Branding fell from favor in the 18th century, but students were still flogged or tied to chairs.

In the early 19th century, school reformer Horace Mann reported that he saw 328 floggings in one school during the course of a week. As the principles of humanitarianism spread and the era of mass schooling arrived, Mann and others replaced or supplemented the elite academies with taxpayer-supported "common schools," which admitted young students from all walks of life. (Later, attendance become compulsory.) In the Gilded Age, as immigrants and migrants flooded the cities, public elementary schools proliferated. Finally, the Progressives championed the view of adolescence as a stage of childhood, and high schools (the first of which opened in the 1820s) multiplied as well.

It appears that more students meant more violence. In 1837, Mann noted that almost 400 schools across Massachusetts had to be shut down because of disciplinary problems. In most institutions, keeping order took precedence over teaching. One observer in 1851 likened the typical American school to "the despotic government of a military camp." In the colleges, where the teen-age students were bigger and less docile, violence was even worse. Princeton University, to take just one example, witnessed six major riots between 1800 and 1830, including the burning of the library in 1802 and a rash of campus explosions in 1823 that caused half of one class to be expelled.

School violence persisted into the 20th century, taking different forms according to the climate of the day. In politically charged times, students became violent in the name of political causes. In 1917, for example, when New York City introduced a "platoon" system to deal with an influx of pupils, students rebelled—literally. Between 1,000 and 3,000 schoolchildren picketed and stoned P.S. 171 on Madison Avenue and attacked nonstriking classmates. Similar riots erupted across the city, resulting in furious battles between student mobs and the police. Likewise, the civil rights movement and anti-Vietnam War protests brought different forms of "political" violence to places ranging from Little Rock Central High in Arkansas to Kent State University in Ohio.

More politically sedate times didn't translate into student acquiescence, however. In the post–World War II years, urban strife and suburban anomie gave rise to school violence of the sorts broadly rendered by Hollywood in the 1955 films *Rebel Without a Cause* and *Blackboard Jungle*. The nation waxed hysterical over "juvenile delinquency," as the vogue phrase had it—alienated adolescents unaccountably sullen in the bountiful Eisenhower years. Though history had recorded public concern over bands of violent teen-agers ever since the beginning of the republic, the fear of "gangs" (a term coined in the 1930s) caught the nation's fancy. *Time* magazine headlined a story, "Teen-agers on the Rampage," which detailed a weeklong outbreak of violence in high schools from Maine to California. Congress held hearings on the delinquency epidemic, calling comic-book artists to testify about whether their drawings inspired children to violence.

Youth rebelliousness surged in the 1960s. While crime grew overall, juvenile crime grew faster. Sociologists, social workers, and policy wonks turned their attention en masse to offenses ranging from vandalism to gang-related crime, from drug use to student-upon-student assaults. Schools implemented safety plans, bringing in adult hall monitors and setting up bodies for hearing student grievances. Urban schools hired professional security agents—and later adopted the surveillance cameras, metal detectors, locker searches, and other measures more commonly seen in prisons. But a major study conducted in 1978 confirmed what experience had been teaching. Teen-agers were more likely to be victims of crime at school than anywhere else.

10 If student violence has now been a major concern for decades now, what 10 seems to distinguish '90s violence is the suburban- or rural-school massacre. West Paducah, Ky.; Jonesboro, Ark.; Pearl, Miss.; Moses Lake, Wash.; Springfield, Ore.; and now Littleton, Colo.—in each case, young students, armed with guns, committed multiple murders in or near the school itself. To be sure, similar atrocities have occurred in the past. In 1927, a 55-year-old school-board official detonated three bombs in the Bath, Mich., schoolhouse, killing 45 people. And to be sure, the string of recent killings in fact reveals nothing, statistically speaking, about our society. Yet they remind us that the number of children killed by guns skyrocketed in the '80s and while tailing off in the '90s remains far higher than in decades past. According to one recent study, the growing trend of violent altercations ending in death is attributable "almost entirely" to the proliferation of guns among children.

The study, by James A. Mercy and Mark L. Rosenberg, tracked data between 1973 and 1991. They point out that "A surprisingly large proportion of adolescents report that they routinely carry guns and bring them to school"—14 percent of boys, according to one study, and 7.9 percent of students overall.

History makes it clear that children and teen-agers are no strangers to violent impulses. There have always been, and always will be, maladjusted or deranged students who unleash those impulses. That they do so is inevitable. How they do so may be within our control.

Freewriting Assignment

During the 1950s, the phrase *juvenile delinquency* was coined. What is a juvenile delinquent? What does the term imply?

Critical Reading

1. Greenberg presents a historical overview of violence in schools to support his argument that students of the past were just as violent as students today, and perhaps even more so. How persuasive is his information? Does he seem credible? Did his information change your perception of violence in schools? Explain.

2. In paragraph 2, Greenberg comments that if school violence wasn't a problem in the seventeenth century, it is "only because few children went to school." Evaluate the effectiveness of this argument.

3. Evaluate Greenberg's statement that "the string of recent killings in fact reveals nothing, statistically speaking, about our society" (paragraph 10). What does he mean by this statement?

4. What assumptions does Greenberg make about his audience? Cite some examples from the text that reveal those assumptions.

5. What connections does Greenberg make between student violence and the overall culture of the time? Does culture shape behaviour? Explain.

Critical Writing

6. *Persuasive Writing*: Are schoolchildren inherently innocent, or naturally violent, as Greenberg implies? Write an essay in which you explore this idea. Refer to information from Greenberg's essay, as well as your personal experience.

7. *Research and Analysis*: Arrange to interview seasoned educators from several school levels (early elementary, middle, late elementary, or secondary) to develop a profile of students today and students from past decades of their teaching experience. Have student behaviours and attitudes changed since, say, the 1970s? If so, in what ways? What might account for the perceived change? If not, ask them to discuss the perception that kids today have changed. Detail their answers and develop conclusions of your own based on their responses.

8. *Personal Narrative*: Were you a "good" or "bad" kid in school? Did you get into trouble, serve frequent detentions, or even get suspended? Discuss your behavioural role in school and the motivation behind it. Why did you behave the way you did? Was it out of boredom, peer pressure, fear of parental reprimand, physical punishment, or simple anger? Explain.

Group Projects

9. Greenberg points out that in the seventeenth century, those we call teenagers were considered adults. Discuss with your group the concept of

childhood and adolescence in our society. In light of the fact that many U.S. states are pushing for legislation to allow courts to try those teenagers as adults who commit serious crimes, are our constructions of the separation between "child" and "adult" outmoded? Write down your group's key discussion points and share them with the class.

The Human Cost of an Illiterate Society

Jonathan Kozol

*Jonathan Kozol (1936–) was born in Boston and gradu-
ated from Harvard University. He has taught at Yale University, Trinity College, and the University of Massachusetts
at Amherst as well as several public schools. He is well
known for his writing on social and educational issues,
often calling for educational reform and more realistic examination of societal problems. His books include* Death
at an Early Age *(1967),* Free Schools *(1972),* On Being
a Teacher *(1981),* Illiterate America *(1985),* Rachel and
Her Children: Homeless Families in America *(1986),
and* Savage Inequalities: Children in America's Schools
(1991). The following selection is an excerpt from Illiterate America. *Kozol does not explore the causes of illiteracy
in this selection, as he does elsewhere in this book, but instead looks at a wide range of effects, or costs, of illiteracy,
both for society and the individual. Before beginning to
read, think for a moment about what it might mean to be
illiterate. Try to imagine how many ways your life would
be different if you couldn't read. Regardless of how imagi-
native you are, you are likely to be shocked by all the ways
illiteracy affects an illiterate person and society as a whole.*

PRECAUTIONS. READ BEFORE USING.
Poison: Contains sodium hydroxide (caustic soda-lye).
Corrosive: Causes severe eye and skin damage, may cause blindness.
Harmful or fatal if swallowed.
If swallowed, give large quantities of milk or water.

Do not induce vomiting.
Important: Keep water out of can at all times to prevent contents from violently erupting . . .

—warning on a can of Drano

1   Questions of literacy, in Socrates' belief, must at length be judged as matters of morality. Socrates could not have had in mind the moral compromise peculiar to a nation like our own. Some of our Founding Fathers did, however, have this question in their minds. One of the wisest of those Founding Fathers (one who may not have been most compassionate but surely was more prescient than some of his peers) recognized the special dangers that illiteracy would pose to basic equity in the political construction that he helped to shape.

"A people who mean to be their own governors," James Madison wrote, "must arm themselves with the power knowledge gives. A popular government without popular information or the means of acquiring it, is but a prologue to a farce or a tragedy, or perhaps both."

Tragedy looms larger than farce in the United States today. Illiterate citizens seldom vote. Those who do are forced to cast a vote of questionable worth. They cannot make informed decisions based on serious print information. Sometimes they can be alerted to their interests by aggressive voter education. More frequently, they vote for a face, a smile, or a style, not for a mind or character or body of beliefs.

The number of illiterate adults exceeds by 16 million the entire vote cast for the winner in the 1980 presidential contest. If even one third of all illiterates could vote, and read enough and do sufficient math to vote in their self-interest, Ronald Reagan would not likely have been chosen president. There is, of course, no way to know for sure. We do know this: Democracy is a mendacious term when used by those who are prepared to countenance the forced exclusion of one third of our electorate. So long as 60 million people are denied significant participation, the government is neither of, nor for, nor by, the people. It is a government, at best, of those two thirds whose wealth, skin color, or parental privilege allows them opportunity to profit from the provocation and instruction of the written word.

5   The undermining of democracy in the United States is one "expense" that sensitive Americans can easily deplore because it represents a contradiction that endangers citizens of all political positions. The human price is not so obvious at first.

19

Since I first immersed myself within this work I have often had the following dream: I find that I am in a railroad station or a large department store within a city that is utterly unknown to me and where I cannot understand the printed words. None of the signs or symbols is familiar. Everything looks strange: like mirror writing of some kind. Gradually I understand that I am in the Soviet Union. All the letters on the walls around me are Cyrillic. I look for my pocket dictionary but I find that it has been mislaid. Where have I left it? Then I recall that I forgot to bring it with me when I packed my bags in Boston. I struggle to remember the name of my hotel. I try to ask somebody for directions. One person stops and looks at me in a peculiar way. I lose the nerve to ask. At last I reach into my wallet for an ID card. The card is missing. Have I lost it? Then I remember that my card was confiscated for some reason, many years before. Around this point, I wake up in a panic.

This panic is not so different from the misery that millions of adult illiterates experience each day within the course of their routine existence in the U.S.A.

Illiterates cannot read the menu in a restaurant.

They cannot read the cost of items on the menu in the *window* of the restaurant before they enter.

10 Illiterates cannot read the letters that their children bring home 10 from their teachers. They cannot study school department circulars that tell them of the courses that their children must be taking if they hope to pass the SAT exams. They cannot help with homework. They cannot write a letter to the teacher. They are afraid to visit in the classroom. They do not want to humiliate their child or themselves.

Illiterates cannot read instructions on a bottle of prescription medicine. They cannot find out when a medicine is past the year of safe consumption; nor can they read of allergenic risks, warnings to diabetics, or the potential sedative effect of certain kinds of nonprescription pills. They cannot observe preventive health care admonitions. They cannot read about "the seven warning signs of cancer" or the indications of blood-sugar fluctuations or the risks of eating certain foods that aggravate the likelihood of cardiac arrest.

Illiterates live, in more than literal ways, an uninsured existence. They cannot understand the written details on a health insurance form. They cannot read the waivers that they sign preceding surgical procedures. Several women I have known in Boston have entered a slum hospital with the intention of obtaining a tubal ligation and have emerged a few days later after having been subjected to a hysterectomy. Unaware of their rights, incognizant of jargon, intimidated by the unfamiliar air of fear and atmosphere of ether that so many of us find oppressive in the confines even of the most attractive and expensive medical facilities, they have signed their names to documents they could not read and which nobody, in the hectic situation that prevails so often in those overcrowded hospitals that serve the urban poor, had even bothered to explain.

Childbirth might seem to be the last inalienable right of any female citizen within a civilized society. Illiterate mothers, as we shall see, already have been cheated of the power to protect their progeny against the likelihood of demolition in deficient public schools and, as a result, against the verbal servitude within which they themselves exist. Surgical denial of the right to bear that child in the first place represents an ultimate denial, an unspeakable metaphor, a final darkness that denies even the twilight gleamings of our own humanity. What greater violation of our biological, our biblical, our spiritual humanity could possibly exist than that which takes place nightly, perhaps hourly these days, within such over-burdened and benighted institutions as the Boston City Hospital? Illiteracy has many costs; few are so irreversible as this.

Even the roof above one's head, the gas or other fuel for heating that protects the residents of northern city slums against the threat of illness in the winter months become uncertain guarantees. Illiterates cannot read the lease that they must sign to live in an apartment which, too often, they cannot afford. They cannot manage check accounts and therefore seldom pay for anything by mail. Hours and entire days of difficult travel (and the cost of bus or other public transit) must be added to the real cost of whatever they consume. Loss of interest on the check accounts they do not have, and could not manage if they did, must be regarded as another of the excess costs paid by the citizen who is excluded from the common instruments of commerce in a numerate society.

15 "I couldn't understand the bills," a woman in Washington, D.C., 15 reports, "and then I couldn't write the checks to pay them. We signed things we didn't know what they were."

Illiterates cannot read the notices that they receive from welfare offices or from the IRS. They must depend on word-of-mouth instruction from the welfare worker—or from other persons whom they have good reason to mistrust. They do not know what rights they have, what deadlines and requirements they face, what options they might choose to exercise. They are half-citizens. Their rights exist in print but not in fact.

Illiterates cannot look up numbers in a telephone directory. Even if they can find the names of friends, few possess the sorting skills to make use of the yellow pages; categories are bewildering and trade names are beyond decoding capabilities for millions of nonreaders. Even the emergency numbers listed on the first page of the phone book—"Ambulance," "Police," and "Fire"—are too frequently beyond the recognition of nonreaders.

Many illiterates cannot read the admonition on a pack of cigarettes. Neither the Surgeon General's warning nor its reproduction on the package can alert them to the risks. Although most people learn by word of mouth that smoking is related to a number of grave physical disorders, they do not get the chance to read the detailed stories which can document this danger with the vividness that turns concern into determination to resist. They can see the handsome cowboy or the slim Virginia lady lighting up a filter cigarette; they cannot heed the words that tell them that this product is (not "may be") dangerous to their health. Sixty million men and women are condemned to be the unalerted, high-risk candidates for cancer.

Illiterates do not buy "no-name" products in the supermarkets. They must depend on photographs or the familiar logos that are printed on the packages of brand-name groceries. The poorest people, therefore, are denied the benefits of the least costly products.

20 Illiterates depend almost entirely upon label recognition. Many 20 labels, however, are not easy to distinguish. Dozens of different kinds of Campbell's soup appear identical to the nonreaders The purchaser who cannot read and does not dare to ask for help, out of the fear of being stigmatized (a fear which is unfortunately realistic), frequently comes home with something which she never wanted and her family never tasted.

Illiterates cannot read instructions on a pack of frozen food. Packages sometimes provide an illustration to explain the cooking preparations; but illustrations are of little help to someone who must "boil water, drop the food—*within* its plastic wrapper—in the boiling water, wait for it to simmer, instantly remove."

Even when labels are seemingly clear, they may be easily mistaken. A woman in Detroit brought home a gallon of Crisco for her children's dinner. She thought that she had bought the chicken that was pictured on the label. She had enough Crisco now to last a year—but no more money to go back and buy the food for dinner.

Recipes provided on the packages of certain staples sometimes tempt a semiliterate person to prepare a meal her children have not tasted. The longing to vary the uniform and often starchy content of low-budget meals provided to the family that relies on food stamps commonly leads to ruinous results. Scarce funds have been wasted and the food must be thrown out. The same applies to distribution of food-surplus produce in emergency conditions. Government inducements to poor people to "explore the ways" by which to make a tasty meal from tasteless noodles, surplus cheese, and powdered milk are useless to nonreaders. Intended as benevolent advice, such recommendations mock reality and foster deeper feelings of resentment and of inability to cope. (Those, on the other hand, who cautiously refrain from "innovative" recipes in preparation of their children's meals must suffer the opprobrium of "laziness," "lack of imagination. . . .")

Illiterates cannot travel freely. When they attempt to do so, they encounter risks that few of us can dream of. They cannot read traffic signs and, while they often learn to recognize and to decipher symbols, they cannot manage street names which they haven't seen before. The same is true for bus and subway stops. While ingenuity can sometimes help a man or woman to discern directions from familiar landmarks, buildings, cemeteries, churches, and the like, most illiterates are virtually immobilized. They seldom wander past the streets and neighborhoods they know. Geographical paralysis becomes a bitter metaphor for their entire existence. They are immobilized in almost every sense we can imagine. They can't move up. They can't move out. They cannot see beyond. Illiterates may take an oral test for drivers' permits in most sections of America. It is a questionable concession. Where will they go? How will they get there? How will they get home? Could it be that some of us might like it better if they stayed where they belong?

25   Travel is only one of many instances of circumscribed existence. 25
Choice, in almost all its facets, is diminished in the life of an illiterate adult. Even the printed TV schedule, which provides most people with the luxury of preselection, does not belong within the arsenal of options in illiterate existence. One consequence is that the viewer watches only what appears at moments when he happens to have time to turn the switch. Another consequence, a lot more common, is that the TV set remains in operation night and day. Whatever the program offered at the hour when he walks into the room will be the nutriment

23

that he accepts and swallows. Thus, to passivity, is added frequency—indeed, almost uninterrupted continuity. Freedom to select is no more possible here than in the choice of home or surgery or food.

"You don't choose," said one illiterate woman. "You take your wishes from somebody else." Whether in perusal of a menu, selection of highways, purchase of groceries, or determination of affordable enjoyment, illiterate Americans must trust somebody else: a friend, a relative, a stranger on the street, a grocery clerk, a TV copywriter.

"All of our mail we get, it's hard for her to read. Settin' down and writing a letter, she can't do it. Like if we get a bill . . . we take it over to my sister-in-law . . . My sister-in-law reads it."

Billing agencies harass poor people for the payment of the bills for purchases that might have taken place six months before. Utility companies offer an agreement for a staggered payment schedule on a bill past due. "You have to trust them," one man said. Precisely for this reason, you end up by trusting no one and suspecting everyone of possible deceit. A submerged sense of distrust becomes the corollary to a constant need to trust. "They are cheating me . . . I have been tricked . . . I do not know . . ."

Not knowing: This is a familiar theme. Not knowing the right word for the right thing at the right time is one form of subjugation. Not knowing the world that lies concealed behind those words is a more terrifying feeling. The longitude and latitude of one's existence are beyond all easy apprehension. Even the hard, cold stars within the firmament above one's head begin to mock the possibilities for self-location. Where am I? Where did I come from? Where will I go?

30 "I've lost a lot of jobs," one man explains. "Today, even if you're 30 a janitor, there's still reading and writing . . . They leave a note saying, 'Go to room so-and-so . . .' You can't do it. You can't read it. You don't know."

"The hardest thing about it is that I've been places where I didn't know where I was. You don't know where you are . . . You're lost."

"Like I said: I have two kids. What do I do if one of my kids starts choking? I go running to the phone . . . I can't look up the hospital phone number. That's if we're at home. Out on the street, I can't read the sign. I get to a pay phone. 'Okay, tell us where you are. We'll send an ambulance.' I look at the street sign. Right there, I can't tell you what it says. I'd have to spell it out, letter for letter. By that time, one of my kids would be dead . . . These are the kinds of fears you go with, every single day . . ."

"Reading directions, I suffer with. I work with chemicals . . . That's scary to begin with . . . "

"You sit down. They throw the menu in front of you. Where do you go from there? Nine times out of ten you say, 'Go ahead. Pick out something for the both of us.' I've eaten some weird things, let me tell you!"

35   Menus. Chemicals. A child choking while his mother searches for a word she does not know to find assistance that will come too late. Another mother speaks about the inability to help her kids to read: "I can't read to them. Of course that's leaving them out of something they should have. Oh, it matters. You believe it matters! I ordered all these books. The kids belong to a book club. Donny wanted me to read a book to him. I told Donny: 'I can't read,' He said: 'Mommy, you sit down. I'll read it to you.' I tried it one day, reading from the pictures. Donny looked at me. He said, 'Mommy, that's not right.' He's only five. He knew I couldn't read . . .'"

A landlord tells a woman that her lease allows him to evict her if her baby cries and causes inconvenience to her neighbors. The consequence of challenging his words conveys a danger which appears, unlikely as it seems, even more alarming than the danger of eviction. Once she admits that she can't read, in the desire to maneuver for the time in which to call a friend, she will have defined herself in terms of an explicit impotence that she cannot endure. Capitulation in this case is preferable to self-humiliation. Resisting the definition of oneself in terms of what one cannot do, what others take for granted, represents a need so great that other imperatives (even one so urgent as the need to keep one's home in winter's cold) evaporate and fall away in face of fear. Even the loss of home and shelter, in this case, is not so terrifying as the loss of self.

"I come out of school. I was sixteen. They had their meetings. The directors meet. They said that I was wasting their school paper. I was wasting pencils . . ."

Another illiterate, looking back, believes she was not worthy of her teacher's time. She believes that it was wrong of her to take up space within her school. She believes that it was right to leave in order that somebody more deserving could receive her place.

Children choke. Their mother chokes another way: on more than chicken bones.

40   People eat what others order, know what others tell them, struggle not to see themselves as they believe the world perceives them. A

25

man in California speaks about his own loss of identity, of self-location, definition:

"I stood at the bottom of the ramp. My car had broke down on the freeway. There was a phone. I asked for the police. They was nice. They said to tell them where I was. I looked up at the signs. There was one that I had seen before. I read it to them: ONE WAY STREET. They thought it was a joke. I told them I couldn't read. There was other signs above the ramp. They told me to try. I looked around for somebody to help. All the cars was going by real fast. I couldn't make them understand that I was lost. The cop was nice. He told me: 'Try once more,' I did my best. I couldn't read. I only knew the sign above my head. The cop was trying to be nice. He knew that I was trapped. 'I can't send out a car to you if you can't tell me where you are.' I felt afraid. I nearly cried. I'm forty-eight years old. I only said: 'I'm on a one-way street . . .'"

The legal problems and the courtroom complications that confront illiterate adults have been discussed above. The anguish that may underlie such matters was brought home to me this year while I was working on this book. I have spoken, in the introduction, of a sudden phone call from one of my former students, now in prison for a criminal offense. Stephen is not a boy today. He is twenty-eight years old. He called to ask me to assist him in his trial, which comes up next fall. He will be on trial for murder. He has just knifed and killed a man who first enticed him to his home, then cheated him, and then insulted him—as "an illiterate subhuman."

Stephen now faces twenty years to life. Stephen's mother was illiterate. His grandparents were illiterate as well. What parental curse did not destroy was killed off finally by the schools. Silent violence is repaid with interest. It will cost us $25,000 yearly to maintain this broken soul in prison. But what is the price that has been paid by Stephen's victim? What is the price that will be paid by Stephen?

Perhaps we might slow down a moment here and look at the realities described above. This is the nation that we live in. This is a society that most of us did not create but which our President and other leaders have been willing to sustain by virtue of malign neglect. Do we possess the character and courage to address a problem which so many nations, poorer than our own, have found it natural to correct?

The answers to these questions represent a reasonable test of our belief in the democracy to which we have been asked in public school to swear allegiance.

Questions on Meaning

1. Define what Kozol means by "human cost." You might start your thinking by considering how this cost is different from the literal monetary costs that are also described at different points in the essay.
2. Kozol relates illiteracy to the concept of subjugation. Brainstorm what your think he means by this. Who are the subjugators? What is their motivation for subjugating illiterate people?
3. In a sentence or two, express the primary theme of this essay.

Questions on Rhetorical Strategy and Style

1. One characteristic of Kozol's style is passages that link concrete examples with larger abstractions or generalizations. For example, in paragraph 24, in the context of the difficulties of an illiterate person traveling, Kozol writes, "Geographical paralysis becomes a bitter metaphor for their entire existence. They are immobilized in almost every sense we can imagine." Another example occurs in paragraphs 12 and 13, where Kozol speaks of women given a hysterectomy without being informed of the meaning of this surgery as "a final darkness that denies even the twilight gleamings of our own humanity." Analyze this passage and explain why Kozol calls this the "ultimate denial."
2. Kozol frequently uses description as a rhetorical device for developing the essay. Read back through the essay and identify at least three examples of illiterate people whose problem Kozol describes in detail. How does each of these examples contribute to the effectiveness of the essay overall?
3. How successful is Kozol in building his argument about the costs of illiteracy? What specific characteristics of the essay contribute to your evaluation?

Writing Assignments

1. To better understand the difficulty illiterates face in many types of communication, use your imagination to solve the following problem. You are the director of a new program at your college or university for teaching reading at no cost to adult illiterates in the community. You have funding to hire teachers and pay for classrooms and materials, but very little money left over to publicize the

program. How do you inform illiterates in the community about your reading classes? How do you give them basic information such as where to come and what times and how to get there? Brainstorm with others to reach the most effective solution that overcomes the problems of communication.

2. Kozol says our political leaders sustain the problem of illiteracy through "malign neglect." What does he mean by this phrase? Why is this neglect "malign"? Consider other social problems, such as homelessness or lack of good health care for people in poverty. Do you see "malign neglect" with these problems too? Write an essay in which you explore the reasons why leaders might be neglectful in these ways.

3. In paragraph 3 Kozol states that illiterate persons can only "cast a vote of questionable worth" because their decision is not based on "serious print information" but on "a face, a smile, or a style." Some social critics would say the same is true of many people who can read: that they vote based on television images and sound bytes rather than careful reading of the issues. If true, this only heightens the resulting national tragedy to which Kozol refers. What do you think about this idea? Do most people take the time to study the issues in depth before voting? Ask a few other people about how much they read before the last election. Think about what you learn from their comments, and formulate your own thesis about what really happens in an election and what you think *should* happen. Write a persuasive essay that develops your thesis.

Guns, Sex, and Education

Jamie O'Meara

Guns and schools—put these two nouns together and immediately you conjure up tragedies such as Columbine High School in the U.S. or Myers High School in Taber, Alberta. Naturally, most people would concur that firearms have no place in our schools. But in this article from Saturday Night, *Jamie O'Meara argues that in order to counter children's natural curiosity, gun education should, in fact, be part of our schools' curricula. Gun education, he argues, including handling and even firing guns, is the only way to remove the mystique of firearms and the only way to get kids to think about guns in a responsible manner.*

Jamie O'Meara is the editor-in-chief of Hour, *an alternative weekly newspaper in Montreal. This article first appeared in* Saturday Night *on May 20, 2000.*

Critical Thinking

Do you feel that guns have a place in our schools under controlled circumstances? What might be the benefits of introducing firearms into the current curricula of our high schools?

1 The first thing I noticed was its weight. It wasn't just cold, it was heavy, like the rock you pick up when you're six years old, with visions of windowpanes dancing in your head. By itself, it's just a rock. In your hand, it has power. That's how the gun felt.

It was a 9-mm military-issue Browning semi-automatic, I think, obtained from a friend who had joined the army cadets. Because of its weight, I had a hard time levelling it at the car battery we'd put halfway up the slope of the abandoned gravel pit at the back of our rural Ontario farm. This was where my brother and I spent a good part of our summers, with our .22-calibre rifles and .177 pellet guns, keeping the pop-bottle population under control. This gun, though, felt different than the ones we'd been shooting since we were kids. Fascinatingly so.

Borrowing my stance from every cop show ever made, I lined up my plastic prey and squeezed the trigger five times in quick succession. The first shot hit the battery and the next four thumped into the earth about twenty feet in front of me. A box of fifty rounds later, I was no closer to hitting my target with any regularity and, frankly, my hand was beginning to hurt. I packed the gun away and returned it to my buddy. (He, after exhausting its cachet among our friends, tossed it in a local river.)

All in all: boring.

5   And that may be a hard concept to grasp if, like most North Americans, you were raised on a steady diet of *Rambo*, *The Terminator*, and *Mad Max*: they showed that guns are fun, the implements of adventure. If you're holding one, people do what you want them to do. All of that's pretty attractive to young people, for whom power and control often seem in scarce supply. So why would a kid voluntarily give up the chance to play with a handgun?

Certainly not because of parental warnings. Lock the booze cabinet with double-plated armour and that's not going to save your Smirnoff. Threaten blindness and the wrath of all saints and that's not going to stop adolescents from masturbating. And tell children that guns are dangerous and that's not going to stop them from wanting to use one if it's accessible—in the gun cabinet, from a store, or in the schoolyard. All you can hope to do is teach them to act responsibly if the occasion arises.

Which is why guns belong in our schools.

Any parent knows that the best way to defuse the curiosity of a child is to address it head on, to transform the mysterious into the mundane. If memory serves, there is no place more mundane than school. Adding a firearm component to the current curricula in regions where guns are prevalent would achieve two things: it would satisfy the inherent inquisitiveness that children have about guns; and it would allow educators to monitor the reactions children have to the weapons—something that might have been of inestimable value to the faculty at Columbine High School in Colorado.

In Canada, it may be argued that guns aren't prevalent enough—in homes or on the streets—to warrant a proactive approach to gun education. Tragedies such as the one last year in Taber, Alberta, and the recent spate of youth shootings in Toronto indicate otherwise.

10   Put a kid on a firing range under strict controls, oblige him to fire hundreds of rounds at a circular target over lengthy periods of time, and what happens? Dirty Harry becomes a junior biathlete, without the skis. The kids who maintain an interest can be funnelled into gun clubs, where they can work through their attraction under the watchful eyes of trainers adept at spotting potential problems.

As long as guns have a mystique, they'll seem powerful. As long as kids feel there's power in guns, they'll be tempted to get their hands on them. And sooner or later someone who possesses a gun is going to want to use it. The solution is to address this desire early on and supply children with the rules of conduct. It's the same principle that lies behind sex education.

Think about it: sex education is taught so that kids will have a better understanding of how their bodies work, why they feel sexual desires, and how to act (or not) on those desires. Basically, we equip our kids with sexual knowledge so that they'll have the confidence to act responsibly. The same argument holds true for gun education: that, armed with knowledge and familiarity, kids will be better equipped to think about guns in a responsible manner. (In fact, the classic argument against sex education—that by providing kids with dangerous information they can't handle, we're encouraging them to run out and recklessly try it for themselves—is exactly the objection you're likely to hear raised against gun instruction.)

We accept the natural sexual curiosity of children and teenagers, and have legislated protection for them in the form of education, rather than pretending that the curiosity doesn't exist. Children are also curious about guns. We should give them the same protection. We don't want our kids shooting first and asking questions later.

Freewriting Assignment

Where do children form their ideas about guns if not in school? How do you think O'Meara would respond to this question?

Critical Reading

1. In paragraph 12, O'Meara compares sex education to gun education and argues that as with sex, "armed with knowledge and familiarity, kids will be better equipped to think about guns in a responsible manner." Do you feel this is a fair comparison? Compare it to the arguments put forth in the Viewpoints section of this book's chapter on Education.
2. O'Meara opens his essay with a personal narrative of his first experience with a gun as a child. What point is he trying to make with this example? Is this an effective way to reach his audience?
3. O'Meara argues that guns will seem powerful to young people as long as they have a "mystique." Can you think of other issues or examples in society that could benefit from being demystified through the education system? Explain.
4. According to the author, why might a firearm component on the school curriculum of Columbine High School have been of "inestimable value"?

31

Critical Writing

5. *Personal Narrative*: This essay begins with a personal narrative about O'Meara's first experience with a handgun. Recall your own first experience with something forbidden, and write a personal narrative describing how you handled it. What was your attitude toward the subject prior to your experience? Did the experience defuse your curiosity or "demystify" your attitude?

6. *Research and Analysis*: Investigate the connection between aggression and children playing with toy guns. Recent studies have suggested that there is no connection, and that in fact, banning toy guns can lead to even more violence. Research this issue and summarize your findings in an essay.

7. *Persuasive Writing*: Write a brief essay from a viewpoint opposite to O'Meara's—that is, persuade your reader that gun education has no place in the academic curriculum. Be sure to respond to all of his points, and include other support for your position.

Group Projects

8. O'Meara claims that films like *Rambo*, *The Terminator*, and *Mad Max* show that "guns are fun, the implements of adventure." Select three characters from a film or television show you would associate with guns. Describe the way that the character relates to guns. What is the prevalent attitude? Discuss with your group the message that each show sends out about guns. What conclusions might you draw from your findings? Does what you've discovered affect your attitude toward O'Meara's conclusions?

9. Despite the relative rarity of guns in Canada, O'Meara argues, tragedies such as Taber, Alberta in 1999 and recent youth shootings in Toronto indicate that our attitudes toward guns deserve attention. Canada prides itself on being much less a gun culture than the United States, and books and films, such as Michael Moore's *Bowling for Columbine*, help to promote this perception. How are the personal ownership and use of firearms perceived in Canada? How does this contrast with the way they are perceived in the U.S.? Research these questions with your group, summarize your findings, and present your conclusions to the class.

10. With your group, explore a number of gun catalogues online. How do these sites present firearms? How do different companies try to make their products stand out? What kind of language do they use to describe their products? Share your findings with the class.

Identity

"I'm Not Racist But . . ."

Neil Bissoondath

Born in Trinidad, Neil Bissoondath (1955–) moved to
Canada at age 18 to attend York University. Upon receiv-
ing a degree in French, Bissoondath taught both French and
English before beginning his writing career. In choosing to
be a full-time writer, he followed in the footsteps of his
internationally known uncles, Shiva and V.S. Naipaul.
Bissoondath's first book, the short story collection Digging Up
the Mountains *(1985), received significant critical praise,*
and his nonfiction critique of multiculturalism, Selling
Illusions: The Cult of Multiculturalism in Canada *(1994),*
stirred a good deal of controversy. His book The Innocence
of Age *(1992) won the Canadian Authors Association Prize*
for fiction. Most of Bissoondath's work, both fiction and non-
fiction, deals with the dislocation, alienation, and racial ten-
sion of non-white immigrants in Canadian society. In the
following essay, the author questions the legitimacy of label-
ing all insensitive ethnic language as racism.

1   Someone recently said that racism is as Canadian as maple syrup.
I have no argument with that. History provides us with ample
proof. But, for proper perspective, let us remember that it is also
as American as apple pie, as French as croissants, as Jamaican as ackee,
as Indian as aloo, as Chinese as chow mein, as. . . . Well, there's an
entire menu to be written. This is not by way of excusing it. Murder
and rape, too, are international, multicultural, as innate to the darker
side of the human experience. But we must be careful that the inevitable
rage evoked does not blind us to the larger context.

The word "racism" is a discomforting one: It is so vulnerable
to manipulation. We can, if we so wish, apply it to any incident involving people of different colour. And therein lies the danger. During

the heat of altercation, we seize, as terms of abuse, on whatever is most obvious about the person. It is, often, a question of unfortunate convenience. A woman, because of her sex, easily becomes a female dog or an intimate part of her anatomy. A large person might be dubbed "a stupid ox," a small person "a little" whatever. And so a black might become "a nigger," a white "a honky," an Asian "a paki," a Chinese "a chink," an Italian "a wop," a French-Canadian "a frog."

There is nothing pleasant about these terms; they assault every decent sensibility. Even so, I once met someone who, in a stunning surge of naiveté, used them as simple descriptives and not as terms of racial abuse. She was horrified to learn the truth. While this may have been an extreme case, the point is that the use of such patently abusive words may not always indicate racial or cultural distaste. They may indicate ignorance or stupidity or insensitivity, but pure racial hatred—such as the Nazis held for Jews, or the Ku Klux Klan for blacks—is a thankfully rare commodity.

Ignorance, not the willful kind but that which comes from lack of experience, is often indicated by that wonderful phrase, "I'm not racist but. . . ." I think of the mover, a friendly man, who said, "I'm not racist, but the Chinese are the worst drivers on the road." He was convinced this was so because the shape of their eyes, as far as he could surmise, denied them peripheral vision.

Or the oil company executive, an equally warm and friendly man, who, looking for an apartment in Toronto, rejected buildings with East Indian tenants not because of their race—he was telling me this, after all—but because he was given to understand that cockroaches were symbols of good luck in their culture and that, when they moved into a new home, friends came by with gift-wrapped cockroaches.

Neither of these men thought of himself as racist, and I believe they were not, deep down. (The oil company executive made it clear he would not hesitate to have me as a neighbour; my East Indian descent was of no consequence to him, my horror of cockroaches was.) Yet their comments, so innocently delivered, would open them to the accusation, justifiably so if this were all one knew about them. But it is a charge which would undoubtedly be wounding to them. It is difficult to recognize one's own misconceptions.

True racism is based, more often than not, on willful ignorance, and an acceptance of—and comfort with—stereotype. We like to think, in this country, that our multicultural mosaic will help nudge us into

34

a greater openness. But multiculturalism as we know it indulges in stereotype, depends on it for a dash of colour and the flash of dance. It fails to address the most basic questions people have about each other. Do those men doing the Dragon Dance really all belong to secret criminal societies? Do those women dressed in saris really coddle cockroaches for luck? Do those people in dreadlocks all smoke marijuana and live on welfare? Such questions do not seem to be the concern of the government's multicultural programs, superficial and exhibitionistic as they have become.

So the struggle against stereotype, the basis of all racism, becomes a purely personal one. We must beware of the impressions we create. A friend of mine once commented that, from talking to West Indians, she has the impression that their one great cultural contribution to the world is in the oft-repeated boast that "We (unlike everyone else) know how to party."

There are dangers, too, in community response. We must be wary of the self-appointed activists who seem to pop up in the media at every given opportunity spouting the rhetoric of retribution, mining distress for personal, political and professional gain. We must be skeptical about those who depend on conflict for their sense of self, the non-whites who need to feel themselves victims of racism, the whites who need to feel themselves purveyors of it. And we must be sure that, in addressing the problem, we do not end up creating it. Does the *Miss Black Canada Beauty Contest* still exist? I hope not. Not only do I find beauty contests offensive, but a racially segregated one even more so. What would the public reaction be, I wonder, if every year CTV broadcast the *Miss White Canada Beauty Pageant?* We give community-service awards only to blacks: Would we be comfortable with such awards only for whites? In Quebec, there are The Association of Black Nurses, The Association of Black Artists, The Congress of Black Jurists. Play tit for tat: The Association of White Nurses, White Artists, White Jurists: visions of apartheid. Let us be frank, racism for one is racism for others.

10   Finally, and perhaps most important, let us beware of abusing the   10
word itself.

Questions on Meaning

1. How does Bissoondath distinguish between what he considers simply unpleasant terms for women or ethnic minorities and true racism? To what extent do you agree or disagree with him?
2. How does Bissoondath characterize the Canadian government's attempts to foster multiculturalism? Why, according to the author, do these attempts fail to address true racism?
3. What does Bissoondath mean when he says that "we must be sure that, in addressing the problem [of racism], we do not end up creating it"? Do you agree with his reasoning? Why or why not?

Questions on Strategy and Style

1. Persuasion appeals sometimes to reason, sometimes to emotion, and sometimes to both. How would you characterize Bissoondath's primary appeal? Is this strategy successful, in your opinion? Explain your response.
2. What is Bissoondath's definition of racism? To what extent does this definition strengthen his argument about misusing the term?
3. Cite two examples used in this essay and explain how they support the author's argument.

Writing Assignments

1. Write a letter to Bissoondath, responding to his essay. Address the distinction he makes between real and imagined racism, and provide support for your position regarding this distinction.
2. Review your institution's policies on diversity, sexist/racist behavior, and offensive speech. Based on Bissoondath's essay, evaluate the effectiveness of those policies in curbing true racism.
3. Research the history of one of the racial/ethnic terms found in paragraph 2, and write an essay describing the evolution of that term from its origins to the present.

If Girls Can Succeed Only at the Expense of Boys, Maybe We Need Segregated Schools

Link Byfield

Throughout the last half of the nineteenth century and the first half of the twentieth century, public education systems across North America separated the boys from the girls. Today many educators and families are arguing for a return to this mode of education. The traditional reasons, such as students not worrying about how they dress or whom they impress when the distraction of the opposite sex is removed, are being replaced by a new concern over the different learning styles of the genders. For instance, some argue that girls prefer a quieter, more intimate learning approach, whereas boys prefer an approach that is more energetic and fast-paced. In the following article, Link Byfield explores this issue and argues that modern composite high schools aren't working; therefore, sex-segregated schools for those students and parents who would prefer them should be an option in the public system.

Link Byfield published the newsmagazine Alberta Report *for 18 years. He is now chairman of the Citizens Centre for Freedom and Democracy.*

Critical Thinking

What is the impact of gender-segregated schools? How might they be empowering for students and teachers? How might they be limiting?

[1] Anyone who has been convinced these past 10 years that the school system favours boys will have been heartened by last week's news that it doesn't. Girls, it turns out, are now doing as well as boys in math and science, and have widened their long-standing lead in reading and writing. This comes from the national School Achievement Indicators Program (SAIP), conducted jointly by Statistics Canada and the Council of Ministers of Education.

Reprinted from the *Alberta Report*, March 13, 2000, United Western Communications, Ltd.

The happy part is that girls may be doing better. The bad news is that boys may be doing worse.

The gender comparisons in SAIP's massive report occupy only part of one chapter, consisting of measurements taken only four years apart. So, while the information is probably useful, it's far from conclusive. Besides, it's always hard to, know—especially in complex interprovincial data-crunching exercises like this—whether the results are really comparative over time, or even within each year.

All the same, some things do become clear. High school girls on average are matching boys in the technology-related subjects of math and sciences, and are far ahead in language skills. The number of boys graduating is declining. The number of girls graduating is rising, to the point where there are now more girls finishing than boys.

Which leads to an interesting question. Is this progress or regress? Must advances among girls come at the expense of boys? Or is there some way of turning this from a zero-sum game into a win-win, where both sexes come out ahead? And now that we can turn off [the] feminist alarm, which for 10 years has been ringing down the hallways that girls are being cheated, is anyone going to worry about the flagging proficiency of boys?

Readers may remember the hue and cry in the 1990s that girls were being frustrated by a male-oriented instructional system. Boys are more competitive, risk-oriented and dominant, and teachers (even women teachers) were said to favour them. Girls were ignored. In addition, the courses themselves were written and presented in a straight linear and logical fashion, not in the more intuitive, co-operative and circuitous manner that supposedly suits the female mind. Appended to which was the usual litany of complaints about girls feeling threatened and harassed by the sexually robust high school atmosphere created by boys, who of course run everything.

If any of this is true, and for all I know some of it is, the only fair solution would be to divide schools, or at least classrooms, by sex. That was how I was schooled after Grade 5, and it seemed to work well enough. My wife started high school in segregated classes, she remembers, and when the boys and girls were mixed the following year almost every one's marks dropped. So why not divide them?

But that would offend the "socialization imperative" which in every public education debate turns out to be the bottom line. The fear is that unless we are endlessly and constantly mixing people—boys and girls, religious and non-religious; smart and less-smart, rich and poor; dark-skinned and pale, normal and handicapped—society will be riven by misunderstanding, ignorance, selfishness and distrust. This strange pessimism about human nature always becomes the sacrosanct absolute of government-funded education. "We will force them to meet each other and we will make them like each other." That is the attitude.

Well, if today's high schools are anything to go by I'd say it isn't working. For one thing, it's now girls who seem to run everything. In one high school I noticed, for instance, that the entire student council consisted of girls. The good girls (the ones who will probably become teachers themselves) run the council, and the bad girls—the ones who dress, act and talk like hookers (pardon the bluntness)—run the culture. The boys just tune out.

I'm sure there are schools much better than this—schools fighting hard for dress codes and some which emphasize boys' interests as much as girls'. But my impression, for what its worth, is that all too many high schools are moshpits of vulgarity where youth is free to run itself according to the values it has absorbed from MuchMusic and 12 years of automatic passing and parent-free sex instruction.

10 Whenever I enter a composite high school, I'm struck by how thoroughly 10 unnatural the environment is. The large modern high school is unlike anything else in human experience except perhaps the large modern university. It's nothing like any workplace in the world, and certainly unlike any home. These institutions should be smaller. Students should show more respect for teachers and for each other. There should be a more studious, less anarchic atmosphere.

One way of breaking them up would be to develop sex-segregated schools for those students and parents who prefer them. A few already exist; more of them might be started. Maybe boys' performance is declining because the public system is now geared consciously for girls. Let's allow both sexes to suit themselves. Not only might they learn better, it could improve their respect for each other.

Freewriting Assignment

In paragraph 8, Byfield states that in high schools today, "it's now girls who seem to run everything . . . The good girls . . . run the council, and the bad ones…run the culture." Respond to this statement.

Critical Reading

1. Identify the author's thesis and evaluate each of his supporting elements. Does the author allow for alternative points of view? Does he try to see multiple sides of the issue? Explain.
2. What is "the socialization imperative" referred to in paragraph 7? Do you agree with the author that it represents a "strange pessimism about human nature"?
3. What evidence does Byfield use to demonstrate that gender-mixed schools aren't working?

4. In paragraph 10, the author states that composite or mixed-gender high schools have an "unnatural" environment. What does he mean by this? Based on your own experience, would you agree with this assertion?

5. Byfield sums up the attitude of government-funded education as follows: "We will force them to meet each other and we will make them like each other." Imagine that you are an administrator promoting mixed-gender schools. How might you rephrase this sentiment in a more positive way?

Critical Writing

6. *Exploratory Writing:* Byfield mentions the fears about a "male-oriented instructional system" (paragraph 5). Do you feel that your own high school was geared more for boys or for girls? Use specific examples in your response. How did this affect your secondary school experience?

7. *Exploratory Writing:* Think of examples of nonacademic situations in which the genders are segregated—prisons or athletic competitions, for example. What are the reasons for the segregation? Could any of these reasons be applied to an academic setting? Alternatively, in one or more of your chosen examples should the genders be integrated?

Group Projects

8. In your group, debate the issue of sex-segregated schools. Divide your group into two and debate the usefulness of gender-segregated education. One of these smaller groups should speak in favour of the practice and the other should argue against it. What might be some of the advantages and disadvantages of sex-segregated schools?

9. Contact local schools in your area that are practising sex-segregation. If possible, interview some teachers or administrators and write a group report evaluating the effectiveness of segregation. Share your findings with the class.

Never Too Buff

John Cloud

While men with lean and muscular bodies have always been admired, the idea that men obsess about their body image as much as women may seem ludicrous to some people. We tend to assume that most men simply do not care about their appearance the way women do. Not so, according to psychiatrists Harrison Pope, Katharine Phillips, and psychologist Roberto Olivardia. Their research reveals a disturbing trend: just as many young women aspire to be supermodel thin, an increasing number of young men yearn for the steroid-boosted and buff bodies typical of today's action heroes and weightlifters. In the following article, John Cloud reports on this groundbreaking research, and what it might mean for boys and men in the years ahead.

Harrison Pope, a professor of psychiatry at Harvard Medical School, and Katharine Phillips, a professor of psychiatry at Brown University, in conjunction with Roberto Olivardia, a clinical psychologist at McLean Hospital in Massachusetts, have researched male body image for the past 15 years. Their book, The Adonis Complex, *published in 2000, concludes that "something awful has happened to American men over the past few decades"—they have become obsessed with their bodies. Journalist John Cloud discusses some of the key highlights of their research in this article, which first appeared in* Time *magazine on April 24, 2000, one week before their book was published.*

Critical Thinking

Try to imagine the "perfect" male body. What does it look like? Is your image influenced by outside forces, such as the media, your gender, or your age? How do real men you know compare to the image in your mind?

1   Pop quiz. Who is more likely to be dissatisfied with the appearance of their   1
chests, men or women? Who is more likely to be concerned about acne, your teenage son or his sister? And who is more likely to binge eat, your nephew or your niece?

If you chose the women and girls in your life, you are right only for the last question—and even then, not by the margin you might expect. About 40 percent of Americans who go on compulsive-eating sprees are men. Thirty-eight percent of men want bigger pecs, while only 34 percent of women want bigger breasts. And more boys have fretted about zits than girls, going all the way back to a 1972 study.

A groundbreaking new book declares that these numbers, along with hundreds of other statistics and interviews the authors have compiled, mean something awful has happened to American men over the past few decades. They have become obsessed with their bodies. Authors Harrison Pope and Katharine Phillips, professors of psychiatry at Harvard and Brown, respectively, and Roberto Olivardia, a clinical psychologist at McLean Hospital in Belmont, Mass., have a catchy name to describe this obsession—a term that will soon be doing many reps on chat shows: the Adonis Complex.

The name, which refers to the gorgeous half man, half god of mythology, may be a little too ready for Oprah, but the theory behind it will start a wonderful debate. Based on original research involving more than 1,000 men over the past 15 years, the book argues that many men desperately want to look like Adonis because they constantly see the "ideal," steroid-boosted bodies of actors and models and because their muscles are all they have over women today. In an age when women fly combat missions, the authors ask, "What can a modern boy or man do to distinguish himself as being 'masculine'?"

For years, of course, some men—ice skaters, body builders, George Hamilton—have fretted over aspects of their appearance. But the numbers suggest that body-image concerns have gone mainstream: nearly half of men don't like their overall appearance, in contrast to just 1 in 6 in 1972. True, men typically are fatter now, but another study found that 46 percent of men of normal weight think about their appearance "all the time" or "frequently." And some men—probably hundreds of thousands, if you extrapolate from small surveys— say they have passed up job and even romantic opportunities because they refuse to disrupt workouts or dine on restaurant food. In other words, an increasing number of men would rather look brawny for their girlfriends than have sex with them.

Consider what they're spending. Last year American men forked over $2 billion for gym memberships—and another $2 billion for home exercise equipment. *Men's Health* ("Rock-hard abs in six weeks!" it screams every other issue) had 250,000 subscribers in 1990; now it has 1.6 million. In 1996 alone, men underwent some 700,000 cosmetic procedures.

At least those profits are legal. Anabolic steroids—the common name for synthetic testosterone—have led to the most dramatic changes in the male form in modern history, and more and more average men want those changes for themselves. Since steroids became widely available on the black market in the 1960s, perhaps 3 million American men have swallowed or injected them—mostly in the past 15 years. A 1993 survey found that 1 Georgia high school boy in every 15 admitted having used steroids without a prescription. And the Drug Enforcement Administration reports that the percentage of all high school students who have used steroids has increased 50 percent in the past four years, from 1.8 percent to 2.8 percent. The abuse of steroids has so alarmed the National Institute on Drug Abuse that on Friday it launched a campaign in gyms, malls, bookstores, clubs and on the Internet to warn teenagers about the dangers. Meanwhile, teenagers in even larger numbers are buying legal but lightly regulated food supplements, some with dangerous side effects, that purport to make you bigger or leaner or stronger.

As they infiltrated the body-building world in the '70s and Hollywood a decade later, steroids created bodies for mass consumption that the world had literally never seen before. Pope likes to chart the changes by looking at Mr. America winners, which he called up on the Internet in his office last week. "Look at this guy," Pope exclaims when he clicks on the 1943 winner, Jules Bacon. "He couldn't even win a county body-building contest today." Indeed, there are 16-year-olds working out at your gym who are as big as Bacon. Does that necessarily mean that today's body builders—including those 16-year-olds—are 'roided? Pope is careful. "The possibility exists that rare or exceptional people, those with an unusual genetic makeup or a hormonal imbalance," could achieve the muscularity and leanness of today's big body builders, he says.

But it's not likely. And Pope isn't lobbing dumbbells from an ivory tower: the professor lifts weights six days a week, from 11 a.m. to 1 p.m. (He can even mark historical occasions by his workouts: "I remember when the Challenger went down; I was doing a set of squats.") "We are being assaulted by images virtually impossible to attain without the use of drugs," says Pope. "So what happens when you change a million-year-old equilibrium of nature?"

10 A historical loop forms: steroids beget pro wrestlers—Hulk Hogan, for 10 one, has admitted taking steroids—who inspire boys to be just like them. Steroids have changed even boys' toys. Feminists have long derided Barbie for her tiny waist and big bosom. The authors of *The Adonis Complex* see a similar problem for boys in the growth of G.I. Joe. The grunt of 1982 looks scrawny compared with G.I. Joe Extreme, introduced in the mid-'90s. The latter would have a 55-in. chest and 27-in. biceps if he were real, which simply can't be replicated in nature. Pope also points out a stunning little feature of the three-year-old video game Duke Nukem: Total Meltdown, developed by GT Interactive Software. When Duke gets tired, he can find a bottle of steroids to get him going. "Steroids give Duke a super adrenaline rush," the game manual notes.

To bolster their argument, the Adonis authors developed a computerized test that allows subjects to "add" muscle to a typical male body. They estimate their own size and then pick the size they would like to be and the size they

43

think women want. Pope and his colleagues gave the test to college students and found that on average, the men wanted 28 lbs. more muscle—and thought women wanted them to have 30 lbs. more. In fact, the women who took the test picked an ideal man only slightly more muscular than average. Which goes a long way toward explaining why Leonardo DiCaprio can be a megastar in a nation that also idealizes "Stone Cold" Steve Austin.

But when younger boys took Pope's test, they revealed an even deeper sense of inadequacy about their bodies. More than half of boys ages 11 to 17 chose as their physical ideal an image possible to attain only by using steroids. So they do. Boys are a big part of the clientele at Muscle Mania (not its real name), a weight-lifting store that *Time* visited last week at a strip mall in a Boston suburb. A couple of teenagers came in to ask about tribulus, one of the many over-the-counter drugs and body-building supplements the store sells, all legally.

"A friend of mine," one boy begins, fooling no one, "just came off a cycle of juice, and he heard that tribulus can help you produce testosterone naturally." Patrick, 28, who runs the store and who stopped using steroids four years ago because of chest pain, tells the kid, "The s__ shuts off your nuts," meaning steroids can reduce sperm production, shrink the testicles and cause impotence. Tribulus, Patrick says, can help restart natural testosterone production. The teen hands over $12 for 100 Tribulus Fuel pills. (Every day, Muscle Mania does $4,000 in sales of such products, with protein supplements and so-called fat burners leading the pack.)

Patrick says many of his teen customers, because they're short on cash, won't pay for a gym membership "until they've saved up for a cycle [of steroids]. They don't see the point without them." The saddest customers, he says, are the little boys, 12 and 13, brought in by young fathers. "The dad will say, 'How do we put some weight on this kid?' with the boy just staring at the floor. Dad is going to turn him into Hulk Hogan, even if it's against his will."

15   What would motivate someone to take steroids? Pope, Phillips and Olivardia   15
say the Adonis Complex works in different ways for different men. "Michael," 32, one of their research subjects, told *Time* he had always been a short kid who got picked on. He started working out at about 14, and he bought muscle magazines for advice. The pictures taunted him: he sweated, but he wasn't getting as big as the men in the pictures. Other men in his gym also made him feel bad. When he found out they were on steroids, he did two cycles himself, even though he knew they could be dangerous.

But not all men with body-image problems take steroids. Jim Davis, 29, a human-services manager, told *Time* he never took them, even when training for body-building competitions. But Davis says he developed a form of obsessive-compulsive disorder around his workouts. He lifted weights six days a week for at least six years. He worked out even when injured. He adhered to a rigid regimen for every session, and if he changed it, he felt anxious all day. He began

44

to be worried about clothes, and eventually could wear only three shirts, ones that make him look big. He still felt small. "I would sit in class at college with a coat on," he says. You may have heard this condition called bigorexia—thinking your muscles are puny when they aren't. Pope and his colleagues call it muscle dysmorphia and estimate that hundreds of thousands of men suffer from it.

Even though most boys and men never approach the compulsion of Davis or Michael (both eventually conquered it), they undoubtedly face more pressure now than in the past to conform to an impossible ideal. Ripped male bodies are used today to advertise everything that shapely female bodies advertise: not just fitness products but also dessert liqueurs, microwave ovens and luxury hotels. The authors of *The Adonis Complex* want guys to rebel against those images, or at least see them for what they are: a goal unattainable without drug use.

Feminists raised these issues for women years ago, and more recent books such as *The Beauty Myth* were part of a backlash against the hourglass ideal. Now, says Phillips, "I actually think it may be harder for men than women to talk about these problems because it's not considered masculine to worry about such things." But maybe there is a masculine alternative: Next time WWE comes on, guys, throw the TV out the window. And order a large pizza. ◆

Freewriting Assignment

Pope, Phillips, and Olivardia report that, in general, men would like to add 28 pounds more muscle to their frames but believe women would prefer even more—at least 30 pounds more muscle. What, in your opinion, accounts for this perception? Does it seem reasonable?

Critical Reading

1. Evaluate the comment made by Pope, Phillips, and Olivardia that young men are increasingly obsessed with body image because they feel that muscle is all men have "over women today." Do you agree or disagree with this statement? Explain.
2. Analyze the author's use of statistics to support his points. Do their conclusions seem reasonable based on the data they cite? Why or why not?
3. Visit the Muscle Memory Web site and look at the photographs of some of the Mr. America winners over the past 50 years at **www.musclememory .com/articles/MrAmerica.html**. How do they compare to today's body builders? Explain.
4. According to the author, what cultural messages tell children that steroid use is okay? Describe some of the ways children receive these messages.

Critical Writing

5. *Analytical Writing*: Write a detailed description of your ideal male image (what you desire in a male or what you would most want to look like as a male). How does your description compare with the conclusions drawn by the psychiatrists and psychologist in the article? Did outside cultural influences direct your description? Explain.

6. *Personal Narrative*: Looking back at your experience in high school, write a narrative about the males who were considered the most "buff." What qualities made these particular males more desirable and more enviable than their peers? How much of their appeal was based on their physical appearance? How much on something else?

7. *Persuasive Writing*: Pope, Phillips, and Olivardia comment that media pressure is connected to the emergence of men's new obsession with body image. Write an essay discussing whether this is true or not true. Support your perspective using examples from Cloud's article and your own experience.

Group Projects

8. Create and administer your own survey regarding the ideal male appearance. As a group, come up with a list of qualities—such as intelligence, body build, facial features, sense of humour, and physical strength—that can be ranked in order of importance. Try to come up with 8–12 qualities or characteristics. Distribute your poll among men and women on your campus (indicate whether the poll is given to a man or a woman). Tabulate the results and present your findings to the class. (For an interesting comparison, groups may also want to distribute a similar list of female characteristics and qualities.)

9. Have everyone in the group bring a copy of a men's magazine (*Details, GQ, Esquire*). Different group members may want to focus on different aspects of the magazines—such as advertising, articles, fashion, or advice columns. Do the models in the magazine fit the description in Cloud's article? What do the articles suggest men should aspire to look like? How many articles on improving appearance are featured? After reviewing the magazines, discuss your findings and collaborate on an essay about how men's fashion magazines help define the "ideal" male.

10. Working in small groups, arrange to visit your campus gym or local health club. Split up and take notes about what kinds of men you see working out there. What patterns of behaviour do you see—for example, are there more men working with weights than doing aerobics? Write brief descriptions of the men's workout attire. Do they seem concerned with how they look? Why or why not? After your visit, get together and compare notes. Write a report on your findings and present your conclusions to the class.

Brains, Brawn, and Beauty: A Place for Feminist Academics in Aesthetic Body Sports, or Working Towards a Physical Feminism

Carolyn Ives

Carolyn Ives has a B.A. and an M.A. in English from the University of Saskatchewan. Since 1994 she has taught at many institutions, including the University of Alberta, Edmonton; NAIT Edmonton; Thompson Rivers University in Kamloops, British Columbia; and, currently, Grant MacEwan College. Among her interests are gender studies, late medieval English and Scottish literature, professional and technical communication, and bodybuilding. In the following essay, she explores the challenges of women in a male-dominated sport and confronts the paradox of being an academic feminist involved in a sport some view as objectifying women.

1   Imagine that you are at a bodybuilding show. You watch as the tanned, oiled up athletes take the stage and then start their posing. For some reason, the bodybuilder who is third from the left strikes you as oddly familiar. Then it hits you: that bodybuilder is one of your university teachers!

Now, when I said "bodybuilder," you probably imagined a man—I'll bet you didn't imagine a woman. Herein lies a connection: while women fought so hard to be recognized as serious academics[1] in universities over the past several decades, so have they fought to be recognized as serious competitors in the physique sport arena. Add

Reprinted from *Forms of Writing: A Rhetoric, Handbook, and Reader*, Fifth Canadian Edition (2009), by permission of the author.

the fact that aesthetic physique sports[2] are marginalized even by the rest of the athletic world (there is no Olympic event, and even Arnold Schwarzenegger is trying to distance himself from his bodybuilding past), and female physique athletes are left trying to sort out where they fit in. It's no wonder that some women competitors use or even abuse steroids to try to appear more masculine—and then get breast implants to appear more feminine. Even more of a paradox is that both figure and fitness athletes are expected to wear glittery posing suits and stilettos on stage, traditionally feminine apparel, sometimes with sexual connotation, while sporting bodies that many would call masculine in their levels of muscularity.

Now, if that woman athlete is also an academic, the room for controversy may be even greater, as neither her colleagues nor her students will likely understand or respect her sport, perceiving her as being too overtly sexual, of being—ironically—anti-feminist. Somehow, disciplining the mind still is valued more highly than disciplining the body. It's no surprise, however, that women sometimes have to challenge social norms of what is considered "appropriate" in order to succeed, not just in academia, but in other arenas, also. This leaves me to question what place, if any, can exist for women, both in and out of universities, who wish to use their brains and brawn (and, depending on the physique sport, perhaps also their beauty, however problematic that may be) in an attempt to overcome barriers and dispel misconceptions.

Now, even before these competitors ever hit the stage, they must negotiate the arena that is the gym. There have been numerous studies and interviews that examine the place for women within the gym, but as Sassatelli explains that "the toned body has become a commercial icon" (228), she also argues that within the site of the gym, "a place which has its own rules and where a vast array of meanings and identities are negotiated" (229), the fit body represents "a conspicuous sign of personal worth" (244). However, in the experiences of many women weightlifters, that worth has been relegated to men only. Indeed, many men at my gym become resentful when we local women physique athletes use equipment that traditionally only men use, or when we lift as much as they do. In fact, Dworkin points out that "The proportion of men to women in the weight room at any given time is approximately 80/20 or 90/10" (132). She also discusses the women she's interviewed who "dare" to lift weights: "it is clear that there is a rejection of femininity when it is perceived as the equivalent of frailty or dependency.

Words such as "power," "strength," "independence," and even outright "rebellion" are often used to describe weightlifting" (144).

5   This sense of rebellion, however, pervades more than the gym: some women in physique sports sometime go to extremes to get noticed both on and off stage as well. Apparently confused about their identities, they scatter their energies in many directions: they want to be athletes, but often they resort to "adult" modeling to fund their sport. In fact, some well-known Canadian bodybuilders are even more famous for their porn sites. This misdirection creates difficulties for those competitors who hold professional positions and want to be taken seriously as athletes. The lines between body sport and body exploitation become blurred, but this line must be clearly drawn for women physique athletes in professional positions: for an academic, for example, there must be no suggestion of overt sexuality. I'll give you a personal example. Our local newspapers often feature local athletes from various sports. When our bodybuilders and figure competitors are preparing for competition, they often appear in the newspaper with explanations of their training schedule and details about the competition. For one such interview, the photographer asked us to put on our posing suits and lie across a car. His request wasn't completely unreasonable, as our posing suits are regulation competition attire, and the car was one from our sponsor, whom we wanted to publicly thank. Still, I could not bring myself to pose in a bikini in the local paper, nor could I lie across the hood of the sports car. Therefore, covered completely in my workout gear and sitting neatly on the car, I didn't look much like a physique competitor, but I worried less about what my colleagues and students would think.

    However, on the positive side, these same women who expose their bodies for fame and money outside of their sport are at the same time challenging societal expectations of femininity: they are muscular, and they are strong—traditionally masculine qualities. Still, they pose in rhinestoned bikinis and stilettos, and they often undergo breast implant surgery to appear more feminine, more physically balanced on stage and in photos. In fact, the sport of figure has been recently criticized as becoming a muscular beauty pageant, an accusation that damages the credibility of the sport and the sensibilities of the competitors who train for hours a day and follow strict diets all year in order to challenge and sculpt their bodies to be able to stand on stage with pride. In their search for a feminist theory of physical liberation, Roth and Basow explain that "the masculine ideal is one of physical strength, large size, and aggressiveness. The feminine ideal, on the other hand, is beautiful, small, thin, and perhaps most importantly, weak" (249). However, women who compete in physique sports combine the positive attributes of both the masculine and the feminine, potentially reconstructing a new, stronger feminine ideal, exactly what Roth and Basow want, but by allowing themselves to be reduced to sexual objects, these competitors and their bodies' feminine aspects become imminently exploitable. Since competing is costly, many of these women believe they have no choice. Also, since social norms dictate that a female body is a sexual body, for some it seems a reasonable compromise to allow that sexual objectification to justify their masculine physiques.

How, exactly, did women's bodybuilding get here, in this precarious and problematic position? Just as early feminists were, early women bodybuilders were pioneers, often enduring harassment and abuse from men at the gym. The main difference, as Jagger points out, is that while early feminists strove for equality of rights, physical bodies and physical strength never entered into the equation (qtd. in Roth and Basow 246). Women physique athletes strove to find their place in society, both in and out of the gym (Klein Ch. 7). They challenged social perceptions of femininity and built strong, muscular bodies—and in competition, they were judged on muscular size, shape, symmetry, and overall aesthetics, just as the men bodybuilders were. Over the decades, however, in order to win, those bodies had to become even bigger. This drove many to steroid abuse in order to achieve that. As the general public became less interested in these competitions, claiming that these new bodily constructions were "unnatural" and not attractive, a new physique competition gained popularity: figure. Figure athletes tend to be smaller, sometimes less genetically gifted in terms of muscle-building. Some women start with figure and work their way to bodybuilding as they develop more mass; others turn to figure when they are too injured for fitness or want a different look than that of the bodybuilders. Surprisingly, though, the main difference between figure and bodybuilding, however, isn't size, at least at the amateur level (at some novice competitions here in BC, there are women who compete in both categories)—the real difference is in presentation. While bodybuilders traditionally pose in plain suits and bare feet, figure athletes are required to wear stiletto heels, and they are judged not only on their physiques, but also on their overall presentation, including decorative suits, hair, and make-up. This competition has ballooned in numbers, as the average woman sees it as a more attainable look, and, most importantly, it's more socially acceptable for women to look like figure athletes than it is for them to look like bodybuilders. While women bodybuilders have the potential to be subversive within the male-dominated sport, figure athletes instead reinforce (not while working out in the gym, but while made up on stage) the social norms that prevent equality, both physical and otherwise.

The popularity of figure has made people within the sport question is validity, which is somewhat unfair, as many figure athletes train just as hard as bodybuilders, but it has also dramatically increased ticket sales. It's worth noting that since the inception of the figure competition, women body-builders have begun wearing prettier suits and paying more attention to their hair and make-up as well. Increasingly, the figure competitors have also become bigger, like the bodybuilders, raising concerns within the sport about steroid abuse, even to the point that in an unprecedented move, the International Federation of Bodybuilding (IFBB) announced in December 2004 that it wanted to see women physique athletes in all fields of competition come in approximately 20% smaller, starting the following year. Although this proclamation has since disappeared from the IFBB website as the site has been updated several times since then, it still exists on Wikipedia under "Female Bodybuilding"; furthermore, discussion about it remains on several bodybuilding discussion boards where it has been hotly debated. Some posters defended the move, arguing that the IFBB is only looking out for the best interests of those competitors who might abuse supplements and harm their health in order to win, while others complained that the move is clearly sexist, arguing there would have been total outrage if the IFBB had made the same proclamation for the men.

Whatever the reasons for the ruling, we saw evidence of its effects in the CBBF Canadian Fitness and Figure Nationals just this year (July 2007). Several of the class winners were smaller than many of the winners from previous years, and many spectators claimed to be surprised by some of the judges' choices. In a few figure classes, previous winners did not even place in the top five. Therefore, women are allowed to compete on the same stage as the men, but they aren't allowed to get "TOO big." The men, however, are praised for looking as big and freaky as they can. Only in the world of bodybuilding is the term

"Freak" a compliment, again challenging social perceptions of beauty. Shara Vigeant, an Alberta bodybuilder, argues that this inability to easily categorize women physique athletes is partially responsible for the general public's discomfort (Vigeant, para 3).

10   I suspect that the other part of the problem, perhaps even the main problem with the place for women in physique sports, is that while society has begrudgingly accepted that women are equal to men in terms of intellectual capability, at least in principle, society is not ready to accept the physical equality of women. People who are uncomfortable with women bodybuilders say they are unattractive because they look unnatural. It wasn't that long ago that women's voting was unnatural, that women working was unnatural, that women in the academy were unnatural. It's probably worth noting that this same cry for what's "natural" and "biologically right" is the root of homophobia and other types of discrimination, also. Social constructions of normalcy are keeping women from reaching their true potential in the gym, in much the same way it kept women out of the work force for decades, and then out of the academy, etc. In fact, I can't count the number of times when I have been training a woman who won't lift more than five pounds because she is afraid of getting too big, of looking too strong. Are we going to ever be prepared to accept physically strong women as natural? If the federations who govern aesthetic body sports can allow women to get past the beauty pageant element of the competitions, then perhaps women physique athletes will be able to carve out new identities for all women—so it will be okay for women to be smart and strong, and women academics won't have to be "closet" physique athletes for fear of losing professional respect. And a "strong woman" will be more than just a metaphor.

Works Cited

Dworkin, Shari L. "A Woman's Place is in the . . . Cardiovascular Room?? Gender Relations, the Body, and the Gym." *Athletic Intruders: Ethnographic Research on Women, Culture, and Exercise*. Ed. Anne Bolin and Jane Granskog. Albany, NY: SUNY, 2003. 131–158.

Klein, Alan M. "Sally's Corner: The Women of Olympic." *Little Big Men: Bodybuilding, Subculture, and Gender Construction*. Albany, NY: State UNY, 1993. 159–193.

Roth, Amanda and Susan A. Basow. "Femininity, Sports, and Feminism: Developing a Theory of Physical Liberation." *Journal of Sport and Social Issues*. 28.3 (2004): 245–265.

Sassatelli, Roberta. "Interaction Order and Beyond: A Field Analysis of Body Culture within Fitness Gyms." *Body Modification*. Ed. Mike Featherstone. London: Sage, 2000. 227–248.

Vigeant, Shara. "Female Bodybuilding." Alberta Bodybuilding. Retrieved October 7, 2006, from <http://www.albertabodybuilding.com/abffeature8. htm>.

End Notes

1. The term "academic" in this context refers to university teachers and researchers.

2. These include bodybuilding, fitness, and figure. Bodybuilding competitors may be men or women; competitors are judged on muscularity, leanness, symmetry, and posing. Fitness and figure competitions include only women in Canada (through the Canadian Bodybuilding Federation, or CBBF), although some organizations in the USA include male fitness competitors. Figure athletes are judged on physique and general appearance, but they do not have to be quite as large or as lean as the bodybuilders. Fitness athletes are also judged on physique, but they must also perform a fitness routine, which includes several strength and flexibility moves combined with dance and gymnastics.

Questions on Meaning

1. According to the author, what conditions exist in the gym that make it difficult for female weightlifters and physique athletes to fit in? How do these conceptions lead to blurred "lines between body sport and body exploitation" and compromise the health and well-being of these athletes?
2. Why does the sport of figure athletics not enjoy the same status as female bodybuilding? What does Ives mean when she says that figure athletes are engaged in a "search for a feminist theory of physical liberation"? What would such a theory realize for these women?
3. How does being a figure athlete herself compromise the author's professional and academic status, particularly given her identity as a feminist? Do you agree that in our society we value a disciplined mind more than a disciplined body? If so, why does this fact trouble female professional people more than male professionals?

Questions on Rhetorical Strategy and Style

1. Why does the author make certain to identify herself as a figure athlete as well as an academic professional? Identify the places in the essay where she brings her own identity into her account. Why might she appear somewhat reserved in expressing her personal views and experiences?
2. How would you characterize the tone of this essay? In what ways does the author present herself as a credible person? What evidence appeals to the emotions? To a sense of reason? How effective is her use of expert opinion?
3. In the last paragraph of the essay, Ives makes the connection between this form of discrimination and other forms. Why does she introduce this point and choose not to develop it?

Writing Assignments

1. While the situation Ives speaks of may not have changed significantly, one could argue that the conditions for female athletes have improved. Write an opinion essay describing the advances women in sports have made.

2. Write a commentary responding to the following statement from our selection: "Social constructions of normalcy are keeping women from reaching their true potential . . . ." In what ways has this statement proved true?

Gals and Dolls: The Moral Value of "Bad" Toys

Marni Jackson

Marni Jackson (1947–) currently lives in Toronto, where she writes a weekly column on reading and writing for The Globe and Mail *and co-hosts the TVO book program "Imprint." She also teaches creative writing at Ryerson Polytechnic University. Jackson has written for many magazines, including* Saturday Night *and* Toronto Life; *her magazine journalism has earned her many awards, including two National Magazine Awards for humor. She is the author of two books,* The Mother Zone: Love, Sex, and Laundry in the Modern Family *(1992) and* Pain: The Fifth Vital Sign *(2002). In addition to her journalism, Jackson has also collaborated on theatrical productions with the Clichettes.* She Devils of Niagara *and* Half Human, Half Heartache *have appeared in theaters in Toronto and across Canada. In the following essay, Jackson takes a humorous look at gender-specific toys such as Barbie, arguing that perhaps these toys are not quite as dangerous as some think they are.*

1   In the days before I actually had a child, child-rearing was a clearcut proposition: simply Raise Them Right. Minimal TV, no hooker-type dolls or plastic Uzis, and a constant flow of high-fibre ideas from the morally evolved parent to the vulnerable, blank-slate child. I felt sorry for parents who didn't have the gumption to stick to this plan. Then I had a son, and the rest is—well, not so much history as culture.

Not since the days of Spock have we had so much parental advice in the air—how to raise kids, how to ruin them, how to "juggle work and family." This is why it's so refreshing to read someone like Alice Miller, the psychoanalyst-turned-writer whose books explore the childhood roots of violence and creativity. She doesn't have a theory about raising kids. In fact, she argues that *any* system of moral values imposed on children is potentially damaging, because too often the rules are there to serve the emotional needs of the parents, not the children. In the name of morality, we try to keep the unruly passions of children—not to mention memories of our own childhood—safe, tidy, and under control. Most pedagogy, good or bad, sends a hidden message to the child: "Your desires and feelings are not good enough. Feel this, think that, instead." If children require so much correction, then deep down—so they reason—they must be bad. Sooner or later the child who only hears this message learns to assemble an other-pleasing, false self around a core of inexplicable shame.

This doesn't mean that Miller thinks children ought to fingerpaint with their food and otherwise disport themselves as gods. Post-Spockian permissiveness is just another form of pedagogy, really. But the experience of her own patients convinced her that it was the ones who were raised rigidly, with an overabundance of "good values," who were most likely to grow into benumbed adults, lost to themselves and predisposed to violence. The violence erupts in response to long-stifled childhood anger, which began as a perfectly human response to a voice that said "Don't be who you are, be good." The moral here—if we dare draw one—is that excessive handwringing about the values we are giving our kids may be as much about peer vanity as anything else. Values are not external; they are intrinsic to the sort of relationship we have with our children, arising out of the ordinary, humdrum way a family works and plays. The boy or girl who receives fair treatment, as opposed to "moral" correction, quickly develops an exquisite sense of justice—one that is more likely to shame the parent, rather than the other way round. (I'm moralizing here, of course.) Even young children bring a surprising amount of savvy and shit-detection to the moral bargaining table. To assume otherwise is to inflate our roles as parents into the architects and owners of our children's souls.

Now, Miller was talking about some fairly rigid, loveless households—Hitler's and Goebbels', for instance. She wasn't necessarily addressing the problem of whether or not to buy your son a Nintendo, or to give your niece a Wet 'n' Wild Barbie. Nevertheless, I detect a lot of dubious pedagogy in our much-cogitated attitudes towards "good" and "bad" toys.

I know what happened with toy guns in our household. I went from a serene pre-child conviction that guns would never cross our threshold to the ridiculous but amiable compromise my seven-year-old son and I have reached. Childish logic is impeccable. If you give him an innocent green water pistol for the bathtub, then why not the hideous toy M-16 in the backyard? If he can brandish a popsicle stick, why not a space laser? So he now owns a bow and arrow and a non-combat rawhide whip (history? art?), but he knows I have a "thing" about realistic guns, so he doesn't ask for them. He watches plenty of TV (all right, too much), but after flat-out indoctrination on my part—moral interference in the name of what I can or cannot stand to over-hear—he now flips past the more violent kids' shows, of his own volition. Of course, our definitions of "violent" are continually being refined. But he's kind by nature, and always has been. I try not to improve on that too much.

There was a time, not so long ago, that Barbie dolls were considered the worst sort of sex-stereotype propaganda. Barbie, with her foot permanently arched in the shape of a high heel, her long, scissoring legs, her high, hard, de-nippled breasts. It's true she's unswervingly represented a career gadfly, a weak-chinned Caucasian princess and a fashion flibbertigibbet—11 1/2 inches of beige plastic that has been accused of encouraging eating disorders, mindless consumerism and low self-esteem in little girls. Small wonder that to the Birkenstock generation, Barbie was bad.

But little girls are not pushovers. They know what they like and they like Barbie. Now 31 years old (but ever ageless and firm of chin), Barbie has triumphed over pedagogy, to the tune of over $500-million annually. Last year was the biggest year for Barbie sales in history. Some 98 percent of Canadian girls aged four to ten have a Barbie—or four—in their bedrooms. Like Coca-Cola, she has insinuated her hourglass, bottle-shaped self into 67 countries around the world. None of this will surprise parents with daughters, but it was news to me.

I went into several department stores to get a blast of Barbie, a feel for Barbie, and there she was—row upon row of her and her almost identical pals, including li'l sister Skipper, brown-skinned Christie, freckle-faced sporty Midge, Hispanic Nia, red-haired vixen Ashley. Her countless outfits run the gamut from the tiny tubes of her pantyhose to wild salsa dresses, purses that turn into skirts and skirts that turn into hair bows. Her eminently loseable accessories include teacups, toe paint, Ferraris, guitars and running shoes.

After twenty years of feminism, you may ask, why don't little boys play with Barbies? What *is* it about girls and dolls, anyway? Boys play with He-men and Ninja turtle figures but the marriage between girls and their Barbies seems more enduring. Girls' sense of pink and blueness also seems more acute, more precocious, although I base this only on the fact that I bought my son some plain but *purplish* boots last year. They didn't bother him until he came home from school one day and announced he couldn't wear them because they were "girls' boots." Who had decreed this? "The girls in my room."

10 Are girls more proprietorial about identifiable girl things because 10 they've already detected an imbalance in the adult world, between boy toys (tanks and guns) and female fun? Or is it something simpler— that at a certain age, children want some kind of sex identity. Just because adults have bequeathed them a culture that offers only testosterone-poisoned orange He-men and anorexic beige Barbies, must we insist on snuffing out any sign of gender?

An eight-year-old girl in the neighborhood lugged over her five Barbies, in two pink vehicles, for my inspection. While twirling and braiding the long blonde tresses on one of them, she explained that although she doesn't want to *be* Barbie, she really likes to play with her. "We make up stories that are like real life and then we make the Barbies act them out," she said with admirable succinctness. "Her body isn't very realistic," she admits, pointing the ballistic bosom of one towards me. "In fact, the only realistic thing about it is her ears." If she were designing them, she would go for more variation. "Like, it would be neat to have a tattooed Barbie, or one with a bigger head. Her head is too small for her body." And Ken's definitely in a rut. "I wouldn't mind a bald Ken, for example."

The sad truth is, Barbie has left the bland, rug-haired Ken behind in a spangled cloud of dust. Ken sales only amount to 35 percent of their combined total—and in fact, his shelf presence suggests more like a ratio of ten Barbies to one Ken. Ken is looking more and more like a rented gigolo, or the guy who takes Barbie's outfits to the cleaners and back. His accessories are laughable (a slice of pizza, a kite, a basketball) and his weekend outfits are a bore (blue pin-striped smock and navy pants). The only thing you can do with him, apart from suicidal dives off the couch, is change his hair color from a terrible fecal-mustard color to an obviously touched-up brown. While Barbie has a choice of five stylish wedding gowns, Ken's lone wedding tuxedo is deplorable, a nylon unitard with an ill-fitting white jacket and a shiny bow tie. His loafers are interchangeable little boats. No wonder Barbie seems to prefer the company of her on-the-go girlfriends.

When I saw Ken strapped stiffly into the passenger seat of Barbie's huge new pink RV trailer, with plates that say "Barbie," I felt a stab of compassion for him. As I was gazing at this harsh spectacle, a couple wandered down the aisle. "Oh there's Ken," said the woman. "We were always so mean to Ken with our Barbies, we used to do terrible things to him. I don't know why." Laughing, they moved down the aisle to inspect a Baby Uh-Oh ("Give her a drink and uh-oh! . . . time to change her diaper!").

However retrograde she appears to be, I sense Barbie is a survivor. Her maddeningly firm little bosom and fashion-victim personality, her fickle careers are all voodoo tricks to ward off parental approval. If we had given Barbie a social conscience and sensible shoes, she might have moldered away at the bottom of the toy bin. As it is, girls play with their uneducational Barbies as they always have, playing out the "mean babysitter" scenario, madly acting away, with no parent-pleasing values to inhibit their stories. Therapists may envy the Barbie blankness—she too can create a private, privileged space where any and every feeling is permitted. May Barbie be "bad" as long as she reigns, for it is her lack of redeeming social value that helps keep her true to the child's sense of play, instead of the parents' worst fears.

Questions on Meaning

1. What does Jackson mean when she distinguishes between "external" values and those values that are "intrinsic to the sort of relationship we have with our children" (paragraph 3)? Why does she believe that it is intrinsic values that shape children's characters?

2. What reasons does Jackson offer for children's preferences for gender-specific toys and clothing? Why do you think that children gravitate toward such items despite parental influences?

3. Why, according to Jackson, are Ken dolls so much less popular than Barbie and her female friends? What do these sales figures say about girls' preferences?

Questions on Strategy and Style

1. What is the effect on children, according to Jackson's source Alice Miller, of imposing moral values on children? What does Miller say are the true childhood causes of adult behavior?

2. Jackson offers several examples of children's responses to gender-specific toys. Choose one of those examples and explain how it supports her position regarding these "bad toys."

3. Jackson's analysis of girls' loyalty to Barbie leads her to take a position regarding such gender-specific toys. What is that position? To what extent do you think her analysis supports that position?

Writing Assignments

1. Write a paper analyzing your own moral upbringing. What moral values did your parents try to instill in you? As an adult, how do you feel those moral values have affected your character? To what extent did family relationships, rather than imposed values, contribute to your character?

2. Think of toys that were popular during your own childhood. Did parents consider those toys bad or good? To what extent did your (and your playmates') responses to those toys depend on your parents' attitudes? To what extent did those toys influence your development? Write an essay describing your experience with these toys.

3. Research sociological and psychological analyses of the Barbie phenomenon, and write an essay analyzing the various interpretations of Barbie's popularity and her influence on girls' development.

Man Trouble

Andre Mayer

Andre Mayer is a Toronto-based writer whose work has appeared in Toronto Life, The Globe and Mail, Report on Business Magazine and eye Weekly. As yet, he has no books to plug.

As a blissfully married and, I like to think, reasonably well-adjusted man, I must own up to a certain obliviousness to the so-called struggles of my gender. I appreciate that there are men who feel aggrieved. I sympathize, but I can't relate.

In fact, the only thing more astonishing than the notion of disgruntled masculinity is any discussion of gender at all. Maybe I'm living in a post-feminist utopia, but I don't know many people who identify themselves by their sex (except when looking for a public washroom).

Which is why it's so startling to open a book like What Makes a Man: 22 Writers Imagine the Future, a just-published collection of essays edited by American author and social activist Rebecca Walker. In it, she and other scribes explore the enormous and, in some cases, untenable expectations placed on modern men. In the leadoff piece, Walker recounts the day her 11-year-old son came home from school convinced that "girls will like me if I play sports." What I see as an innocent remark, Walker views with utter gravitas—momentous enough to inspire a book. She sees her son's realization as symptomatic of society's disposition. Men must repress their gentler impulses in order to take up arms against each other in an unrelenting fight for dominance, a cut-throat competition that begins with school athletics and begets the narcissistic quest for the best cheekbones, the best job and the most money, and reaches its apex on the geopolitical scale with the most fearsome military. "This war against what is considered feminine that is wounding our sons and brothers, fathers and uncles, is familiar to women," Walker writes, "but now we see that it is killing the other half of the planet, too. But instead of dying of heartache and botched abortions and breast cancer and sexual trauma and low self-esteem, this half is dying of radiation from modern weaponry, suicidal depression, and a soul-killing obsession with the material."

Walker is not alone in her anxiety. Her book is merely the latest chapter in a growing literature beset by the waning status of men. Author Susan Faludi may have galvanized the issue in 2000 with her fulsome bestseller Stiffed: The Betrayal of the American Man. She attributed the decline of men's self-worth to the shrinking military of the postwar era and the rampant downsizing in corporate America, as well as the rise of feminism. The fact that men feel diminished has led to proportionately higher secondary school dropout rates and lower university enrollment rates compared with women.

5   These are relatively new developments, but San Diego-based   5
author Warren Farrell believes the devaluation of men is more entrenched. He likes to remind readers that in the military, a man is more likely to die in war than his female counterpart, and that prostate cancer, one of the worst killers of men, gets much less funding than breast cancer, a predominantly female affliction.

Farrell is widely thought to have fathered the men's movement; his 1974 book The Liberated Man is the masculine corollary to The Feminine Mystique. A feminist during the rights movement of the 1960s, Farrell changed his ideological orientation in the '70s to examine the unspoken plight of men. In his 1993 book The Myth of Male Power, Farrell outlined the 25 worst professions based on a combination of salary, stress, work environment, outlook, security and physical demands. He called the results—which included cross-country truck driver, sheet-metal worker and construction worker—the "death professions." He found that of these 25 jobs, 24 of them were 95 to 100 percent male. Where feminists speak of a glass ceiling, Farrell talks of a glass cellar. "In the industrialized world, there has never been a time when men have been so unappreciated," says Farrell. "For about 30 years, it hasn't really been a battle of the sexes, but a war in which only one side has shown up. And women have been shooting the bullets and men have been putting their heads in the sand hoping the bullets will miss."

Farrell has an affinity for pat analogies, and not everyone buys his reasoning. "Men have and still hold the power—political, economic, cultural—in every way. They own the property, they control the businesses," says Kay Armatage, an associate professor of women's studies at the University of Toronto. "So the notion of discrimination against men is ridiculous, as far as I'm concerned. However, you can argue that they pay a certain price for their power, for their ownership, for their domination." Sending young males to war isn't discriminatory, Armatage contends; combat is an activity men have always initiated and engaged in.

Whatever the reasons, there is evidence of a deep dissatisfaction among men. It's generally accepted, for example, that men commit 80 percent of the suicides in Canada. The standard explanation is that men don't like to talk about their feelings; if pushed to the emotional brink, they would sooner die by their own hand than reach out for someone else's. (That said, a 1999 research study by Health Canada noted that "while men commit suicide more frequently, women attempt suicide more often but are more likely to fail in their attempts.") The notion of men and their inscrutable emotions is a favourite subject of female advice columnists, but as the stats demonstrate, the cliché holds more than a whisper of truth.

Alan Mirabelli, executive director of the Vanier Institute of the Family, feels that more and more men are opting to talk it out. "[They have] realized that to bottle it up and carry the stress leads to a direct line to Prozac or the psychiatrist's couch. And that's not the way they want to live their lives. They want to find a way to enjoy life, and if that means being vulnerable to some extent but not carrying that stress, so be it." It's not a perspective all men share. The model is still the strong dominant male. Although there are more "sensitive males," their liberalism is continually challenged by our culture—most often by advertisers, who ridicule men for weakness or indecision.

10 "Men get a conflicting message," Mirabelli says. "On the one 10 hand, women want them to be gentle, but at the same time, they want them to be strong. Which is it? Or is there room for both?"

The reality is that both sexes grapple with conflicting cues. "Simone de Beauvoir said, 'Women are not born, they're made,'" Armatage submits. "In exactly the same way, men aren't born, they're made. Obviously, those gender constructions for men and women are equally forceful, although in different directions." One thing both sides agree on is that as a society, we default to outmoded stereotypes, that women are gentle and nurturing but also self-doubting and needy, and men are strong and protective but prone to infidelity and violence.

If you want to experience the frontier of male disaffection, spend a Tuesday evening with the FACT group. The advocacy organization Fathers Are Capable, Too agitates for equal shared parenting time, and each week it convenes a support group in the basement of All Saints' Kingsway Anglican Church in Toronto's west end. The room is garlanded with bunny paintings and alphabet charts; a Little Tikes climbing apparatus sits at the front of the room. During the day, it's a childcare facility; Tuesday nights, it becomes a soapbox for collective rancour toward the family courts.

The dozen or so men—and one woman—assembled on this night sit facing David Osterman and Gene Colosimo, the FACT directors who typically lead the meetings. The faces are long and worn with misery; these are people whose existence is no longer defined by their career accomplishments or even their families. The measure of these men is how long they've been in court. One man, Terry Lear, has spent 17 years in litigation—so far.

The meeting begins when a newbie floats a candid question. "I need an honest opinion on what chance I've got if I go to court," says the tall, gangly fellow, who looks to be in his late 20s. Embittered chuckles ensue. The man is separated from his wife, with whom he has an eight-month-old son. FACT's position on the justice system is firm: judges inexorably grant custody to women, and lawyers exist merely to draw out the proceedings and pocket the exorbitant fees. The organization lobbies various levels of government to rectify this perceived injustice but, for the most part, all FACT members can do is console one another. FACT's message can be distilled in two words: make do. Osterman encourages him to attempt a reconciliation with his wife rather than proceed to litigation.

15 The young guy is skeptical. Right now, he gets to see his son for 15 only two hours a week, in his wife's apartment, under her supervision. "You will get as much access as she allows you," quips Colosimo, who has no patience for platitudes. "You're the hostage, she has a gun, and you're trying to work out a deal." Over the course of the evening, Colosimo will dispense a litany of caustic refrains, many of which are imbued with a subtle misogyny. "Love is grand, but divorce is 100 grand," he says, simpering. You can tell he's used that one before; it

elicits knowing laughter. His repertoire also includes "She got the goldmine, he got the shaft" and "It's cheaper to keep her."

An outsider might find Colosimo insufferably mordant, but his cynicism is earned. He separated from his wife in 1991, and the custody battle over their daughter cost him $80,000; his wife spent as much as $160,000. He kept up the child-support payments for a while, but his ex-spouse wouldn't allow him access to their daughter. After two years, Colosimo stopped paying. In doing so, he became a deadbeat dad, but he felt he couldn't sustain the arrangement. He hasn't seen his daughter in 10 years, which is about as long as he's been out of work. The lawyer's fees and support payments had reduced him to penury, and the mental strain had driven him to severe depression. Three therapists told him he was unfit to work; he quit his job in appliance repair in 1993.

Colosimo puts on a doughty bravado in the meetings, but his wounded humanity comes out in the poems he has written about his estrangement from his daughter, who is now in her teens. "Divorce was quite a revelation/Not just a split but devastation," he declaims in the church parking lot after the meeting. "They took my child, my joy, my soul/ And left my life a gaping hole." As he recites these lines, his gaze is almost pleading. Of all the issues plaguing the male sex, the perceived discrimination in child-custody battles remains the most damaging. In 1988, mothers won sole custody of their children in 75 percent of divorce proceedings; this past May, the federal Department of Justice reported that, for the first time, less than 50 percent of custody cases went directly to women. Most judgments opted for joint custody. This would appear to be an improvement, but FACT director Brian Jenkins says it's misleading. The concept of joint custody is actually broken down into separate categories: "joint physical custody" and "joint custody with primary residency." The former is a total sharing of responsibility, the latter means that although the parents make major decisions together, the child spends most of his or her time living with one parent. According to Jenkins, the parent who provides primary residency tends to hold sway; in most cases, it's still the woman.

"Men who lose their connection to children lose their connection to society," Osterman notes. As Colosimo likes to remind FACT members, eight men commit suicide in Canada every day. The likelihood of suicide rises considerably among divorced men. According to 1995 Statistics Canada figures, the national suicide rate among divorced men was 42.5 per 100,000, four times the overall men's rate. The ideology of family courts can be debated endlessly, but the fact remains that a distressing number of men find divorce so financially and emotionally taxing that they consider death their only recourse.

The blinkered stereotypes that complicate child-custody battles are also perpetuated in mass culture. Look no further than Homer Simpson. Crude, insensitive, moronic and quite possibly the worst father in television history, he's the icon of male inadequacy.

20 Two Canadian researchers, Paul Nathanson and Katherine 20
Young, found enough instances of misandry—a more refined word for male-bashing—in television, film, comic strips and books to write a fairly thick tome. Published in 2001, Spreading Misandry: The Teaching of Contempt for Men in Popular Culture delineates stereotyping throughout the 1990s. Nathanson and Young take aim at movies like Sleeping With the Enemy, The Color Purple and The Hand That Rocks the Cradle for portraying men as either violent reprobates, hopeless patsies or women in a male guise.

"The people who make these movies aren't necessarily trying to make that point, and the people who consume these products aren't necessarily conscious of it," says Nathanson. "You come out of a movie and you either like or you don't like it. But very few people think, 'Well, what does that say about me?' That takes a level of conscious reflection that a lot of people don't have. Some women have it, because they've been trained for 30 years to look for misogynistic elements. But for men, at least in the 1990s, it was a little harder to do that."

One of their targets is the forgettable sitcom Home Improvement. In it, actor Tim Allen played Tim "The Tool Man" Taylor, a sheepish joe who wielded tools at work and simply acted like one at home. Alternately macho and dim-witted, Tim continually shot off his mouth, only to be summarily scolded by his wife, Jill (played by Patricia Richardson). The spate of daytime talk shows also reinforced our worst fears about men. Whether it was Oprah, Geraldo, Sally Jesse Raphael or Montel, topics like domestic violence and male perfidy were recurring themes.

According to Nathanson and Young, misandry was first promoted in political and academic circles to redress a history of female oppression. Eventually it radiated out into the wider culture. Nathanson says the cumulative effect of these stereotypes is that they warp men's sense of who they are. "If you don't provide boys with a positive identity, then they're going to embrace the negative one," he says.

Ironically, amid the flurry of unwitting male stereotypes, our culture began to reclaim many of them. If some men were feeling ill at ease about their collective image, the Maxim-ization of pop culture did them no favours. Thanks to the outbreak of lad mags, increasingly loutish pop stars (Oasis, Kid Rock, countless rappers), crass television series like Beavis and Butt-head, guy-oriented talk-radio stations (Toronto's MOJO) and even whole television networks dedicated to men's programming (Spike TV), it's become all right—downright amusing, in fact—to be boorish, hedonistic and blatantly sexist, all those qualities glibly associated with the male id.

25 David Shackleton produces a lad mag, of sorts—he's the editor and 25 publisher of Everyman, a quarterly journal devoted to men's issues. What you won't find in its pages, however, are airbrushed pictures of bosomy supermodels, tips on building adamantine abs or how to uncouple a bra with one hand. With its low-budget paper stock, black-and-white appearance and humourless, didactic tone, Everyman is not for every man. It's a zine for disillusioned males, dealing with topics like divorce and family law. The periodical has a circulation of 500 copies, which Shackleton prints in his Ottawa home.

He became involved in the magazine in 1994—eventually taking it over from co-founder Andrew McDonald—after a shocking personal revelation. In 1987, Shackleton's first wife left him. He concedes that the split was upsetting but inevitable. It was her methodology, however, that truly rankled him. Instead of laying out the reasons in person, she left the house with their dog—under the pretence of seeing the veterinarian—and then called to tell him she wanted a divorce. When he asked her why she had chosen to break up in such an impersonal manner, she said she feared he might get violent.

Having never exhibited an aggressive tendency, Shackleton was stunned that his wife of seven years had so profoundly misunderstood him. The more disturbing inference, however, was that all men have a propensity for brutality.

"Up until then, I'd been kind of living out the cultural script of, you know, career success, et cetera. I started to look around at the stereotype that men are violent. And what I saw was that the whole gender story that was in play in society was the story of female victimhood, and it didn't ring true to me," he says. "I felt that there was a whole piece missing." Shackleton believed that any discussion of how men were feeling was viewed as either anti-feminist or simply petty. "I got a sense why we were so caught up in women's experience about gender and why we're silent and unresponsive to men's stories. I found myself steering my life more and more into that work."

In 1993, Shackleton quit a well-paying engineering job at Nortel Networks to devote himself to the male cause. "I decided the world didn't need more technical products," he says. "What we needed was some more social insight." Shackleton, who has remarried twice, divides his time between publishing Everyman, hosting gender workshops and doing speaking engagements. (Male advocacy is not a lucrative field, so Shackleton supplements his income with desktop publishing and technical consulting of the sort he did at Nortel.) One of his recent speeches was at Stories of Healing, a two-day conference this past June organized by the Men's Network and Kitchener-Waterloo Counselling Services. Held in the auditorium of a Waterloo, Ontario, community centre, the annual assembly is a forum for abused and otherwise beleaguered males, as well as counsellors, to share tales of personal renewal.

30 On the morning of the second day, Shackleton stood before a 30 still-somnolent crowd and narrated his story. A tall fellow with a close-cropped white beard, Shackleton has a muted intonation; although he's thoughtful and articulate, his voice will occasionally become tremulous. Outlining his points on an overhead projector, Shackleton explained that his investigation of gender roles has led him to one overriding theory. He doesn't deny that historically, women have been victims of male tyranny, but he says that men and women actually have a mutually oppressive relationship. Men subjugate women with physical, economic and political power; women, on the other hand, subjugate men with sexual, emotional and moral power. Shackleton's belief: for all of men's overbearing qualities, women have the power to shame. You could sense a collective tension in the room. People stiffened in their plastic chairs. Shackleton is quite used to offending people, and he took the acute silence in stride. Even so, when it came time for questions, he gazed around the room with nervous anticipation. One man stood up to

69

the microphone and extolled Shackleton's wisdom and courage. The majority of participants, however, took issue with his essential point. Another male counsellor approached the microphone and said, "Among my friends in their 20s, 30s and 40s, I don't know anyone who thinks that way." Shackleton smiled uneasily and mumbled something about welcoming differing opinions. Event organizer Randy Scott ended the discussion on a cheerfully contrite note, thanking Shackleton for his time but offering nothing in the way of an endorsement.

I could appreciate the heartbreak that inspired Shackleton's rhetoric, but his conclusions seemed misguided. I found it difficult to liken shaming to physical abuse in terms of severity. Perhaps the most awkward thing about Shackleton's speech was that it dispensed fault at an event honouring personal triumph. "I was really hoping we'd moved past that sort of thinking," muttered one participant when I asked her about the presentation. "We don't need any more assigning of blame." I have to concur. If men are feeling plagued by negative stereotypes, reacting with equally hoary female stereotypes seems, at the very least, counterproductive.

If you ask Warren Farrell, a battle-hardened women's and men's libber, he'll tell you the way forward is to take a more mature approach. "We've had a women's movement blaming men, when what we should have had is neither a women's movement blaming men nor a men's movement blaming women. We should have been having a gender transition movement moving from the old, rigid roles that were survival-based to new, more flexible roles." That ultimately means unlearning the gender myths, particularly the fiction that men can't articulate their feelings. For too long, they've been told, and dumbly accepted, that they're incapable of doing so. For men and women, the key to transcending this ridiculous drama is to play against type.

Media

On Sale at Old Navy: Cool Clothes for Identical Zombies!

Damien Cave

Mass-market retail stores like Old Navy, Gap, Pottery Barn, and Ikea have enjoyed enormous popularity in recent years. Part of their appeal is that they market the concept of "cool." But are these stores just marketing conformity under the guise of "cool"? Are they crushing our individuality? Are we moving rapidly to the day where we will all dress the same way, own the same furniture, and want the same things? Writer and Phillips Foundation fellow Damien Cave thinks so. This article first appeared in the November 22, 2000, issue of the e-zine Salon.

1 Thomas Frank walks by the candy-cane-adorned displays of Old Navy, passing the sign exclaiming "priced so low, you can't say no," and into the chain's San Francisco flagship store. The all-devouring Christmas rush hasn't started yet, but it's clear from the frown on Frank's face that he's not being seduced by the cheap but stylish clothes, the swirling neon and the bass-heavy hip-hop pounding in his ears.

"Oh God, this is disgusting," Frank says. This reaction isn't surprising. The bespectacled Midwesterner is a pioneering social critic—one of the first writers to document how, starting in the '60s, American businesses have co-opted cool anti-corporate culture and used it to seduce the masses. His arguments in the *Baffler*, a pugnacious review Frank founded in 1988, and in 1997's "The Conquest of Cool" read like sermons, angry wake-up calls for consumers who hungrily ingest hipper-than-thou ("Think Different") marketing campaigns without ever questioning their intent.

Old Navy and other cheap but tasteful retailers provide perfect fodder for Frank's critique. Their low prices and hip-but-wholesome branding strategy are supposed to present a healthy alternative to the conspicuous consumption of a Calvin Klein. But critics like Frank and Naomi Klein, author of "No Logo," argue that the formula is really nothing more than the wolf of materialism wrapped in cheaper sheep's clothing.

Consumers are being scammed, says Klein, arguing that stores like Old Navy and Ikea are duping millions, inspiring mass conformity while pretending to deliver high culture to the masses. "It's this whole idea of creating a carnival for the most homogeneous fashions and furniture," says Klein. "It's mass cloning that's being masked in a carnival of diversity. You don't notice that you're conforming because everything is so colorful."

5   Klein and Frank say that few consumers recognize just how conformist their consumption habits have become. And certainly, it's hard to argue that Ikea's and Old Navy's items haven't become icons of urbanite and suburbanite imagination. Watch MTV, or rent "Fight Club," to see Ikea's candy-colored décor, then truck down to your local Old Navy flagship store. When you arrive, what you'll find is that hordes of people have beaten you there. At virtually every opening of Old Navy's and Ikea's stores—in the New York, Chicago and San Francisco areas, for example—tens of thousands of people appeared in the first few days. Even now, long after the stores first opened, lines remain long.

What's wrong with these people? Nothing, say defenders of the companies. The popularity of brands like Ikea and Old Navy, they argue, derives from the retailers' ability to offer good stuff cheap. "They provide remarkable value," says Joel Reichart, a professor at the Fordham School of Business who has written case studies on Ikea. "They're truly satisfying people's needs."

Despite his irritation with the way companies like Old Navy market themselves, Frank acknowledges that businesses have always sought to offer cheap, relatively high-quality merchandise and concedes that there is some value in their attempts. He even admits that consumerism is good for the economy.

But he and other critics argue that in the end we're only being conned into thinking that our needs are being satisfied. What's really happening, they argue, is that clever marketers are turning us into automatons who equate being cool with buying cheap stuff that everyone else has. Under the stores' guise of delivering good taste to the general public, any chance we have at experiencing or creating authenticity is being undermined. Ultimately, our brave new shopping world is one in which we are spending more time in the checkout line than reading books, watching movies or otherwise challenging ourselves with real culture.

"Shopping is a way of putting together your identity," laments "Nobrow" author John Seabrook. And the "homogenized taste" of today's Old Navy and Ikea shoppers proves, he says, that Americans either are consciously choosing to look and live alike or are determined not to notice that that is what they're doing.

10   According to Christine Rosen, a professor in the Haas School of Business at UC-Berkeley, people who fill their closets, homes and lives with Old Navy and Ikea—or Pottery Barn or a host of other slick stores—are simply new examples of the trend toward conformity that started when the first "brands"

appeared in the 1910s and '20s. "We're Pavlovianly trained to respond to this," she says.

And we're also just too damn lazy. That's the theory floated by Packard Jennings, an anti-consumerism activist who says that stores like Old Navy are designed to numb the brain and remove all semblance of creativity from the purchasing process. "Ikea pre-arranges sets of furniture in its stores, thereby lessening individual thought," he says. Once people are in the store, they can't resist. "Entire households are purchased at Ikea," he says.

Indeed, Janice Simonsen, an Ikea spokeswoman, confirmed that a large part of the chain's demographic consists of "people who come in and say, 'I need everything.'" Meanwhile, those who don't want everything usually end up with more than they need, says Fordham's Reichart. "The way they design their stores"—with an up escalator to the showroom and no exit until the checkout—"you end up going through the entire store," he says.

Old Navy plays by the same sneaky rules. When Frank and I entered the San Francisco store, clerks offered us giant mesh bags. Ostensibly, this is just good service, but since the bags are capable of holding at least half a dozen pairs of jeans and a few shirts, it's obvious that they're also meant to encourage overconsumption.

Frank called the bags "gross" but not out of line with other state-of-the-art retailing practices. But according to Klein, the sacks, in conjunction with Old Navy's penchant for displaying T-shirts in mock-1950s supermarket coolers, prove that the company is aiming to do something more. The idea behind this "theater for the brand" architecture is to commodify the products, to make them "as easy to buy as a gallon of milk," Klein says. "The idea is to create a Mecca where people make pilgrimages to their brand," Klein says. "You experience the identity of the brand and not the product."

Disney, which opened its first store in 1987, was the first to employ this strategy. And since then others have appeared. Niketown, the Body Shop, the Discovery Store—they all aim to sell products by selling a destination.

Old Navy and Ikea, however, are far more popular than those predecessors—and, if you believe the more pessimistic of their critics, more dangerous. Not only are the two chains remaking many closets and homes into one designer showcase, says Klein, but they are also lulling consumers to sleep and encouraging them to overlook some important issues.

Such as quality. People think they're getting "authenticity on the cheap," says David Lewis, author of "The Soul of the New Consumer." But the truth may be that they're simply purchasing the perception of quality and authenticity. "Because [Ikea and Old Navy] create these self-enclosed lifestyles," Klein explains, "you overlook the fact that the products are pretty crappy and fall apart." Adds Jennings, "Things may be cheaper, but you keep going back to replace the faulty merchandise."

Then there is the trap of materialism. Survey after survey suggests that people who place a high value on material goods are less happy than those who do not, says Eric Rindfleisch, a marketing professor at the University of Arizona. The focus on bargains, incremental purchases and commodification plays to a uniquely American blind spot.

"We operate with a duality," explains Rindfleisch, who has conducted studies linking materialism with depression. "Americans know that money doesn't buy happiness, but most people somehow believe that increments in pay or goods will improve our lives. It's a human weakness—particularly in America."

20   The most insidious danger may be more abstract. The anti-consumerism   20 critics argue that by elevating shopping to cultural status, we are losing our grip on real culture. We live in a time where college kids think nothing of decorating their rooms with Absolut vodka ads and fail to realize that they're essentially turning their rooms into billboards. Meanwhile, museum stores keep getting larger, Starbucks sells branded CDs to go with your coffee and because Ikea and other stores now look like movie theaters or theme parks, we don't just shop, "we make a day of it," as Klein puts it.

This only helps steer us away from other endeavors. When people spend so much time buying, thinking and talking about products, they don't have time for anything else, for real conversations about politics or culture or for real interaction with people.

Ultimately, the popularity of Old Navy, Ikea and their ilk proves that we're stuck in what Harvard professor Juliet Schor calls "the cycle of work and spend." Breaking that cycle may not be easy, but if one believes critics like Frank, it's essential if we are to control our own culture, instead of allowing it to be defined by corporations.

The cycle may not be possible to break. Frank, for one, is extremely pessimistic about our chances for turning back the tide of conformity and co-opted cool. Maybe that's one reason why he wanted to get out of Old Navy as fast as he could.

But I'm not so sure. When "Ikea boy," Edward Norton's character in "Fight Club," watched his apartment and his Swedish furniture explode in a blaze of glory, I wasn't the only one in the theater who cheered. ◆

Critical Thinking

1.   In paragraph 2, Cave notes that American businesses have "co-opted cool anti-corporate culture." What does he mean? What is "anti-corporate" culture, and why is it "cool"? What started it, and how are businesses using it to their advantage? In what ways is this ironic? Before responding, read "The Rebel Sell" [p. 130]. Are Cave's assertions supported by the theoretical framework provded by Heath and Potter?

2. In paragraph 20, Cave observes that "college kids think nothing of decorating their rooms with Absolut vodka ads and fail to realize that they're essentially turning their rooms into billboards." What decorating choices have you made to your personal space? In what ways has your decorating style been influenced by outside forms of advertising? Explain.

3. What techniques do mass-market stores employ to squeeze the maximum profit from consumers who enter them? Were you aware of these techniques? Have you fallen victim to them yourself? Explain.

Research Projects

4. In paragraph 9, author John Seabrook comments, "Shopping is a way of putting together your identity." Consider the ways your shopping habits put together your identity. Arrange to go shopping with a few friends at several popular stores. As you shop, consider whether you or your companions seem to be influenced by some of the techniques described in this essay. Consider not just what you buy, but where you shop, why you shop, and with whom. Note whether your companions criticize certain products, and why. How do your shopping companions influence each other's choices? Finally, how does branding appeal to their desire to buy particular things as part of presenting a personal identity? Write an essay describing the experience, and what you learned about marketing culture from your observations.

5. Visit the Web sites of the stores that Cave cites in his essay (**www.pottery barn.com, www.ikea.com, www.oldnavy.com**, etc.) and review their merchandise from the perspective of a cultural analyst. Acting like a social anthropologist, write an essay describing what North American consumers are like—for example, what they buy, their personal style preferences, and what they desire based on what you see on the websites you analyzed. Can you determine any common themes? Does anything seem surprising? What might a person from another country, such as China or El Salvador determine about North American consumers based on the offerings at these stores? Explain.

New Country, New Journalists

Adrienne Clarkson

Canada's demographic profile has changed over the past 20 years. Our traditionally European-based immigrant population has become more diverse, its origins, cultures, and ideologies more varied, stemming from national histories very different from that of the West. How has the Canadian media evolved to meet this new reality? Do journalists really know who their contemporary audience is, or are they writing for a generally mainstream Western readership with whom they share a social history and a set of cultural assumptions? If the Canadian media are not taking our "multiracial, multifaith" immigrant population into account, how can new Canadians be expected to see themselves as an integral part of the national identity?

Her Excellency the Right Honourable Adrienne Clarkson pursued a long and distinguished career as a journalist before being appointed Governor General of Canada. This article is based on an address presented at the Annual Conference of the McGill Institute for the Study of Canada, on February 14, 2003. It was first published in Queen's Quarterly.

Critical Thinking

When someone is immigrating to this country, what does he or she need to know in order to become "Canadian"? Is it possible to retain the culture of one's country of origin and yet still be able to fully participate in the culture of a new country?

Every society has a discreet, almost unconscious coding of shared understanding—insider humour, insider cynicism, an unspoken attachment to values, and a sense of belonging. We feel pride in our society's achievements, even when these occurred long before we were born, just as we feel shame for injustices that took place before we came into the world and into this society. But like the rest of the world, Canada's people today are a much more connected, complicated community than we were only twenty years ago. And

Reprinted from *Queen's Quarterly* 110, no. 2 (2003).

the country's journalists, even more than other citizens, must be better attuned than ever to the subtleties of our many shared messages.

Propaganda, ideology, and bias are extremely easy to promote in any kind of information medium, if you know how. And by "information" I mean not only newspapers, television, radio, and the Internet, but also advertising. People need diverse and quality sources of information in order to make sense not only of their own lives but also of their community. As a society, we have to worry, therefore, if our citizens are not dealt a full deck of information. And this is the job of the journalists and editors, broadcasters, publishers, and media owners.

It has been said that journalists share a vocation of unhappiness and discontent. If that is so, I think that's precisely what makes them competent, and often superb, at what they do. Why on earth would you want a happy journalist? Kierkegaard said that people hardly ever make use of the freedom they already have; in place of freedom of thought, they settle for freedom of speech as compensation. Journalists, therefore, should examine themselves and think about whether or not they actually have the freedom of thought that gives them the privilege to communicate with others freely. That is a professional struggle. It is what we mean when we say that we expect them to aspire to the highest possible professional standards.

There is now a patchwork quilt of information out there that makes it very difficult for people to discern exactly what is really happening. I mentioned advertising as an aspect of information that is important for the public now. Remember that McLuhan told us thirty years ago that advertising creates a parallel world. But it may not be a parallel world for the majority of the population, who are struggling to piece together a patchwork quilt of information. Are we deliberately making it more difficult or less difficult for them to discern between what is really happening in the news and what has been carefully constructed to fit into part of the news and grab attention for commercial purposes?

A recent automobile ad features a little automotive object of desire gliding through a number of different situations in shots lasting about one second each. It ends up in a field with hundreds and hundreds of fighter airplanes going over it. What kind of message is actually being delivered by that car ad? It is designed to say that we will stop at nothing to have that new model. To those of us who have grown up in this country, long exposed to the subtle messages and inside jokes of popular culture and the advertising world, it may be an amusing juxtaposition between luxury on four wheels and the power and might of military force. But to others' minds, others not understanding either English or French very well, it could be an image of terror blandly accepted. Confusion and misunderstanding can be the order of the day, rather than factual information and the gathering of enough information to create thought.

And this is where the question of the makeup of the audience becomes extremely important. By this I do not mean gender, race, or demographic makeup;

I mean that we must try to understand exactly how people in Canada have evolved. Where does the audience come from? From what parts of the public? How do they think? You can say, "Well we can't be saying all things to all people." But it is still very healthy to challenge yourself to try and think about who is actually reading, watching, listening to the media.

Why? Because I believe that much of the information we get—and how it is purveyed by the media—is based upon an old idea of Canada. It is based on an idea of a Canada of middle-class values, some historical memory, and a Canada seen as fully functioning in at least one of the official languages. It is a Canada where a stable democratic system is taken for granted. In other words, we basically see the audience in our own image of ourselves, more or less affluent, more or less committed to a status quo. We see the audience as people who have some education in our kinds of schooling, as people curious to know about day-to-day events, though mainly interested in the outside world when it bursts into flame, floods, or loses electrical power.

Yes, that kind of "original" audience does exist. But even it is not getting all the information it needs. For instance, when we get news of an election in a foreign country, we are always told who won or lost. But we are rarely given hard information as to the number of seats gained by any particular party or what those parties really represent. As a result, our understanding of the world outside our own country is glib, frequently dismissive. And when we search for the information we need, we have to rely on foreign websites, articles in foreign publications, or on programs from abroad—information that often arrives a few days, a week, or even a month later in Canadian newspapers and magazines.

But that "original" audience—as ill-served as it is—was the audience of Canada twenty years ago. The audience you are looking for today is different— an audience that needs attention, that needs to be informed, needs to be given the absolute basics of our way of life, including our criticism of our way of life.

Today, we have a new kind of society in Canada. We live in the year 2003, and we are a multiracial, multifaith immigrant population on an aboriginal base. We have a society, a way of life, and a form of government that have served us well for the last several centuries and into which we have up to now successfully and rather efficiently integrated immigrants. We have many flaws in our system, but on the whole it has worked quite well. Can it continue to do so at that level?

Our original so-called multicultural society was built of immigrants from Europe, all of whom could be expected within a relatively short time—perhaps a generation around the beginning of the twentieth century and often half a generation in the postwar period—to achieve an economic and social status on a par with other Canadians. But, as Carol Goar of the Toronto Star recently pointed out in an article reporting on a conference on immigrants in Toronto, our new immigrants are different. The bulk of the 200,000 to 250,000 people we take in a year, expecting to become citizens, are different. They come from countries where war, strife, and destitution have been the norm. They come from different religious traditions. Many of them came here to escape horrific events in their homelands. These are the people who are urgently in need of information about how they can truly participate in their new society and become Canadian.

All information media must play a part in helping that process to happen—and not by relating only "good news" stories or somehow teaching citizenship lessons subliminally. Through good journalism, people learn things through a sort of osmosis. And, as people are watching hours and hours of television every day, that particular medium has a special obligation to these newcomers and their children.

Even such a small thing as the weather report can have a deep effect on newcomers. I have noticed a growing and regrettable tendency within the last 25 years to describe snow as "bad weather," when in fact it is normal weather for Canada. This may seem like a tiny detail, but why should we publicly deny our climate in this way? Why should we say to ourselves or to others that having snow constitutes bad weather? Why should we pass on that kind of valuation of it to people who are coming here from countries where the average temperature is 40 degrees?

The "old immigration" from Europe had trades or could farm or had strong survival skills in Western culture. The people we now receive need different education, different acculturation, and certainly different approaches to information. Consider what that advertisement with the little car and the dozens of fighter planes would mean to somebody who has arrived here from a disputed border area in Southeast Asia or from bloody civil strife in Africa. An ad shown during a newscast is part of that newscast; the information is all knitted together. And of course the better the advertising is, the more likely that it will have an effect on the viewer. I like to remember what Stephen Leacock said about advertising—that it is the science of arresting the human intelligence long enough to get money from it.

15 We have said as a country that we are going to bring over 200,000 immigrants a year to Canada. And what we have done in fact is invited these people to come and take part in our society and become citizens. It is incumbent upon us, therefore, to think about what we do to help them "catch up" to other citizens who've been here for decades or even generations.

I believe that all the media are absolutely critical in this respect. They play a crucial role in building the new Canada and in the acculturation of those who have come here to make Canada their home. In fact, I believe that what you do as journalists is as important and critical as public education is in helping our new kind of immigrants to understand and become a really functioning part of our society. And remember, public education, important as it is, is a provincial responsibility—while many news outlets have a national audience. This means a greater responsibility, not just a greater market.

In order to be part of this country, you have to be a fully functioning citizen. Citizenship has its responsibilities as well as its rights. As an immigrant myself, I feel very strongly about this. And as Governor General, I am firmly convinced that it is the only way in which our nation can continue to live according to its beliefs, to its traditions, to its history, and to its often hard-won democratic processes. What I believe is that, by assuming citizenship, the new citizen of Canada takes on the entire history of the country.

So as a new Canadian you can be very proud of the sacrifices that Canada made in the First and Second World Wars. But you also have to acknowledge and accept the shame and tragedy of the residential schools for aboriginal children or the dislocation of Japanese-Canadians sixty years ago. We cannot continue to have a country if the huge numbers of people we involve in becoming citizens slough off any responsibility for what the country did before they got here.

Many of the immigrants we are now bringing to this country fully understand what it is to have a complex, tortured history. They have chosen to leave it and take up life in Canada. In remaking themselves as citizens of our country, they must learn to understand what we, as a country, have gone through in our evolution up to now. Citizenship is not a buffet table of rights, privileges, and perhaps some inconveniences—like the cranberry sauce you won't take with the turkey. If a country is to have a continuous history, then it must have a history that all members of it comprehend and—most importantly—in which all members feel implicated.

20   I remember somebody once watching me singing the national anthem in   20
French and asking me afterwards, in a polite and rather gingerly way, how I could sing the line "Land of our ancestors." And I replied that I really mean that line. Canada is the country of my ancestors, my adopted ancestors, the ones who struggled to create the kind of country to which I was able to come, of which I became a citizen, and of which I am now Governor General. My ancestors fought in 1837. They're the ancestors who created Confederation. All of that belongs to me and to each and every one of us when we are citizens of Canada.

For those of us who are immigrants, it doesn't mean an either/or situation. It's not that we forget where we came from, or what the food there tastes like, or when the festivals are. It means only that we have added another level of texture, a different kind of complexity, to our individual circumstances as citizens. But it is this kind of complex person that good journalism must reach, and indeed perhaps even shape. They may be new arrivals now, but their impact will be felt over generations. And you can bet that they will be actively involved in creating the Canadian society of the future.

It is these people to whom the world of media and information must be responsible—if we truly believe in freedom of thought. This is where freedom of the press should be operating. This is where freedom of the press can give people the keys to whole new worlds. And so if it is true that journalists share a "vocation of unhappiness and discontent" then this is where the journalist's unhappiness and discontent can create justice for others.

Freewriting Assignment

How much of what you define as Canadian is based on your perceptions of the news media's portrayal of this country? Do you think that current Canadian journalism takes into account our large immigrant population?

Critical Reading

1. Clarkson claims that "propaganda, ideology, and bias are extremely easy to promote in any kind of information medium." What do these terms mean, and how do they differ from one another?
2. What is Clarkson's "old idea of Canada?"
3. Clarkson refers to Marshall McLuhan's statement that "advertising creates a parallel world." Describe this world. How does it differ from the world of your experience?
4. Clarkson refers to the idea that "journalists share a vocation of unhappiness and discontent." What does she mean by this?
5. Would you agree that our understanding of the world outside of Canada is "glib, frequently dismissive"? Would that include our understanding of the United States?
6. The author refers to Stephen Leacock's comment that advertising "is the science of arresting the human intelligence long enough to get money from it." In your own words, what does this statement mean?
7. In paragraph 11, Clarkson claims that the 200 000 to 250 000 people who immigrate to Canada each year are "different." What does she mean by this?

Critical Writing

8. *Research and Evaluation*: Interview several people who have immigrated to Canada, preferably of different generations and origins. Find out how they feel about the way that the news and current events of their home countries are represented in the Canadian media. How difficult is it for them to find news of their country of origin? Summarize your findings in an essay.

9. *Exploratory Writing*: Write a paper on the meaning of citizenship. What defines a citizen? What is the responsibility of the state to its citizens, and conversely, what are the rights and responsibilities of a citizen? Explain.

Group Projects

10. Clarkson says that in the past 25 years we have come to describe snow as "bad weather," when in fact it is normal weather for Canada. Have each member of your group watch or listen to a different Canadian weather forecast over a period of a few days. Record how the meteorologists editorialize about their forecasts. Note which adjectives are used to describe the weather; what does this imply about our perception of our climate and even its role in our national identity? Present your findings to the class.

11. How does a country decide who would make a good citizen? Members of your group should take the Canadian Citizenship Practice Test at **www .yourlibrary.ca/citizenship/**. Score yourselves on the complete test. How do you perform as a group? Do you feel the questions are equally relevant? If not, which ones would you eliminate? What questions might you add?

The Hidden Life of SUVs

Jack Hitt

Jack Hitt (1957–) publishes widely in such prestigious peri-odicals as Harper's, *the* New York Times Magazine, *and* Mother Jones. *His recent essays in the* New York Times Magazine *include a report on bizarre conspiracy theories about the authenticity of the Apollo lunar landing, and a study of pseudoscience that suggests the Chinese discovered America. His books include* Off the Road: A Walk Down the Pilgrim's Road into Spain *(1994) and* In a Word: Dictionary *(1992). He contributes frequently to National Public Radio's* This American Life, *and has edited* Harper's Forum Book, *(1991) and* Perfect Murder: Five Great Mystery Writers Create the Perfect Crime *(1991).*

1 What's in a name? What do you make of a passenger vehicle called a Bronco?

Or one dubbed a Cherokee? How about a Wrangler? Are they just chrome-plate expressions of sublimated testosterone flooding the highways? Check out the herd that grazes the average car lot these days: Blazer, Tracker, Yukon, Navigator, Tahoe, Range Rover, Explorer, Mountaineer, Denali, Expedition, Discovery, Bravada. Besides signaling that we're not Civic or Galant, they indicate there's some-thing else going on here.

These are, of course, all names of sport utility vehicles, the miracle that has resurrected Motown. Think back to the dark days of the previ-ous decade when the Japanese auto industry had nearly buried Detroit. In 1981, only a relative handful of four-wheel-drives traveled the road, and the phrase "sport utility vehicle" hadn't entered the language. Today, they number more than 14 million, and that figure is growing fast. If you include pickups and vans, then quasi trucks now constitute about half of all the vehicles sold in America. Half. They're rapidly displacing cars on the highways of our new unbraking economy.

Go to any car lot and jawbone with a salesman, and you'll find that big is once again better. Any savvy dealer (clutching his copy of Zig Ziglar's *Ziglar on Selling*) will try to talk you up to one of the latest behemoths, which have bloated to such Brobdingnagian dimensions as to have entered the realm of the absurd.

5   Ford, in fact, unveiled a new monster, the Excursion [in 1999]. With a corporate straight face, its literature touted as selling points that the Excursion is "less than 7 feet tall . . . and less than 20 feet long" and is "more fuel efficient . . . than two average full-size sedans."

The Big Berthas have even spawned new vocabulary words. The biggest of the big, for instance, can no longer fit comfortably in a standard-size garage or the average parking space. So salesmen will often sell you on one of the "smaller" SUVs by praising its "garage-ability."

What, then, explains the inexorable advance of these giant SUVs into our lives? Why do we want cars that are, in fact, high-clearance trucks with four-wheel drive, an optional winch, and what amounts to a cow-catcher?

The answer, in part, lies in the vehicles themselves. Cars are not fickle fashions. They are the most expensive and visible purchases in an economy drenched in matters of status and tricked out with hidden meanings.

Some people will tell you that the shift from car to truck can be explained simply: We Americans are getting, um, bigger in the beam. We aren't comfortable in those Camrys, so we trade up to a vehicle we can sit in without feeling scrunched. Here's a new buzzword for Ziglar disciples: fatassability.

10   But I think the key is found not so much in their size or expense (although both keep ballooning) but in those ersatz Western names. The other day, I saw an acquaintance of mine in a boxy steed called a Durango. Say it out loud for me: "Durango." Can you get the syllables off your tongue without irony? In the post-*Seinfeld* era, can anyone say Durango without giving it an Elaine Benes enunciation at every syllable? Doo-RANG-Go.

The true irony comes from the fact that this thoroughly market-researched word no longer has any core meaning. No one comprehends its denotation (Colorado town) but only its vague connotations (rugged individualism, mastery over the wilderness, cowboy endurance). The word does not pin down meaning so much as conjure up images.

These names are only the end product of the intense buyer-profiling that the car companies and the marketing firms continuously carry out. By the time they make it to the lot, these cars are streamlined Frankensteinian concoctions of our private anxieties and desires. We consumers don't so much shop for one of these SUVs as they shop for us.

A typical focus-group study might be one like the "cluster analysis" conducted by college students for Washington, D.C.–area car dealers in 1994 and reported in *Marketing Tools*. The analysts coordinated numerous databases, mail surveys, and census information to profile the typical "Bill and Barb Blazers," whose consumer apprehensions can shift from block to block, but can be pinpointed down to the four-digit appendix on the old zip code.

Each Bill and Barb then got tagged as "Young Suburbia" or "Blue-Collar Nursery" or "Urban Gentry." Translation, respectively: "college-educated, upwardly mobile white" or "middle-class, small-town" or "educated black" people. The students next identified what images poke to the underlying appeal of an SUV for each group (prestige, child space, weekend leisure). Then they developed targeted ads to run in the media most favored by each group: the *Wall Street Journal, National Geographic,* Black Entertainment Television.

15 Many of the ads they developed were directed at women. For 15
example, the one meant for upscale homeowners depicted a "woman architect standing next to her four-door [Blazer] at a Washington-area construction site" and "conveyed her professional leadership in a city with one of the highest rates of labor force participation for women."

Sport utility vehicles are quickly becoming women's cars. In fact, current statistics show that 40 percent of all SUV sales are to women, and the proportion is growing. (More men, on the other hand, are buying bigger, tougher pickup trucks.) But one wonders what's going on in the mind of that female architect or that soccer mom, high above the world in her soundproof, tinted-glass SUV, chatting on her cellular phone as she steers her mobile fortress down the street.

When GMC decided to launch the Denali (an SUV named for the Alaskan mountain), the auto-trade papers discussed the subtleties of that outdoorsy name: Even though most buyers "will never venture into territory any less trampled than the local country club parking lot," wrote Ward's *Auto World*, "the important goal of the Denali mar-keting hype is to plant the image in customers' minds that they can conquer rugged terrain. The metaphor of Alaska is particularly apt because SUVs, especially the larger of the species, depend on the myth that we have new frontiers yet to pave. Perhaps we're trying to tame a different kind of wilderness. Indeed, in an age of gated com-munities the SUV is the perfect transportation shelter to protect us from fears both real and imagined."

In one focus group, female drivers confessed they hesitated even to exit the interstate "because they are afraid of what they are going to find on some surface streets."

G. Clotaire Rapaille, a French medical anthropologist and stu-dent of the consumer mind, practices a more advanced marketing technique called "archetype research." In one session he has con-sumers lie on the floor and lulls them into a relaxed alpha state with soothing music. Then he asks them to free-associate from images of different vehicle designs and write stories about what they hoped the design would become. Overwhelmingly, Rapaille told the *Wall Street Journal,* his participants had the same reaction: "It's a jungle out there. It's Mad Max. People want to kill me, rape me. Give me a big thing like a tank."

20 More and more, SUVs give us that tanklike security, and part of the feeling derives from their literal altitude. Down there is the old working class, the new peasants who haven't figured out how to snatch a six-figure income out of our roaring economy—the little people who don't own a single Fidelity fund. There's a brutal Darwinian selec-tion at work: They huddle down in their wretched Escorts and their Metros—not merely because they are poor but because they deserve to be.

These are the new savages: people who drive cars. The scrape and fetch about in their tiny compacts, scuttling along on surface streets. But above it all, in their gleaming, skyscraping vehicles, is the new high society—the ambitious, the exurban pioneers, the downtown frontiersmen.

It's been said that the most distinctive feature of the American character is that we continually define ourselves as pilgrims facing a new frontier. In their darkest hearts, the members of the new-money bourgeoisie have convinced themselves that we live in an unforgiving wilderness of marauders and brutes. The hidden meaning of our new conveyances can be found right on the surface. Once upon a time, Trailblazers, Explorers, and Trackers tamed the Wild West. Now, through the sorcery of focus groups, the bull-market gentry have brought the Pathfinders and Mountaineers back into their lives in the belief that they need to conquer the savage land one more time.

Questions on Meaning

1. What's in a name? Why do American car dealers give adventure names to SUVs? How do they come up with these adventure names?
2. Who buys these big vehicles and why? What are these owners afraid of?
3. How do advertisers use students and others to decide what SUVs should be and do? What does an SUV say about its driver? Why are so many SUV drivers women?

Questions on Rhetorical Strategy and Style

1. The essay is written in exaggerated language to match the exaggerated size and cost of the SUV. Give examples of this exaggerated language. Who comes up with this language? The essay uses humor for what purpose?
2. The first line of the essay is ironic because it quotes Romeo in the romantic play *Romeo and Juliet*. The first two lines contrast romance with wild west adventure in a "Bronco" SUV. What effect does this introduction have on a reader?
3. The essay ends by explaining that these autos appeal to people who fear the underclasses. Why does this ending change the tone of the essay?

Writing Assignments

1. Look up information on the dangers of SUVs. Write about those dangers in light of the expanding sales of these vehicles.
2. Go to a busy intersection. Count the SUVs and count the number of men versus women driving them. Then write about Hitt's claim that women drive these vehicles to be safe.
3. Visit an auto sales lot to discover the prices of these vehicles, or go online to look up the prices. Write about the kinds of incomes necessary to own these big pieces of metal and plastic. You might compare the price to the number of cup holders.

TV News: All the World in Pictures

Neil Postman and Steve Powers

It's 6 p.m. and you turn on the local evening news. You depend on it to keep you informed of the day's events in your area, your nation, and worldwide. But how much do you really learn from that nightly news broadcast? According to Neil Postman and Steve Powers, the answer is not very much. The nightly news, they argue, is really visual entertainment that only creates the illusion of keeping the public informed.

A professor at New York University, the late Neil Postman founded the Steinhardt School of Education's program in media ecology at NYU in 1971. He was chair of the Department of Culture and Communication until 2002. During his career, he wrote 20 books on a wide variety of subjects ranging from education to television to technology's influence on modern life. His most recent books include The End of Education: Redefining the Value of School *(1995) and* Building a Bridge to the 18th Century: How the Past Can Improve Our Future *(1999).*

Steve Powers is an award-winning journalist with more than 30 years of experience in broadcast news. Postman and Powers are co-authors of How to Watch TV News *(2000) from which this essay was taken.*

Critical Thinking

Think about your local television news broadcast. How much does it rely on video clips to tell the story? How are events narrated? How much information do you learn from each clip?

1   When a television news show distorts the truth by altering or manufacturing facts (through re-creations), a television viewer is defenseless even if a re-creation is properly labeled. Viewers are still vulnerable to misinformation since they will not know (at least in the case of docudramas)

Reprinted from *How to Watch TV News* (1992), Penguin Putnam Inc.

what parts are fiction and what parts are not. But the problems of verisimilitude posed by re-creations pale to insignificance when compared to the problems viewers face when encountering a straight (no-monkey-business) show. All news shows, in a sense, are re-creations in that what we hear and see on them are attempts to represent actual events, and are not the events themselves. Perhaps, to avoid ambiguity, we might call all news shows "re-presentations" instead of "re-creations." These re-presentations come to us in two forms: language and pictures. The question then arises: what do viewers have to know about language and pictures in order to be properly armed to defend themselves against the seductions of eloquence (to use Bertrand Russell's apt phrase)? . . .

[Let us look at] the problem of pictures. It is often said that a picture is worth a thousand words. Maybe so. But it is probably equally true that one word is worth a thousand pictures, at least sometimes—for example, when it comes to understanding the world we live in. Indeed, the whole problem with news on television comes down to this: all the words uttered in an hour of news coverage could be printed on one page of a newspaper. And the world cannot be understood in one page. Of course, there is a compensation: television offers pictures, and the pictures move. Moving pictures are a kind of language in themselves, but the language of pictures differs radically from oral and written language, and the differences are crucial for understanding television news.

To begin with, pictures, especially single pictures, speak only in particularities. Their vocabulary is limited to concrete representation. Unlike words and sentences, a picture does not present to us an idea or concept about the world, except as we use language itself to convert the image to idea. By itself, a picture cannot deal with the unseen, the remote, the internal, the abstract. It does not speak of "man," only of a man; not of "tree," only of a tree. You cannot produce an image of "nature," any more than an image of "the sea." You can only show a particular fragment of the here-and-now—a cliff of a certain terrain, in a certain condition of light; a wave at a moment in time, from a particular point of view. And just as "nature" and "the sea" cannot be photographed, such larger abstractions as truth, honor, love, and falsehood cannot be talked about in the lexicon of individual pictures. For "showing of" and "talking about" are two very different kinds of processes: individual pictures give us the world as object; language, the world as idea.

There is no such thing in nature as "man" or "tree." The universe offers no such categories or simplifications; only flux and infinite variety. The picture documents and celebrates the particularities of the universe's infinite variety. Language makes them comprehensible.

5   Of course, moving pictures, video with sound, may bridge the gap by juxtaposing images, symbols, sound, and music. Such images can present emotions and rudimentary ideas. They can suggest the panorama of nature and the joys and miseries of humankind.

Picture—smoke pouring from the window, cut to people coughing, an ambulance racing to a hospital, a tombstone in a cemetery.

Picture—jet planes firing rockets, explosions, lines of foreign soldiers surrendering, the American flag waving in the wind.

Nonetheless, keep in mind that when terrorists want to prove to the world that their kidnap victims are still alive, they photograph them holding a copy of a recent newspaper. The dateline on the newspaper provides the proof that the photograph was taken on or after that date. Without the help of the written word, film and videotape cannot portray temporal dimensions with any precision. Consider a film clip showing an aircraft carrier at sea. One might be able to identify the ship as Soviet or American, but there would be no way of telling where in the world the carrier was, where it was headed, or when the pictures were taken. It is only through language—words spoken over the pictures or reproduced in them—that the image of the aircraft carrier takes on specific meaning.

Still, it is possible to enjoy the image of the carrier for its own sake. One might find the hugeness of the vessel interesting; it signifies military power on the move. There is a certain drama in watching the planes come in at high speeds and skid to a stop on the deck. Suppose the ship were burning: that would be even more interesting. This leads to an important point about the language of pictures. Moving pictures favor images that change. That is why violence and dynamic destruction find their way onto television so often. When something is destroyed violently it is altered in a highly visible way; hence the entrancing power of fire. Fire gives visual form to the ideas of consumption, disappearance, death—the thing that burned is actually taken away by fire. It is at this very basic level that fires make a good subject for television news. Something was here, now it's gone, and the change is recorded on film.

10   Earthquakes and typhoons have the same power. Before the viewer's eyes   10 the world is taken apart. If a television viewer has relatives in Mexico City and an earthquake occurs there, then he or she may take a special interest in the images of destruction as a report from a specific place and time; that is, one may look at television pictures for information about an important event. But film of an earthquake can be interesting even if the viewer cares nothing about the event itself. Which is only to say, as we noted earlier, that there is another way of participating in the news—as a spectator who desires to be entertained. Actually to see buildings topple is exciting, no matter where the buildings are. The world turns to dust before our eyes.

Those who produce television news in America know that their medium favors images that move. That is why they are wary of "talking heads," people who simply appear in front of a camera and speak. When talking heads appear on television, there is nothing to record or document, no change in process. In the cinema the situation is somewhat different. On a movie screen, closeups of a good actor speaking dramatically can sometimes be interesting to watch. When Clint Eastwood narrows his eyes and challenges his rival to shoot first, the spectator sees the cool rage of the Eastwood character take visual form, and the narrowing of the eyes is dramatic. But much of the effect of this small movement depends on the size of the movie screen and the darkness of the theater, which make Eastwood and his every action "larger than life."

The television screen is smaller than life. It occupies about 15 percent of the viewer's visual field (compared to about 70 percent for the movie screen). It is not set in a darkened theater closed off from the world but in the viewer's ordinary living space. This means that visual changes must be more extreme and more dramatic to be interesting on television. A narrowing of the eyes will not do. A car crash, an earthquake, a burning factory are much better.

With these principles in mind, let us examine more closely the structure of a typical newscast, and here we will include in the discussion not only the pictures but all the nonlinguistic symbols that make up a television news show. For example, in America, almost all news shows begin with music, the tone of which suggests important events about to unfold. The music is very important, for it equates the news with various forms of drama and ritual—the opera, for example, or a wedding procession—in which musical themes underscore the meaning of the event. Music takes us immediately into the realm of the symbolic, a world that is not to be taken literally. After all, when events unfold in the real world, they do so without musical accompaniment. More symbolism follows.

The sound of teletype machines can be heard in the studio, not because it is impossible to screen this noise out, but because the sound is a kind of music in itself. It tells us that data are pouring in from all corners of the globe, a sensation reinforced by the world map in the background (or clocks noting the time on different continents). The fact is that teletype machines are rarely used in TV news rooms, having been replaced by silent computer terminals. When seen, they have only a symbolic function.

15   Already, then, before a single news item is introduced, a great deal has been communicated. We know that we are in the presence of a symbolic event, a form of theater in which the day's events are to be dramatized. This theater takes the entire globe as its subject, although it may look at the world from the perspective of a single nation. A certain tension is present, like the atmosphere in a theater just before the curtain goes up. The tension is represented by the music, the staccato beat of the teletype machines, and often the sight of news workers scurrying around typing reports and answering phones. As a technical matter, it would be no problem to build a set in which the newsroom staff remained off camera, invisible to the viewer, but an important theatrical effect would be lost. By being busy on camera, the workers help communicate urgency about the events at hand, which suggests that situations are changing so rapidly that constant revision of the news is necessary.

The staff in the background also helps signal the importance of the person in the center, the anchor, "in command" of both the staff and the news. The anchor plays the role of host. He or she welcomes us to the newscast and welcomes us back from the different locations we visit during the filmed reports.

Many features of the newscast help the anchor to establish the impression of control. These are usually equated with production values in broadcasting. They include such things as graphics that tell the viewer what is being shown, or maps and charts that suddenly appear on the screen and disappear on cue, or the orderly progression from story to story. They also include the absence of gaps, or "dead time," during the broadcast, even the simple fact that the news starts and ends at a certain hour. These common features are thought of as pure technical matters, which a professional crew handles as a matter of course. But they are also symbols of a dominant theme of television news: the imposition of an orderly world—called "the news"—upon the disorderly flow of events.

While the form of a news broadcast emphasizes tidiness and control, its content can best be described as fragmented. Because time is so precious on television, because the nature of the medium favors dynamic visual images, and because the pressures of a commercial structure require the news to hold its audience above all else, there is rarely any attempt to explain issues in depth or place events in their proper context. The news moves nervously from a warehouse fire to a court decision, from a guerrilla war to a World Cup match, the quality of the film most often determining the length of the story. Certain stories show up only because they offer dramatic pictures. Bleachers collapse in South America: hundreds of people are crushed—a perfect television news story, for the cameras can record the face of disaster in all its anguish. Back in Washington, a new budget is approved by Congress. Here there is nothing to photograph because a budget is not a physical event; it is a document full of language and numbers. So the producers of the news will show a photo of the document itself, focusing on the cover where it says "Budget of the United States of America." Or sometimes they will send a camera crew to the government printing plant where copies of the budget are produced. That evening, while the contents of the budget are summarized by a voice-over, the viewer sees stacks of documents being loaded into boxes at the government printing plant. Then a few of the budget's more important provisions will be flashed on the screen in written form, but this is such a time-consuming process—using television as a printed page—that the producers keep it to a minimum. In short, the budget is not televisable, and for that reason its time on the news must be brief. The bleacher collapse will get more time that evening.

While appearing somewhat chaotic, these disparate stories are not just dropped in the news program helter-skelter. The appearance of a scattershot story order is really orchestrated to draw the audience from one story to the next—through the commercial breaks to the end of the show. The story order is constructed to hold and build the viewership rather than place events in context or explain issues in depth.

20   Of course, it is a tendency of journalism in general to concentrate on the surface of events rather than underlying conditions; this is as true for the newspaper as it is for the newscast. But several features of television undermine whatever efforts journalists may make to give sense to the world. One is that a television broadcast is a series of events that occur in sequence, and the sequence is the same for all viewers. This is not true for a newspaper page, which displays many items simultaneously, allowing readers to choose the order in which they read them. If newspaper readers want only a summary of the latest tax bill, they can read the headline and the first paragraph of an article, and if they want more, they can keep reading. In a sense, then, everyone reads a different newspaper, for no two readers will read (or ignore) the same items.

But all television viewers see the same broadcast. They have no choices. A report is either in the broadcast or out, which means that anything which is of narrow interest is unlikely to be included. As NBC News executive Reuven Frank once explained:

> A newspaper, for example, can easily afford to print an item of conceivable interest to only a fraction of its readers. A television news program must be put together with the assumption that each item will be of some interest to everyone that watches. Every time a newspaper includes a feature which will attract a specialized group it can assume it is adding at least a little bit to its circulation. To the degree a television news program includes an item of this sort . . . it must assume that its audience will diminish.

The need to "include everyone," an identifying feature of commercial television in all its forms, prevents journalists from offering lengthy or complex explanations, or from tracing the sequence of events leading up to today's headlines. One of the ironies of political life in modern democracies is that many problems which concern the "general welfare" are of interest only to specialized groups. Arms control, for example, is an issue that literally concerns everyone in the world, and yet the language of arms control and the complexity of the subject are so daunting that only a minority of people can actually follow the issue from week to week and month to month. If it wants to act responsibly, a newspaper can at least make available more information about arms control than most people want. Commercial television cannot afford to do so.

But even if commercial television could afford to do so, it wouldn't. The fact that television news is principally made up of moving pictures prevents it from offering lengthy, coherent explanations of events. A television news show reveals the world as a series of unrelated, fragmentary moments. It does not—and cannot be expected to—offer a sense of coherence or meaning. What does this suggest to a TV viewer? That the viewer must come with a prepared mind—information, opinions, a sense of proportion, an articulate value system. To the TV viewer lacking such mental equipment, a news program is only a kind of rousing light show. Here a falling building, there a five-alarm fire, everywhere the world as an object, much without meaning, connections, or continuity. ◆

Freewriting assignment

Consider the phrase "a picture is worth a thousand words." Do you think it is true? How does it apply to television journalism?

Critical Reading

1. According to Postman and Powers, what is wrong with news programs recreating actual events? How does re-creation affect the viewer? How does it affect the story?
2. Consider the "pictures" in paragraphs 6 and 7. Imagine you are seeing each of these pictures without any explanation accompanying them. How many different ways could these pictures be interpreted? How important are words to the contexts of these pictures?
3. What is the authors' position on news broadcasts? How can you tell?
4. How do you think a broadcast journalist from your local television network would respond to this essay? How argumentative is this essay? Explain.
5. What is the price viewers pay for fragmented video clips? Evaluate the pros and cons of this style of journalism.
6. How does the order in which news stories are presented during the news broadcast "control" the audience? Does the knowledge that you are being manipulated change your opinion of the nightly news? Explain.
7. Analyze the authors' last paragraph that television programs cannot offer a sense of coherence and meaning. Do you agree with this? Why might this be ironic when you consider the reasons why people watch the news?

Critical Writing

8. What is news? Many of us think we know the answer, but what might be newsworthy to one person may seem superfluous to another. Write a short essay on what you expect (or want) from a news program and what you actually get. How much does the tradition of news broadcasts influence your expectations?
9. You are a television news producer who must develop a new local television news program to compete against others in the early evening time slot.

Conduct a survey on what people want to watch on local television news. After gathering your information, design your newscast and explain in detail the reasons for your design. How much does your new program resemble others already on the air? What assumptions do you make about your overall audience? Predict the success of your broadcast, based on your program's rationale.

Group Projects

10. Evaluate television newscasts. Each member of your group should watch several television newscasts from major networks. What differences, if any, are notable between networks? Are there differences between local and national news broadcasts? What assumptions seem to be made about the audiences of the various newscasts? Consider the stories reported, their order, how newscasters are dressed, the set, and the advertisements appearing on each program. Write a group-informed essay in which you describe your discoveries and analyze their relevance.

11. Prepare a survey questionnaire that seeks to find out just what it is that people want to watch on television news. Do they watch it to be entertained, informed, or both? What expectations do they bring to the programs? Do they feel newscasts are reliable sources of information? Each member of the group should survey at least 10 people and be prepared to discuss the responses with the group. Based on the responses, do viewers think the purpose of television news programs is to inform or to entertain?

Can TV Improve Us?

Jane Rosenzweig

Although television is often cited as the source of many social ills—from teen violence to the decline of the family—many people point out that it also teaches, informs, and entertains us. The next article takes the debate one step further by postulating that TV can actually improve us. Jane Rosenzweig describes some of the ways in which television has forced us to think about social issues and has promoted moral values. And although television may not be the ideal vehicle to advocate values, it may be the best one we have.

A former staff editor for the Atlantic Monthly, *Jane Rosenzweig now teaches writing at Yale University. This article was first published in the July/August 1999 issue of the* American Prospect.

Critical Thinking

Think about how television can increase awareness about a particular issue or promote certain values in audiences. What social or moral themes can you recall that were recently featured in popular television programs?

1   It's eight o'clock Wednesday evening and a rumor is circulating at a small-town high school in Massachusetts that a student named Jack is gay. Jack's friends—one of whom is a 15-year-old girl who has been sexually active since she was 13, and another of whom has a mother who has recently committed adultery—assure him it would be okay with them if he were, but admit their relief when he says he isn't. An hour later, in San Francisco, a woman named Julia is being beaten by her boyfriend. Meanwhile, in Los Angeles, a young stripper who has given birth out of wedlock learns that her own mother locked her in a basement when she was three years old, an experience that she thinks may explain her inability to love her own child.

A typical evening in America? If a visitor from another planet had turned on the television (specifically the WB and Fox networks) on the evening of Wednesday, February 10, 1999, with the aim of learning about our society, he would likely have concluded that it is made up pretty exclusively of photogenic young people with disintegrating nuclear families and liberal attitudes about

Reprinted from *American Prospect* (1999).

sex. It's obviously not an accurate picture, but what might our visitor have learned from the programs he watched? Would all the sex, violence, and pathology he saw teach him antisocial behavior? Or might he glean from prime-time dramas and sitcoms the behavior and attitudes that he would do well to adopt if he intended to go native in America?

This is not an idle question—not because aliens might be watching American television, but because people are, particularly impressionable children and teenagers. In a time when 98 percent of U.S. households own at least one television set—a set which is turned on for an average of nearly seven hours a day—the degree to which people learn from and emulate the behavior of the characters they see on TV is an academic cottage industry. Some evidence does support the widespread belief that children and teenagers are affected by violence and other antisocial behavior in the media. When Dan Quayle made his infamous comments in 1992 about Murphy Brown having a baby out of wedlock, he was merely doing what numerous concerned parents, ethnic groups, religious organizations, gun-control advocates, and others were already doing—blaming television for encouraging certain types of behavior.

But if television contributes to poor behavior, might it also be a vehicle for encouraging good behavior? In 1988, Jay Winsten, a professor at the Harvard School of Public Health and the director of the school's Center for Health Communication, conceived a plan to use television to introduce a new social concept—the "designated driver"—to North America. Shows were already dealing with the topic of drinking, Winsten reasoned, so why not add a line of dialogue here and there about not driving drunk? With the assistance of then-NBC chairman Grant Tinker, Winsten met with more than 250 writers, producers, and executives over six months, trying to sell them on his designated driver idea.

5   Winsten's idea worked; the "designated driver" is now common parlance across all segments of American society and in 1991 won entry into a Webster's dictionary for the first time. An evaluation of the campaign in 1994 revealed that the designated driver "message" had aired on 160 prime-time shows in four seasons and had been the main topic of twenty-five 30-minute or 60-minute episodes. More important, these airings appear to have generated tangible results. In 1989, the year after the "designated driver" was invented, a Gallup poll found that 67 percent of adults had noted its appearance on network television. What's more, the campaign seems to have influenced adult behavior: polls conducted by the Roper Organization in 1989 and 1991 found significantly increasing awareness and use of designated drivers. By 1991, 37 percent of all U.S. adults claimed to have refrained from drinking at least once in order to serve as a designated driver, up from 29 percent in 1989. In 1991, 52 percent of adults younger than 30 had served as designated drivers, suggesting that the campaign was having greatest success with its target audience.

In 1988 there were 23,626 drunk driving fatalities. By 1997 the number was 16,189. While the Harvard Alcohol Project acknowledges that some of this decline is due to new laws, stricter anti-drunk driving enforcement, and other factors, it claims that many of the 50,000 lives saved by the end of 1998 were saved because of the designated driver campaign. (The television campaign was only a part of the overall campaign; there were strong community-level and public service components as well.) As evidence, the project cites statistics showing the rapid decline in traffic fatalities per 100 million vehicle miles traveled in the years during and immediately following the most intensive period of the designated driver campaign. Officials at the National Highway Traffic and Safety Administration have stated that the only way to explain the size of the decline in drinking-related traffic fatalities is the designated driver campaign.

Following the success of the Harvard Alcohol Project's campaign, various other advocacy groups—the majority of them with progressive leanings—have begun to work within the existing structures of the television industry in a similar fashion, attempting to influence programming in a positive direction. In truth, there are limits to the effect any public interest group can have on what gets broadcast. Commercial television's ultimate concerns are Nielsen ratings and advertisers. Thus there will always be a hefty quantity of sex and violence on network television. As Alfred Schneider, the former vice president of policy and standards for ABC, asserts in his contribution to the forthcoming anthology *Advocacy Groups and the Television Industry*, "While [television] can raise the consciousness of the nation, it should not be considered as the major vehicle for social relief or altering behavior." But why not?

Other groups remain optimistic, emulating Winsten's method of treating television as a potential ally rather than an adversary and approaching writers and producers likely to be receptive to particular ideas. When writers and producers for the WB network's critically acclaimed new drama *Felicity* were working on the script for a two-part story about date rape, they wanted to make sure they got the details right. They sought the advice of experts from the Kaiser Family Foundation, a nonprofit that focuses on education about health issues; its Program on Entertainment Media and Public Health offers briefings, research services, and a hotline for script writers with health-related questions. "We were really aware of the message we were sending out," the show's executive producer Ed Redlich told me recently. "Given that our audience is teenage girls, we wanted to be correct. At the same time we didn't want it to be an extended public service announcement." As the scripts went through revisions, the show's writers sat down to discuss date rape with representatives from Kaiser, who had previously offered their services to the WB. In whom might a young woman confide after being raped? What kind of advice might a rape counselor provide? What physical tests would the woman undergo? What kind of message would the show be sending if the rapist didn't use a condom?

Meanwhile, WB network executive Susanne Daniels sought input on the *Felicity* scripts from Marisa Nightingale at the National Campaign to Prevent Teen Pregnancy, an advocacy group formed in 1995 with the goal of reducing teen pregnancies by one-third by the year 2005. Nightingale, the manager of media programs, spends her days meeting with writers and producers to offer statistics, information on birth control methods, and suggestions for how to incorporate pregnancy prevention into storylines. "I can't knock on every door in the country and discuss safe sex with teenagers," she says, "but if Bailey and Sarah on [the Fox network's] *Party of Five* discuss it, that's the next best thing."

10   According to a recent Kaiser Foundation survey, 23 percent of teens say   10 they learn about pregnancy and birth control from television and movies. Clearly, we should be mindful of what exactly teenagers are watching. On a recent episode of *Dawson's Creek* two 16-year-olds contemplating sex ran into each other at a drugstore only to discover they were standing in front of a condom display, which led to a frank discussion about safe sex. An episode of *Felicity* featured the title character researching birth control methods and learning the proper way of putting on a condom. Once prepared, Felicity then decided in the heat of the moment she wasn't quite ready to have sex. A young woman's decision to put off having sex is rarely portrayed in prime time, but Felicity is a strong character and her reasoning is probably convincing to a teenage audience. She may well have more influence on teenage girls than a public service announcement.

Of course, making television an explicit vehicle for manipulating behavior has its dangers. My idea of the good may not be yours; if my ideas have access to the airwaves but yours don't, what I'm doing will seem to you like unwanted social engineering. We can all agree that minimizing drunk driving is a good thing—but not everyone agrees on the messages we want to be sending to, say, teenage girls about abstinence versus condoms, about having an abortion, or about whether interfaith marriages are okay. Television's power to mold viewers' understanding of the world is strong enough that we need to be aware that embedding messages about moral values or social behavior can have potent effects—for good or for ill.

For the moment, Hollywood's liberal tilt (yes, it really has one) makes it likely that the messages and values it chooses to incorporate into its television programs will be agreeable to progressives. But how active a role do we want television to play in the socialization of our youth? If advocacy groups can gain access to Hollywood with messages that seem like positive additions to existing fare, then they may someday be able to do the opposite—to instill, say, values of a particular religion or an intolerant political group through television.

Consider the popularity of CBS's *Touched by an Angel*, which has just completed its fifth season and has secured a regular place among the top ten Nielsen-rated programs. The show, which features angels—not winged creatures, but messengers of God who arrive to help mortals in times of crisis—has sparked a mini-trend in prime time. Along with its spin-off *Promised Land* and the WB's *7th Heaven, Touched by an Angel* has carved out a new niche in family hour entertainment: fare that's endorsed by many groups on the religious right (as well as, to be fair, by people not of the Christian right who are seeking wholesome television entertainment).

7th Heaven's producer Brenda Hampton, who created the show for Aaron Spelling's production company (the creative force behind such racier fare as *Beverly Hills 90210* and *Melrose Place*), emphasizes in interviews that she is not influenced by religious groups and that her goal is simply to create entertaining television. But Martha Williamson, the producer of *Touched by an Angel*, is very outspoken about her Christianity. While Williamson, too, emphasizes that she aims primarily to entertain, the program's religious message is unmistakably in the foreground. Williamson says she is regularly contacted by viewers who say the show helped them make a decision—to get in touch with a long-estranged relative or to stop smoking.

15   On its face there's nothing objectionable about this; in fact, it's probably   15
good. And there's no evidence that *Touched by an Angel* is actively converting people, or making unwilling Jews or atheists into Christians. Still, the show does proselytize for a set of values that some viewers might find alienating or offensive. A more extreme version could become Big Brotherish propaganda, beamed into the homes and receptive minds of the seven-hour-a-day TV watchers. At this point, the most offensive thing about *Touched by an Angel* is its saccharine writing (even some religious groups have criticized it on these grounds). But it is perhaps telling that a Republican Congress has awarded Williamson a "Freedom Works Award" for "individuals and groups who seek the personal reward of accepting and promoting responsibility without reliance on or funding from the federal government."

Given that writers have to create 22 episodes each season, it's not surprising that they are receptive to outside groups pitching socially redeeming story ideas. *Dawson's Creek* producer Paul Stupin estimates he sits down with three to five advocacy groups at the beginning of each season and always finds the meetings useful. The fact that large numbers of writers and producers attend briefings sponsored by Kaiser, the National Campaign to Prevent Teen Pregnancy, or Population Communications International (which recently sponsored a "Soap Summit") suggests that others feel the same way.

The strongest evidence that advocates can effect change through partnerships with the television industry comes from the success of the designated driver campaign. While there are as of yet no large-scale studies exploring the effects of public health advocacy through television, a survey conducted by the Kaiser Foundation is enlightening. On April 10, 1997, NBC aired an episode of ER focusing on morning-after contraception, put together with the help of

Kaiser Foundation research. Before the show aired, independent researchers interviewed 400 of the show's regular viewers about their knowledge of options for preventing unwanted pregnancy even after unprotected sex. In the week after the show aired, 305 more viewers were interviewed. The number of ER viewers who said they knew about morning-after contraception went up by 17 percent after the episode aired. The study concluded that up to six million of the episode's 34 million viewers learned about emergency contraception for the first time from the show (and 53 percent of *ER* viewers say they learn important health care information from the show).

Even the limited evidence provided by the *ER* study suggests the scope of television's power to educate and influence. And additional Kaiser studies suggest that the lobbying of public health groups advocating safe sex and birth control is not yet having nearly enough of a beneficial effect. While 25 percent of teenagers say they have learned "a lot" about pregnancy and birth control from TV shows and movies, and 40 percent say they have gotten ideas about how to talk to their boyfriend or girlfriend about sex from TV and movies, 76 percent say that one reason teens feel comfortable having sex at young ages is that TV shows and movies "make it seem normal" to do so.

Another problem: According to Kaiser, while 67 percent of *ER* viewers knew about morning-after contraception when questioned immediately following the show, only 50 percent knew about it when questioned two-and-a-half months later. This suggests that the 17 percent who gained new information about contraception from the episode may not have retained it. Jay Winsten says that because new information fades without repetition, for a single message to take hold the way the designated driver campaign did will require a barrage of appearances on a wide range of TV shows, over an extended period of time.

20   The role of advocacy groups as a resource for Hollywood writers and producers is growing, and it's worth taking seriously. Their approach—presenting ideas to a creative community that is constantly in need of ideas—is proving effective. Yes, the messages are diluted to fit sitcom or drama formats. Yes, for every "good value" that makes its way onto the small screen, a flurry of gunshots on another network will partly counteract it. And yes, when *Time* cites Ally McBeal as a factor in the demise of feminism, it is placing absurdly disproportionate responsibility on a television character, and on the creative community that invented her. Yet if the college women on *Felicity* practice safe sex, or if a prime-time parent talks about drugs—or adoption, or eating disorders, or the Holocaust—with a child, the message is likely to resonate with an audience comprised of people who relate to their favorite television characters as if they knew them.

Is television the ideal forum for a culture to define its values? No. As long as television remains a profit-driven industry, the best we can hope to do—

especially those of us who have views in common with those who create television content (and fortunately for liberals, we tend to)—is to work within the existing system to make it better. We do need to be realistic about the limits of television in packaging messages to fit this format. To turn *Friends* into a show about capital punishment would be ineffective as well as dramatically unconvincing; but to encourage the producers of *Dawson's Creek* to portray young people facing the realistic consequences of adult decisions just might work.

Freewriting Assignment

In paragraph 11, Rosenzweig states that "manipulating behavior has its dangers." In what ways can using television as a vehicle for public service announcements be dangerous?

Critical Reading

1. Assess Rosenzweig's question in paragraph 4, "if television contributes to poor behavior, might it also be a vehicle for encouraging good behavior?" What assumptions does Rosenzweig make about her audience by phrasing the question this way?

2. Based on your overall impression of Rosenzweig's article, what conclusions can you make about the author's social and political leanings? Cite some examples from the text to support your answer.

3. Evaluate the author's use of supporting evidence and examples in this article. Is her evidence fair and balanced? Does it seem credible? Is it accessible to her audience? Explain.

4. Rosenzweig notes that although it was easy for Hollywood to incorporate the issue of drunk driving into its programming, other issues have met with less success. What makes a social issue interesting, and why?

5. Rosenzweig states in a side comment that Hollywood "really has" a liberal tilt (paragraph 12). On what evidence does she base this statement? Do you agree or disagree with her view?

Critical Writing

6. *Creative Analysis*: In her introduction, Rosenzweig questions what visitors from another planet would think about our society based on what they learned from watching television on one specific evening. Pretend you are such a visitor, and you know nothing about North American culture or social values. Based on an evening's television viewing (you may hop between several programs), what conclusions would you make about our culture? Cite specific examples in your analysis.

7. *Personal Narrative*: Has a television program ever made you think about a social or moral issue that you would not otherwise have thought about had you not watched the program? Write a personal narrative about a television program that influenced, or even changed, how you felt about a social or moral issue.

8. *Exploratory Writing*: Rosenzweig comments that television programs may attempt to promote social agendas with which some viewers may not agree. Watch one, or several, of the programs she cites in her article to which people may object. What concerns may some audiences have with these programs? What social agendas do they promote? Write an essay in which you support or argue against the use of television to promote social, political, or religious perspectives.

Group Projects

9. Rosenzweig notes that although the issue of drunk driving was easy for Hollywood to incorporate into its programming, other issues have met with less success. With your group, make a list of the issues that television programming has addressed in your viewing experience. After reviewing the list, expand it to include other important, but less "exciting" issues, such as the hole in the ozone layer or recycling. Develop a story line together for a popular program dealing with one of these less stimulating issues and present it to the class.

10. Using a television weekly programming guide for reference, try to identify the political "tilt" of prime-time programs with the members of your group. In your analysis, include television dramas, news programs, and sit-coms. Based on your results, personal experience, and the information provided by Rosenzweig, participate in a class discussion on the social and political influences of television programming.

Nature

Water Incorporated: The Commodification of the World's Water

Maude Barlow

Maude Barlow lives in Ottawa and chairs the Council of Canadians, a public advocacy organization. She is also a director of the International Forum on Globalization, based in San Francisco, and is the founding co-chair of the Action Canada Network. Most recently, she co-authored Blue Gold: The Battle Against Corporate Theft of the World's Water *(2003). Barlow is considered one of Canada's leading voices against the U.S.–Canada Free Trade Agreement, North American Free Trade Agreement (NAFTA), and the Multilateral Agreement on Investment.*

1 Global consumption of water is doubling every 20 years—more than twice the rate of human population growth. According to the United Nations, more than one billion people on Earth already lack access to fresh drinking water. If current trends persist, by 2025 the demand for fresh water will rise by 56 percent and as many as two-thirds of the world's population will be living with serious water shortages or absolute water scarcity.

Around the world, the most common tactic to meet increased water demand has been to divert rivers and to build environmentally destructive dams. The number of large dams worldwide has climbed from just over 5,000 in 1950 to 38,000 today. Only 2 percent of U.S. rivers and wetlands remain free-flowing and undeveloped, while the country has lost more than half of its original wetlands. In the U.S.,

37 percent of freshwater fish are at risk of extinction, 40 percent of amphibians are imperiled and 67 percent of freshwater mussels are extinct or vulnerable to extinction.

More than 30 countries already face water stress and scarcity. The Earth's water system can support, at most, only one more doubling of demand, estimated to occur in less than 30 years. The U.S. National Intelligence Council, a group that reports to the CIA, warns that water will become the main resource-scarcity problem by 2015 and that the instability created by water shortages "will increasingly affect the national security of the United States."

Fortune magazine notes that "water will be to the 21st century what oil was to the 20th." Who owns water and how much they are able to charge for it will become the question of the century. The privatization of water is already a $400-billion-a-year business. Multinational corporations hope to increase profits from water commodification even further by using international trade and investment agreements to control its flow and supply. One Canadian water company, Global Water Corp., puts it best: "Water has moved from being an endless commodity that may be taken for granted to a rationed necessity that may be taken by force."

5   Over the last few decades, multinational corporations have profited from the provision of water through the Structural Adjustment Programs (SAPs) of the World Bank and International Monetary Fund (IMF), which used these economic restructuring programs to give corporations access to the water systems of developing countries. Today, corporations are using a new generation of trade and investment agreements to gain ownership over the world's ever-dwindling water supplies so that they will become the suppliers of last resort.

The FTAA: At Your Service

In the past, governments unanimously believed that access to basic human services such as water, healthcare and education should not be included in trade agreements because these were essential components of citizenship. However, the North American Free Trade Agreement (NAFTA) and the General Agreement on Tariffs and Trade (GATT) began the process of eroding these basic human rights. Today, the Free Trade Area of the Americas (FTAA) is poised to take this process to a whole new level.

The Free Trade Area of the Americas is the formal name given to the massive expansion of NAFTA ["NAFTA for the Americas," Summer 2001]. The FTAA would impose NAFTA's failed model of privatization and deregulation on 34 nations in North, Central and South America and the Caribbean, creating the world's largest free-trade zone with a population of 800 million and a combined GDP of $11 trillion.

The FTAA's "services agreement" grants private corporations sweeping new authority to overrule government regulations. Under the FTAA, all public services—schools, hospitals, prisons—would be forced to open up for competition from foreign for-profit service corporations. This agreement would forbid any federal government or local government from giving preferential funding to domestic providers of sewer or water services.

The FTAA would increase the number of towns and cities forced into privatizing their water systems and would reduce the ability of governments to ensure that the privatized systems work to protect the environment, consumers and workers.

10 As the water crisis intensifies, governments worldwide—under 10 pressure from multinational corporations—are advocating the commodification and mass transport of water. Proponents of water privatization say that a market system is the only way to distribute water to the world's thirsty. But experience shows that selling water on the open market does not address the needs of poor, under-served people.

On the contrary, privatized water is delivered to those who can pay for it, such as wealthy cities and individuals, agriculture and industries. As one resident of New Mexico's high desert observed after his community's water was diverted for use by the high-tech industry: "Water flows uphill to money."

In cities and towns across the Western Hemisphere, results of water privatization have been almost universal: increased prices and a concurrent loss of access to water, failed promises of infrastructure improvement, loss of indigenous peoples' rights to water, worker layoffs, lack of information on water quality and big profits for the privatizing corporations.

In India, some households pay a staggering 25 percent of their income for water. Poor residents of Lima, Peru, pay private vendors as much as $3 per cubic meter for buckets of often-contaminated water while the affluent pay only 30 cents per cubic meter for treated municipal tap water.

Water-Related Conflicts

The push to commodify water comes at a time when the social, political and economic impacts of water scarcity are rapidly becoming a destabilizing force around the globe. In 1997, Malaysia, which supplies about half of Singapore's water, threatened to cut off its supply after Singapore criticized Malaysia's policies. In Africa, relations between Botswana and Namibia have been severely strained by Namibian plans to construct a pipeline to divert water from the shared Okavango River. In the water-starved Middle East, the late King Hussein of Jordan once said that the only thing he would go to war with Israel over was water because Israel controls Jordan's water supply.

15   More than 5 million people, most of them children, die every year   15
from illnesses caused by drinking poor-quality water. In the industrial maquiladoras along the Mexico-U.S. border, water is so scarce that Mexican babies and children are compelled to drink Coca-Cola and Pepsi instead.

Eighty percent of China's major rivers are so degraded they no longer support fish. China is facing the likelihood of severe grain shortages because of water depletion and the shift of water resources from agriculture to industry and cities. The resulting demand for grain in China soon could exceed the entire world's available exportable supply.

Today, the future of one of Earth's most vital resources is being determined by those who profit from its overuse. At the annual World Economic Development Congress, corporations and financial institutions met with government representatives from more than 84 countries to attend panels on such subjects as "Overcoming Obstacles to Water Investment." The agenda was clear: water should be treated like any other commodity, with its use determined by market principles.

The Global Water Power Play

The World Water Forum (WWF) held in The Hague in March 2000 was chaired by World Bank Vice President Ismail Serageldin. The WWF is part of the continuing activities of the World Water Council (WWC), a coalition of governments, international agencies and private-sector interests. The WWC has formed close working partnerships with private corporations, the Global Water Partnership and Business Partners for Development. The websites and reports of these organizations and corporations make clear that some of the world's largest water privateers are taking the lead in developing global water policies.

With the support of international trade agreements, these companies are setting their sights on the mass transport of water by pipeline and supertanker. Several companies are developing technology to pump fresh water into huge sealed bags to be towed across the oceans for sale.

20 The U.S. Global Water Corp., a Canadian company, has signed an agreement with Sitka, Alaska, to export 18 billion gallons of glacier water per year to China. It would then be bottled for export in one of China's "free trade" zones to take advantage of cheap labor. The company brochure entices investors "to harvest the accelerating opportunity . . . as traditional sources of water around the world become progressively depleted and degraded."

The National Post called Canada's water "blue gold" and Post business columnist Terence Corcoran predicts that "The issue will not be whether to export, but how much money the federal government and provinces will be able to extract from massive water shipments. . . . Using the OPEC model, they will attempt to cartelize the world supply of water to drive the price up."

Based on negotiating documents that have been released, we can begin to paint a picture of the threats to water that are likely to be included in the FTAA.

Under the agreement, the goods that are subject to the agreement's obligations include "waters, including natural or artificial waters, and aerated waters." In 1993, then-US Trade Representative Mickey Kantor said in a letter to a US environmental group, "When water is traded as a good, all provisions of [NAFTA] governing trade in goods apply."

"National Treatment" is a standard trade provision guaranteeing that countries do not "discriminate" by favoring domestic producers over foreign producers. This means that if a locality provides any portion of its water supply through a private company, it cannot favor a locally owned service provider that may have a greater commitment to the area and may be easier for the local community to oversee. Furthermore, once a permit is granted to a domestic company to export water, the corporations of all the other FTAA countries would have the same access rights to the commercial use of that water. For example, if a Bolivian company were granted the right to export Bolivian water, U.S. multinationals would then have the right to help themselves to as much Bolivian water as they wished.

25   NAFTA's "Investor State" provision (which the U.S., among others, would like to see included in the FTAA) gives investors, usually corporations, the right to sue a foreign government directly.

Under this provision, if any FTAA country, state or province permits only domestic companies to export water, corporations in the other countries would have the right to financial compensation for "discrimination."

NAFTA's Chapter 11 allows foreign corporations to sue a country if a government implements legislation that "expropriates" the company's future profits. For example, if a country privatized its water services, hired a foreign provider and then passed laws requiring improved environmental protections or worker safety, the client corporation could argue that the laws were an expropriation of its profits and therefore illegal under the FTAA.

Suing for the Access to Water

Corporations already have begun suing governments to gain access to domestic water sources. The first such NAFTA Chapter 11 case (Sun Belt Water Inc. vs. Canada) was filed in the fall of 1998. Sun Belt Water Inc. of Santa Barbara, Calif., filed suit after losing a contract to deliver Canadian water to California when British Columbia banned the export of bulk water in 1991. Sun Belt is seeking $220 million in damages. However, Sunbelt appears more interested in access to BC's water than the $220 million. As Sun Belt's CEO Jack Lindsay explained, "Because of NAFTA, we are now stakeholders in the national water policy in Canada."

Chapter 11 was also used successfully by the Virginia-based Ethyl Corp. to force Canada to reverse its ban on MMT, a toxic chemical gasoline additive. In June 1997, Canada banned the cross-border sale of MMT because it is, in the words of Canadian Prime Minister Jean Chretien, an "insidious neurotoxin." Under NAFTA, Ethyl sued Canada for $250 million in damages for lost future profits and for damaging the company's "good name." Rather than allow the case to go to a NAFTA tribunal where it feared losing, the Canadian government reversed its ban in July 1998 and paid Ethyl $13 million in compensation for its "trouble."

30   In July 1999, Canadian-owned Methanex Corp. sued the U.S. 30 for $970 million after California Gov. Gray Davis mandated the removal of methyl tertiary butyl ether (MTBE) from gasoline sold in the state by December 31, 2002. The chemical has been associated with human neurotoxicological effects and may cause cancer. Methanex claims that California's ban violates NAFTA by limiting the corporation's ability to sell MTBE.

Water as a Human Right

In January 2000, thousands of citizens of Cochabamba, Bolivia, took to the streets to oppose the takeover of their water systems by a company jointly owned by the U.S.-based multinational Bechtel and the Italian utility Edison ["Bolivia's Water War Victory," Autumn 2000]. The rebellion, which shut the city down for four days, was sparked after the foreign-owned water corporation raised Cochabamba's water rates 35 percent.

Bolivian President Hugo Banzer was eventually forced to lift martial law and Bechtel was compelled to abandon its Bolivian water-privatization scheme.

An international "civil summit" of farmers, workers, indigenous people, students, professionals, environmentalists, educators and nongovernmental organizations from Bolivia, Canada, India, Brazil and the U.S. subsequently gathered in Cochabamba to combine forces in the defense of the vital right to water. At the conclusion of the summit, they issued "The Cochabamba Declaration" which reads, in part:

- Water belongs to the Earth and all species and is sacred to life. Therefore, the world's water must be conserved, reclaimed and protected for all future generations and its natural patterns respected.
- Water is a fundamental human right and a public trust to be guarded by all levels of governments. Therefore it should not be commodified, privatized or traded for commercial purposes. These rights must be enshrined at all levels of government. An international treaty must ensure these principles are non-controvertible.

111

Questions on Meaning

1. To refer to water as a commodity is to identify a trend toward privatization and greater profits resulting from ownership. According to the author, how have corporations gained greater control over water through different types of agreements?

2. What role has NAFTA played in increasing the stakes companies would have in controlling water sources? In Maude Barlow's opinion, what problems are associated with it? Do you feel she could account for some advantages to privatization? Explain.

3. Barlow notes that corporations have been able to sue governments to gain access to water. Explain how this has happened. How does corporate control over water potentially compromise human right issues?

Questions on Rhetorical Strategy and Style

1. Writing teachers often say that an essay should have a hook, something that grabs the reader's attention. What is the effect of the first sentence of this essay? Does it hook you? If so, explain why.

2. The success of this essay rests on whether it creates in the reader a concern over a "water crisis." What evidence does the author provide that will most likely raise a reader's level of concern about water issues?

3. This article is published by the Global Policy Forum. From reading it, are you able to identify the kind of audience for this forum? How so? What does the author of this article assume about readers' knowledge of the issue at hand? Explain what conveys this.

Writing Assignments

1. Discussions about globalization are in the media every day. Some of these discussions are highly contested and have even led to public protests. The more we know about globalization, the better prepared we can be to situate ourselves in the

debate and determine what is at stake for us. One of the values of research is that it enables us to participate more effectively in important issues. Conduct your own research on globalization and write a brief report defining its major issues.

2. This essay opens up on a debate on whether water is to be defined as a commodity or a human right. How something is defined or gets named has much to do with how it is controlled and by whom. For example, in the western states, defining "wetlands" is a hot topic, because a state cannot build a highway in an area with wetlands designation. Write an essay about an environmental debate in your part of the country. In your essay, examine how the terms of the debate are set by the names people give to these topics.

Excerpt from *Slow Food: The Case for Taste*

Carlo Petrini

Carlo Petrini was born in Cuneo, Italy in 1949. He studied sociology in Trento, Italy. He began the slow food movement in the late 1980s in the form of a campaign against McDonalds in Rome. He is the editor of many magazines within the publishing house Slow Food Editore. He writes for La Stampa *and was one of* Time *magazine's influential people in 2004. He is the author of* Slow Food Nation: Why Our Food Should Be Good, Clean, Fair *(2007);* Slow Food Revolution: A New Culture for Dining and Living *(2006); and* Slow Food: The Case for Taste *(2001), from which the following selection comes. In 2002, Petrini received the Sicco Mansholt Prize for Slow Food's activities to promote and defend a new model of sustainable farming. In this selection, Petrini lays out his argument and the human importance of eating good food of your own choosing.*

Educating and Learning

The Praise of the Senses and the Paradox of Taste

1 Beginning in the 1950s, a powerful wave of industrialization and modernization swept over Italy. Historians, sociologists, and anthropologists have studied the effects of the passage from a rural society that had remained almost unchanged for centuries to one that closely followed the pattern of development of the richest nations, led by the United States. The changes in lifestyle, collective mentality, patterns of consumption, and even the landscape have been profound. And

Reprinted from *Slow Food: The Case for Taste*, translated by William McCuaig (2001), by permission of Columbia University Press.

there has been an enormous transformation in the way we take our nourishment.

Until the Second World War, around 60 percent of the limited household budgets of Italians went toward the cost of food, although the average diet remained meager: fewer than 3,000 calories per day per capita, on average. The basic foodstuffs were cereals, milk, wine, and little else. Only at the end of the 1950s did the consumption of meat begin to grow, at a rate that soon became exponential, going from 22 kilograms (48 pounds) per capita in 1960 to 62 kilograms (136 pounds) per capita in 1975. Italians were now eating more cheese, eggs, fresh fruit, sugar, and coffee, while the quantities of corn and rice consumed fell off, and that of wheat held stationary only because of the spread of pasta from its traditional stronghold in the center and south of the peninsula to the north. It was also at this time that the depopulation of the countryside began: 15 to 20 percent of the population changed residence, with many country people relocating to the coasts or the major urban centers, leaving villages and hamlets empty. The sharecropping farmsteads were abandoned, while agricultural businesses turned to monocultures, erasing the mixed farming of the old estates, and with it the autarkic production of foodstuffs.

Statistical research into Italian family budgets, carried out systematically by ISTAT, the national statistical agency, since 1952, pinpoints the new tendencies and the changes in modes of nourishment that resulted from the preponderance of the nuclear family, increased purchasing power, the decrease in heavy physical labor, and the entry of women into the labor market. Consumption was no longer restricted to local produce or local dishes (the spread of pasta was soon followed, for example, by the success of pizza), and thanks to the greater ease of transportation, was soon globalized. Advanced techniques of preservation, including deep freezing (for centuries the only options had been smoking, salting, and drying) made it possible to find "fresh" products anywhere, at any time of year, independently of where they were grown or raised and what the season was. The food distribution system ramified. The cooking styles of the different territories were suddenly in peril, crowded out by a sort of alimentary syncretism. So was family conviviality, which died in the United States with the advent of the TV dinner and later the microwave, as precooked and reheated dinners were eaten in silence before the blue glow of the television screen. Meals got lighter and more amorphous, and the number of them eaten outside the house, at cafeterias, snack bars, fast-food places, and restaurants, grew. Influenced by a new cult of health, the body, and the mirage of eternal youth, people began to follow diets that dictated their choices in the kitchen.

Clearly the changed relationship between contemporary man and food derives from the slashing of the umbilical cord that once bound the world of the peasant farmer to the world of consumption, the producer of food to the diner. In today's society, almost no one procures their daily wine directly from a trusted vine dresser/wine maker anymore, or goes to a farmstead to pick up a week's supply of eggs, a chicken, or a rabbit. Almost no one is personally acquainted with the baker who makes the bread she puts on the table, or the sausage maker who personally takes part in the butchering of pigs and the preparation of salami and other meat products, or the cheese maker who prepares cheese from the milk of his own sheep or goats. The small food stores and the *osterie* that were once to be found in even the smallest villages, and to which people went not only to get their provisions but to keep in touch with village life and meet their neighbors, closed their doors one by one, and in the cities the spread of the supermarkets (which now control 40 percent of the food retail business) is inexorably smothering the small retailers, with all that entails in loss of human rapport, direct selection of merchandise, and exchange of information and acquaintance. We now prefer to buy individual portions of prepackaged, presliced, and often precooked food, and opportunities to feel it, smell it, evaluate it, and compare it—in other words, to know what it is we are choosing and why—are growing ever more rare.

In this way we have lost touch forever with an immense heritage of wisdom relating to the cultivation of fruit and vegetables, the raising of animals, and the preparation of artisanal specialties and even traditional local dishes. There was a time when the family and the social milieu transmitted knowledge of foods, recipes, alimentary customs, and the recurring yearly occasions for special meals. Today this chain of transmission has been severed, and neither the schools nor other social institutions have taken its place. The result is that children and young people in our time (and many adults as well) have never seen a cow or a stable, the courtyard of a farmstead (Italian farms don't look like North American ones) or a wine cellar, up close. They identify the smell of an apple with a brand of shampoo, and imagine that fish grow in the rectangular shape of the "fish fingers" they consume battered and fried. Their tastes are formed by what the food industry puts before them, from French fries to snacks with soft drinks, and stark elementary flavors crowd out complexity and nuance.

Yet on the other hand, we see that this loss of roots has left a void, surreptitiously filled by spectacles of various kinds and ably exploited by advertisers in order to foist industrial products on the public with messages evoking naturalness, genuineness, the link with tradition, and local specificity. Then there is the flood of cookbooks spilling off the shelves of the bookstores and inviting consumers to rediscover "old-time cooking"; the profusion of local festivals and banquets dreamed up in order to celebrate specialties or recipes, many of them highly improbable or outright inventions; the multitude of cooking shows on television, offering an idyllic and historically false vision of the gastronomy of the regions of Italy. The massive and often ill-fitting use of terms like "traditional," "*tipico*" (i.e., specific to a locality), "genuine," and "*territorio*" (in the sense discussed and used throughout this book) indicates a spreading phenomenon.

When choices about what and when to eat are no longer suggested (or dictated) by tradition and social milieu, everyone assumes direct responsibility for what she eats, swayed by advertising, fashion, diet information, common beliefs, and personal tastes and distastes. In this situation, the strategy to follow is a large-scale campaign of consumer education, so that, despite the din of the marketplace, everyone will be in a position to choose a proper, healthy, honest, and enjoyable mixture of foods for himself or herself. We need to reconstruct the individual and collective heritage, the capacity to distinguish—in a word, taste.

The primary instruments that, when trained, can make it possible for anyone to choose an adequate and enjoyable diet are our senses. Slow Food endorses the primacy of sensory experience and treats eyesight, hearing, smell, touch, and taste as so many instruments of discernment, self-defense, and pleasure. The education of taste is the Slow way to resist McDonaldization. It is not so much a question of fighting a fundamentalist war against the spread of the hamburger as it is of informing, stimulating curiosity, giving everyone the opportunity to choose.

To train the senses, refine perception, restore atrophied dimensions of sensory experience—these are the objectives of Slow Food.

By "voting with their feet," consumers can actually do a lot to signal to producers that quality matters. But quality, which is an ensemble of objectively determinable values, even when it comes to food, has to be discovered, then learned and codified. That means gaining the kind of knowledge that allows you to determine how foods and wines are produced, how they evolve and change biologically, how they are preserved, which ingredients stabilize them and which denature them, and what characteristics enable you to classify them. Follow this route and you will acquire the salutary habit of recognizing and assessing what it is you are eating and drinking, and the beneficial effects will surely follow: you will be more demanding and you will discourage the kind of production that relies on short-sighted and indiscriminate purchasing patterns by offering low-grade food. In sum, if quality is our right as consumers, then it is up to us to equip ourselves to recognize it and ask for it.

10   Clearly a correct approach to food and wine is a question of men-   10
tality, of one's overall attitude to life—an attitude that does not repress pleasure but searches it out, making choices in the light of reason, the attitude of those who know how to maintain close rapport with the roots of things, who recognize the importance of material culture and conviviality. Real knowledge, not just superficial impressions, or worse than that, pedantry, opens the door to real communication and the sharing of interests.

Let me put the paradox this way: no matter how important sensory awareness and knowledge of how food gets from the fields to our dinner tables are in justifying our choices about what to eat, the pleasure we get from dinner is not reducible to a mechanical process or an arithmetical sum. Our pleasure is shaped in certain ways by different factors, cultural and sensory, and differences in the societal context and personal history of every person. Precisely because the word "taste" applies to many forms of culture, including art, fashion, and elegance, when used in gastronomy it also absorbs a thousand nuances that can't be chewed and swallowed, and is charged with values that often have little to do with flavor.

Hence the difficulty of challenging a system of food production that makes consumption into a total behavior and the product into an absolute value, proclaiming *gusto, goût, sapore,* and *taste.* . . . If training people's taste buds were all it took to transform their nutritional intake, then the world would live in a realm of complete gratification, total harmony, and the perfect marriage of didacticism and pleasure. Unfortunately things aren't like that, and tasting is not enough. This paradox can be more clearly stated by looking at the origin of fast food, the Adam's rib from which Eve was formed, and with her the end of the earthly paradise. McDonald's was born when the company made choices that differentiated it, starting around the end of the 1950s, from drive-ins and bars and cafés with jukeboxes, associating its hamburgers with familiar and reassuring values and making sure all the restaurants served the same food the same way and that the employees worked as a team. Perhaps it is not an exaggeration to say that in the soft bun and the ground meat patty, the commercial strategy is so forceful that it is the dominant flavor. Against an adversary like that, classically ceremonious tasting sessions with just the right shape of glass and starched white napkins, as fragile as one's own taste buds, will make little headway and could never be the sole vehicle for launching a process of recovering memory and creating new conviviality.

Taste is a pact of fellowship and a program of cultural integration. It should be studied like a restless creature that thrives on diversity, works retroactively to revive memories, and goes forward blindly, promising virtual pleasures. It needs people who speak a Babel of languages and continually discover new foods, babies who grow up and, one day, hand on their own way of experiencing pleasure to other babies. Yet another paradox: in a world organized around hamburgers, popcorn, and French fries and reeking with the smell of deep-frying oil and deodorant, taste represents a new moral imperative. It signifies rigor in choices about production, even before choices about consumption, firmness in defense of our heritage against fleeting and heedless satisfaction. There is not a single Slow Food project that doesn't link pleasure with responsibility and food with awareness, that doesn't bring to mind a philosophical banquet in which eating and debate about the resources and values of the human race go hand in hand. Just yesterday we were talking about specific territories, about kinds of grapes and vegetables that needed protection, and tomorrow we will take up the destiny of a world that is called "Third" and is being culturally exterminated.

These paradoxes lead to very stark choices: if pleasure is a moral right, then an education and an ethics of taste become necessary and indeed indispensable for its attainment. This holds true for adults as they play the role of schoolchildren during one of our workshops

119

dedicated to bread or olive oil; but the main target of this education will have to be the young rebels who prefer McDonald's French fries to homemade ones and are satisfied with the cold, overcooked pasta served at the school cafeteria. The philosophical banquet must speak about the kids, indeed *to* the kids. How Slow Food arrived at this contradiction requires a bit of history.

Questions on Meaning

1. What are the basic precepts of Slow Food? What social conditions does this movement respond to? In Petrini's estimation, why is it important "to resist McDonaldization" and change the way we eat?

2. Petrini says that the industrialized processing of food has transformed our tastes and "left a void" advertisers fill with false messages about naturalness. What is the void he refers to? What signs illustrate that certain conditions have been lost? How does advertising purport to "reconnect" consumers to those traditions?

3. For Petrini, taste is about more that the taste of food itself. As he says, "tasting is not enough." Not enough in what sense? Why does this represent a paradox? How does Petrini define taste? Why is it necessary to cultivate good taste in the broader sense that he intends?

Questions on Rhetorical Strategy and Style

1. Petrini creates a compelling metaphor by likening the advent of fast food with Adam and Eve's expulsion from paradise and the loss of innocence. How does this metaphor hold true?

2. Note that some of the diction that contributes to the tone of Petrini's writing lends it a rather aesthetic and philosophical character. The most obvious example of this comes as he asserts that "taste represents a new moral imperative." What other words and phrases convey to the reader Petrini's sense of urgency as well as the social importance of his subject?

3. Where in the chapter does Petrini emphasize the connection between food and "human rapport" and community? How does he attempt to persuade you that the "chain of transmission" that passed down important values "has been severed"? What makes you trust his perspective?

Writing Assignments

1. Clearly we live in a fast food culture. It suits our lifestyle, for better or for worse. The problem, though, is that our tastes are determined by food companies limiting our choices of what to consume. However, perhaps things are changing to an extent. Write

an essay on the efforts people have made to return choice, variety, and high value to food. One obvious example in the popularity of the farmer's market. Also, the popularity of cooking programs on television. What other signs show that things may be changing for the better?

2. Write a report on the Slow Food Movement and its influence on our taste for food and social structures that Petrini considers critical in the age of fast food and commercialization. Have Americans been eating better, demanding more good food?

3. Write an essay on other types of trends or movements that attempt to reconnect people to nature and empower them by helping them to grant themselves the right to live a better physical and social existence.

The Pain of Animals

David Suzuki

Born in Vancouver, David Suzuki (1936–) has worked as a research scientist, environmentalist, and broadcaster who deals with the relationships among social, economic, and ecological needs. A professor of zoology at the University of British Columbia until 2001, he is currently at the Sustainable Development Research Institute (UBC). In this essay Suzuki details the price that animals pay for human progress.

Medical technology has taken us beyond the normal barriers of life and death and thereby created unprecedented choices in *human* lives. Until recently, we have taken for granted our right to use other species in any way we see fit. Food, clothing, muscle power have been a few of the benefits we've derived from this exploitation. This tradition has continued into scientific research where animals are studied and "sacrificed" for human benefit. Now serious questions are being asked about our right to do this.

Modern biological research is based on a shared evolutionary history of organisms that enables us to extrapolate from one organism to another. Thus, most fundamental concepts in heredity were first shown in fruit flies, molecular genetics began using bacteria and viruses and much of physiology and psychology has been based on studies in mice and rats. But today, as extinction rates have multiplied as a result of human activity, we have begun to ask what right we have to use all other animate forms simply to increase human knowledge or for profit or entertainment. Underlying the "animal rights" movement is the troubling question of where we fit in the rest of the natural world.

When I was young, one of my prized possessions was a BB gun. Dad taught me how to use it safely and I spent many hours wandering through the woods in search of prey. It's not easy to get close enough to a wild animal to kill it with a BB gun, but I did hit a few pigeons and starlings. I ate everything I shot. Then as a teenager, I graduated to a .22 rifle and with it, I killed rabbits and even shot a pheasant once.

One year I saw an ad for a metal slingshot in a comic book. I ordered it, and when it arrived, I practised for weeks shooting marbles at a target. I got to be a pretty good shot and decided to go after something live. Off I went to the woods and soon spotted a squirrel minding its own business doing whatever squirrels do. I gave chase and began peppering marbles at it until finally it jumped onto a tree, ran to the top and found itself trapped. I kept blasting away and grazed it a couple of times so it was only a matter of time before I would knock it down. Suddenly, the squirrel began to cry—a piercing shriek of terror and anguish. That animal's wail shook me to the core and I was overwhelmed with horror and shame at what I was doing—for no other reason than conceit with my prowess with a slingshot, I was going to *kill* another being. I threw away the slingshot and my guns and have never hunted again.

All my life, I have been an avid fisherman. Fish have always been the main source of meat protein in my family, and I have never considered fishing a sport. But there is no denying that it is exciting to reel in a struggling fish. We call it "playing" the fish, as if the wild animal's desperate struggle for survival is some kind of game.

I did "pleasure-fish" once while filming for a television report on the science of fly fishing. We fished a famous trout stream in the Catskill Mountains of New York state where all fish had to be caught and released. The fish I caught had mouths gouged and pocked by previous encounters with hooks. I found no pleasure in it because to me fish are to be caught for consumption. Today, I continue to fish for food, but I do so with a profound awareness that I am a predator of animals possessing well-developed nervous systems that detect pain. Fishing and hunting have forced me to confront the way we exploit other animals.

I studied the genetics of fruit flies for twenty-five years and during that time probably raised and killed tens of millions of them without a thought. In the early seventies, my lab discovered a series of mutations affecting behaviour of flies, and this find led us into an investigation of nerves and muscles. I applied for and received research funds to study behaviour in flies on the basis of the *similarity* of their neu-romuscular systems to ours. In fact, psychologists and neurobiologists analyse behaviour, physiology and neuroanatomy of guinea pigs, rats, mice and other animals as *models* for human behaviour. So our ner-vous systems must closely resemble those of other mammals.

These personal anecdotes raise uncomfortable questions. What gives us the right to exploit other living organisms as we see fit? How do we know that these other creatures don't feel pain or anguish just as we do? Perhaps there's no problem with fruit flies, but where do we draw the line? I used to rationalize angling because fish are cold-blooded, as if warm-bloodedness indicates some kind of demarcation of brain development or greater sensitivity to pain. But anyone who has watched a fish's frantic fight to escape knows that it exhibits all the manifestations of pain and fear.

I've been thinking about these questions again after spending a weekend in the Queen Charlotte Islands watching grey whales close up. The majesty and freedom of these magnificent mammals contrasted strikingly with the appearance of whales imprisoned in aquariums. Currently, the Vancouver Public Aquarium is building a bigger pool for some of its whales. In a radio interview, an aquarium representative was asked whether even the biggest pool can be adequate for animals that normally have the entire ocean to rove. Part of her answer was that if we watched porpoises in the pool, we'd see that "they are quite happy."

10   That woman was projecting human perceptions and emotions 10 on the porpoises. Our ability to empathize with other people and liv-ing things is one of our endearing qualities. Just watch someone with a beloved pet, an avid gardener with plants or, for that matter, even an owner of a new car and you will see how readily we can personal-ize and identify with another living organism or an object. But are we justified in our inferences about captive animals in their cages?

Most wild animals have evolved with a built-in need to move freely over vast distances, fly in the air or swim through the ocean. Can a wild animal imprisoned in a small cage or pool, removed from its habi-tat and forced to conform to the impositions of our demands, ever be considered "happy"?

Animal rights activists are questioning our right to exploit animals, especially in scientific research. Scientists are understandably defensive, especially after labs have been broken into, experiments ruined and animals "liberated." But just as I have had to question my hunting and fishing, scientists cannot avoid confronting the issues raised, especially in relation to our closest relatives, the primates.

People love to watch monkeys in a circus or zoo and a great deal of the amusement comes from the recognition of ourselves in them. But our relationship with them is closer than just superficial similarities. When doctors at Loma Linda hospital in California implanted the heart of a baboon into the chest of Baby Fae, they were exploiting our close *biological* relationship.

Any reports on experimentation with familiar mammals like cats and dogs are sure to raise alarm among the lay public. But the use of primates is most controversial. In September 1987, at the Wildlife Film Festival in Bath, England, I watched a film shot on December 7, 1986, by a group of animal liberationists who had broken into SEMA, a biomedical research facility in Maryland. It was such a horrifying document that many in the audience rushed out after a few minutes. There were many scenes that I could not watch. As the intruders entered the facility, the camera followed to peer past cage doors, opened to reveal the animals inside. I am not ashamed to admit that I wept as baby monkeys deprived of any contact with other animals seized the fingers of their liberators and clung to them as our babies would to us. Older animals cowered in their tiny prisons, shaking from fear at the sudden appearance of people.

15   The famous chimpanzee expert, Jane Goodall, also screened the   15 same film and as a result asked for permission to visit the SEMA facility. This is what she saw (*American Scientist,* November–December 1987):

> Room after room was lined with small, bare cages, stacked one above the other, in which monkeys circled round and round and chimpanzees sat huddled, far gone in depression and despair.
>
> Young chimpanzees, three or four years old, were crammed, two together into tiny cages measuring 57 cm by 57 cm and only 61 cm high. They could hardly turn around. Not yet part of any experiment, they had been confined to these cages for more than three months.
>
> The chimps had each other for comfort, but they would not remain together for long. Once they are infected, probably with hepatitis, they will be separated and placed in another cage. And there they will remain, living in conditions of severe sensory deprivation, for the next several years. During that time they will become insane.

Goodall's horror sprang from an intimate knowledge of chimpanzees in their native habitat. There, she has learned, chimps are nothing like the captive animals that we know. In the wild, they are highly social, requiring constant interaction and physical contact. They travel long distances, and they rest in soft beds they make in the trees. Laboratory cages do not provide the conditions needed to fulfill the needs of these social, emotional and highly intelligent animals.

Ian Redmond (*BBC Wildlife,* April 1988) gives us a way to understand the horror of what lab conditions do to chimps:

> Imagine locking a two- or three-year-old child in a metal box the size of an isolette—solid walls, floor and ceiling, and a glass door that clamps shut, blotting out most external sounds—and then leaving him or her for months, the only contact, apart from feeding, being when the door swings open and masked figures reach in and take samples of blood or tissue before shoving him back and clamping the door shut again. Over the past 10 years, 94 young chimps at SEMA have endured this procedure.

Chimpanzees, along with the gorilla, are our closest relatives, sharing ninety-nine per cent of our genes. And it's that biological proximity that makes them so useful for research—we can try out experiments, study infections and test vaccines on them as models for people. And although there are only about 40,000 chimps left in the wild, compared to millions a few decades ago, the scientific demand for more has increased with the discovery of AIDS.

No chimpanzee has ever contracted AIDS, but the virus grows in them, so scientists argue that chimps will be invaluable for testing vaccines. On February 19, 1988, the National Institute of Health in the U.S. co-sponsored a meeting to discuss the use of chimpanzees in research. Dr. Maurice Hilleman, Director of the Merck Institute for Therapeutic Research, reported:

> We need more chimps. . . . The chimpanzee is certainly a threatened species and there have been bans on importing the animal into the United States and into other countries, even though . . . the chimpanzee is considered to be an agricultural pest in many parts of the world where it exists. And secondly, it's being destroyed by virtue of environmental encroachment—that is, destroying the natural habitat. So these chimpanzees are being eliminated by virtue of their being an agricultural pest and by the fact that their habitat is being

destroyed. So why not rescue them? The number of chimpanzees for AIDS research in the United States [is] somewhere in the hundreds and certainly, we need thousands.

20   Our capacity to rationalize our behaviour and needs is remarkable.   20
Chimpanzees have occupied their niche over tens of millennia of biological evolution. *We* are newcomers who have encroached on *their* territory, yet by defining them as *pests* we render them expendable. As Redmond says, "The fact that the chimpanzee is our nearest zoological relative makes it perhaps the unluckiest animal on earth, because what the kinship has come to mean is that we feel free to do most of the things to a chimp that we mercifully refrain from doing to each other."

And so the impending epidemic of AIDS confronts us not only with our inhumanity to each other but to other species.

Questions on Meaning

1. What is Suzuki's point of view on the use of animals for scientific research? Point to specific statements in the text to support your answer.
2. What useful social purpose is served by keeping whales in aquariums? What harm is done to the animals?
3. Based on the evidence Suzuki presents, what is the greatest harm that results from the use of animals for scientific purposes? Explain.

Questions on Strategy and Style

1. Why does Suzuki begin with the story of his childhood experience hunting with a BB gun?
2. Which of Suzuki's arguments or illustrations is most persuasive? Why?
3. Why does Suzuki stress the biological similarities between people and chimpanzees? What argumentative end is served by the analogy?

Writing Assignments

1. Tell the story of a moment when you realized the difference between right and wrong.
2. Research a pharmaceutical product that you use. The product might be a medicine or a cosmetic. What kinds of tests were used to assure the public that the product was safe for human use?
3. Do you believe that it is morally right or practically necessary to use animals to test medicines for humans? Is it necessary for all medicines or only for those that treat more serious diseases such as AIDS? Write an essay that presents your point of view on animal testing.

Science

Should Human Cloning be Permitted? and Yes, Human Cloning Should be Permitted

Patricia A. Baird and Chris MacDonald (respectively)

Patricia A. Baird

Born in England, Patricia Baird studied medicine in Canada, earning a B.A. in biological sciences and an M.D. with a specialty in pediatrics and medical genetics from McGill University in Montréal, Quebec. She has developed a prenatal diagnostic program for women, and she teaches medical genetics at the University of British Columbia. A scholar as well as a practitioner and professor, she was the first woman to chair the Department of Medical Genetics at the university and is a Fellow of both the Canadian College of Medical Geneticists and the Royal College of Physicians and Surgeons. In 2002 she was awarded the Order of British Columbia in recognition of her work. Baird has published extensively on medical and ethical issues, including genetic testing, the human genome project, industry-sponsored clinical trials, cloning, and public health policy. When the state of California began investigating the prospect of authorizing human cloning, Baird was invited to make a presentation to the legislative committee charged with recommending a position on the issue. In this selection adapted from that testimony for publication in The Annals of the Royal College of

Reprinted from *The Royal College of Physicians and Surgeons of Canada*, June 2000, by permission of the author.

Physicians and Surgeons of Canada, she presents an unequivocal and carefully constructed argument against human cloning.

Should Human Cloning be Permitted?

Introduction and Background

1   The California state legislature has struck a committee to recommend by December 2001 whether human cloning should be permitted. This committee has invited individuals to present their recommendations on what position should be taken on human cloning, and outline their reasons. This article is an abridged version of an invited presentation in January 2000 to that committee.

A Qualitatively Different Type of Reproduction

Producing humans by somatic-cell nuclear-transfer cloning differs from sexual reproduction—it separates reproduction from recombination. Normally, in an outbred species such as humans, we cannot predict what the overall characteristics of an embryo will be. In sexual reproduction, it is unpredictable which combination of the parents' thousands of genes will occur. To date, in creating the next generation, we have had to give ourselves over to chance. But if nuclear transfer is used, the nucleus can be taken from an adult whose characteristics are known—and the process reproduces the biology of the former individual. It becomes possible to select by known characteristics which humans will be copied. The new technology allows the asexual replication of a human being, the ability to predetermine the full complement of a child's nuclear genes, and the easier alteration of the genes of prospective individuals. Cloning is a change in the integrity of our species, and we must think about the long-term consequences.

Public Reaction to Human Cloning

Cloning used to produce a human is rejected by the overwhelming majority of people. Polls on new scientific developments have limitations, but the Economist reported that over 90 per cent of Americans were opposed to human cloning.[1] Other polls have shown similar results.[2,3] Polls, however, are affected by how the questions are asked, so an in-depth approach is needed. Many experts believe that lay people cannot understand complicated scientific topics, but there are data showing that they can assimilate and make judgments about

132

complex issues. The Wellcome Trust did a qualitative focus-group study, and reported that opposition to human cloning was "nearly universal" among participants.[4] Most were against the idea of using cloning for reproductive purposes, stemming from concerns for the children and society, as much as from fears about interfering with nature. When over 90 per cent of citizens in a democracy oppose human cloning, it is difficult for a government to justify a policy that permits it. There are a few people, however, who would pursue cloning because they see potential advantages for themselves.

Foreseeable Requests for Cloning

There are foreseeable situations where individuals may want to pursue cloning, for example, for couples where both are infertile and have neither eggs nor sperm, or where the male produces no sperm. Given that there are new treatment techniques using cells from testicular biopsy, such problems are rare. A second example is where a lesbian couple might wish to use one partner's body cell and the enucleated egg of the other to produce a child together. In these scenarios, there are other options available to form a family—such as sperm donation, egg and embryo donation, or adoption. Other situations where cloning may be pursued is when a couple's child is dying or is killed, and they want to replace him or her by using one of his or her cells in nuclear-transfer cloning; or when a clone could provide a genetically compatible organ for transplantation. There will be instances where people wish to pursue cloning for particular reasons.[5–7]

5   The arguments about physical and psychological harm to clones   5
have also been well delineated.[8,9] For example, with regard to possible physical harms, congenital malformations, handicap, early death, increased risk of cancer, premature aging, and death have all been raised. Possible psychological harms to cloned individuals (replicands) have also been outlined, including diminished individuality, a sense of foreclosed future, or a disturbed sense of identity. An important part of human identity is the sense of arising from a maternal and a paternal line while at the same time being a unique individual. Many children who are adopted, or conceived from donor insemination, show a deep need to learn about their biological origins. Making children by cloning means that they do not have this dual genetic origin; they are not connected to others in the same biological way as the rest of humanity. The first person born this way would have to cope with being the first not to come from the union of egg and sperm. Social,

133

family, and kinship relationships that support human flourishing have evolved over millennia—but there is no way to place replicands. Is the DNA source the twin? The mother? The father?

Widening the Frame

Most debate on human cloning focuses on a weighing of harms and benefits to individuals. This is a dangerously incomplete framing. Looking at the issue as a matter of reproductive technology choice, although it focuses on individual autonomy, reproductive freedom, and protection of children, means that other issues are omitted.[10] We need to shift from the framing as individual choice, to a framing that reveals how permitting cloning affects future generations and society. I am reminded of one of the consultations of the Royal Commission on New Reproductive Technologies with an aboriginal group in Canada. They told the commission about their seventh-generation rule. They said that when they had to make a big decision in their community, they always considered what the consequences were likely to be in the seventh generation. This is a useful perspective to have, because viewing cloning as a personal matter inappropriately minimizes potentially serious social consequences. Individual choices in reproduction are not isolated acts—they affect the child, other people, and future generations. The wider consequences must be considered because we all have a stake in the type of community that we live in. We do not want it to be one where the use of cloning commodifies children, commercializes family formation, or increases social injustice. Cloning raises issues about the future of our species. We have not yet found the wisdom to deal with hunger, poverty, and environmental degradation—we are unlikely to have the wisdom to direct our own evolution.

Nuclear-transfer cloning allows third parties to choose the genotypes of people who will be cloned. Before, when two people mated, no one could control which genes the child received out of a myriad of possibilities. This lottery of reproduction has been a protection against people being predetermined, chosen, or designed by others—including parents.

Cloning directs the production of human beings in an unprecedented way. When a child of a particular genetic constitution is "made," it is easier to look on him or her as a product, rather than a gift of providence. If we can, and some people do, make children "to order," it is likely to change the way we view children.

An impetus to developing nuclear-transfer cloning for producing animals has been that it could then be combined with genetic enhancement—genes could be added to give the animals desired traits. Genes are inserted into cells in culture, then the cells screened to pick the ones that have incorporated the desired genes. These altered cells are used as the donors of nuclei for cloned animals. It is then possible to create transgenic cloned animals with commercially desirable genetic traits (for example, heavier meat yield or production of insulin in the milk).[11]

10   Reproduction by nuclear-transfer cloning makes it possible to think about genetically enhancing humans. A person's cells could be cultured, genes inserted, and those cells taking up the desired genes used to produce a cloned "improved" individual. We could insert genes for viral-disease resistance, or to protect against baldness or degenerative diseases, or insert genes related to height or intelligence. If nuclear-transfer cloning is permitted, what will stop genetic enhancement being used eventually? There would be strong individual motivation to have a taller or disease-resistant child. We would then be taking human evolution into our own hands. Are we wise enough to manage it or the social consequences? Most people will want their child to be brighter, taller, disease-resistant—so this technology could make people more standard, based on individual choices and market forces. If it works, it is likely to become used more often than just occasionally.

Who would have access to cloning or genetic improvements? Everyone? It is likely that those with financial resources would have access, but not other people, because cloning or enhancement would have to be provided as a socially underwritten "good" if it were to be available to everyone. And it is unlikely that most countries would provide publicly supported cloning, given that there are few social benefits and many potential harms.

If cloning or enhancement technology were provided as a public good to ensure equality of access, the government would have to decide in what circumstances people may clone themselves, and what traits were desirable. Docility? Height? Ability to provide a tissue transplant? Unless the market is to decide, criteria as to who may clone themselves, and a regulatory body will be needed.

If cloning is used, will we undermine the unconditional parental acceptance of offspring that is central to nurturing human beings? Parental acceptance is likely to become conditional when we are able

135

to program for certain characteristics. If cloning technology or genetic enhancement is permitted, people with disabilities, or members of racial or ethnic minorities, will be affected differently, and in a way unlikely to lead to greater equality and respect.

There are forces favouring the use of cloning—particular individuals will pursue it, and it will benefit financially those who provide it, so it is likely to be marketed to the public.

15   Many issues arising from cloning cannot be resolved in the framework of individual autonomy and reproductive choice. The focus on autonomy leads us to overlook the collective and transgenerational consequences of leaving the use of reproductive technologies to individual choices.[12] The use of scientific technology focused on individual wishes may result in social harms because individual interests differ from the public good at times. It is analogous to the tragedy of the commons,[13] which is exemplified by ranchers sharing grazing land, or fishers sharing a fishing ground. There is an incentive for individuals to overgraze or overfish because the benefits of doing so accrue to the individual, whereas the costs and harms occur to the community. The aggregate effect of individually beneficial choices may harm the long-term common good, and the cumulative impact of individual choices can result in an unethical system. Public policy-making differs from individual-based decision-making—because the moral unit of a physician is the patient, while the moral unit of public policy is all citizens.[14] If there is a conflict between the total social good and the good of an individual, public policy must uphold the public interest.

All members of the public have a stake in whether cloning is permitted, because if cloned people exist, the changes affect everyone. Even though a majority do not want to allow it, if it is permitted, we would all live in a world where people are cloned. Even though initially, individuals on whom cloning technology had a direct impact would be a minority, their collective experiences would influence social values. In public policy-making, it is inappropriate to subordinate every consideration to the question of whether it helps a couple to have a family. Society has a legitimate role in deciding whether cloning will be used. The far-reaching nature of this choice means more voices must be involved in making decisions. The decisions should not be taken preemptively by a clinical facility or a group of scientists who ignore the wishes of the rest of the community. We need the perspectives not just of those who are knowledgeable in biology or science; we also need the perspectives of sociologists, humanists, and citizens from a variety of life experiences. On something that affects our species' future, it would be valuable to have the perspectives of people from many countries.

Conclusions Regarding Policy

There is no compelling case to make people by asexual means; human reproductive cloning is without potential benefits to almost all citizens, and other options are available in most situations. Many institutions have come to this conclusion; the prospects of making human beings by cloning have elicited concern in many countries, and there have been calls for a worldwide ban on cloning used to produce humans by many political and religious leaders, and by organizations such as the World Health Organization, the World Medical Organization, the American Medical Association, and UNESCO. Nineteen countries in the Council of Europe have signed an agreement that bans human cloning. Medicine, science, and technology are worldwide endeavours, so this is an issue facing humans as a species. For this reason, WHO is making an international effort to co-operate on guidelines for cloning in humans.

History shows that where there is a demand for a new service and the ability of a few to pay for it, unless there is legislation, there will be professionals willing to provide it. There is licensing of fertility clinics in several European countries, but in some other countries, reproductive technologies are highly commercialized and little regulated. If human cloning were permitted in the United States, it would likely proceed in the billion-dollar private reproductive-medicine sector. In this market-driven context, its use is unlikely to be controlled. It is now possible to peruse catalogues if you wish to buy eggs or surrogate pregnancies, so it seems likely that if human cloning is permitted in the United States, it is only a matter of time before pressure from individuals with specific interests would open up the field. Legislation is needed to ban the implantation into a woman of an egg cell that has had its nucleus transferred from a body cell. When such legislation is written, its wording should not inadvertently ban non-reproductive cloning research, or animal cloning research that may be of benefit, and that many people see as acceptable.

How we use cloning is not an individual or medical matter. It is a matter of social policy that cannot be viewed in a narrow framework of reproductive technology and individual choice. How we choose to use this technological capacity will shape society for our children, their children, and after. How it is used is likely to entrench existing inequalities, and create new ones.

20   In conclusion, using nuclear-transfer cloning to allow people to have a child introduces a different way of reproduction for our species. Once we breach this barrier, it leaves us with no place to stop. Given all the problems outlined, the reasons for permitting cloning to produce a person are insufficiently compelling. Even in the few circumstances where the case for human cloning seems justified, there are alternative solutions. We are at an appropriate stopping place on a slippery slope. Not all reasons why a person might wish to copy his or her cells are unethical, but given there are other options open to people wishing to form a family, concerns about individual and social harms from cloning are strong enough that it is not justified to permit it. These issues affecting the creation of the next generation are important for the future of our species; we must deal with them wisely. I hope we can.

References

1. Whatever next? *The Economist* 1997 March 1;79–81.
2. Time/CNN poll. 1997 March.
3. International Food Information Council. *Wirthlin group quorum survey*, 1997 March 21–24.
4. *Public perspectives on human cloning, medicine in society program.* The Wellcome Trust, 1999 June (http://www.wellcome.ac. uk/en/1/awtpubrepcln.html).
5. McGee G. The human cloning debate. Berkeley: Berkeley Hills Books, 1998.
6. Hummer J, Almeder R. Human cloning. Biomedical Ethics Reviews. Totowa: 1998.
7. Andrews L. *The clone age: 20 years at the forefront of reproductive technology.* New York: Henry Holt, 1999.
8. Wilson JQ, Kass L. *The ethics of human cloning.* Washington: American Enterprise Press, 1999:10(2).
9. Cloning human beings. Report of the national bioethics advisory commission. *Hastings Centre Report* 1997:27(5).
10. Baylis F. Human cloning: three mistakes and a solution. Unpublished manuscript.
11. Pennis E. After Dolly, a pharming frenzy. *Science* 1998:279;646-8.
12. Baird PA. Individual interests, societal interests, and reproductive technologies. *Perspectives Biology Medicine* 1997;40(3):440–51.
13. Hardin G. The tragedy of the commons. *Science* 1968;162:1243–8.
14. Lamm RD. Redrawing the ethics map. *Hastings Centre Report* 1999;29(2):28–9.

Chris MacDonald

An associate professor of philosophy at Saint Mary's University in Halifax, Nova Scotia, Chris MacDonald coordinates the university's master's degree program in philosophy. He has also served a post-doctoral fellowship in the department of Bioethics and Dalhousie University and conducted graduate research at the University of British Columbia's Young Centre for Applied Ethics. Throughout his academic career he has been active in public organizations, serving on the executive committee of the Canadian Bioethics Society, and as president of the Canadian Society for the Study of Practical Ethics. He is also a member of the editorial board of the Journal of Business Ethics *and a member of the Ethics Research Network. In addition to co-authoring the Canadian edition of* The Power of Critical Thinking *(2007), MacDonald has published articles on bioethics in a number of journals, including the* American Journal of Bioethics, The Scientist, *and the* Canadian Bioethics Society Newsletter. *When Patricia Baird's article opposing human cloning appeared in* The Annals of the Royal College of Physicians and Surgeons of Canada, *MacDonald wrote the following response, arguing that caution, rather than an outright ban, is the appropriate approach to the issue.*

Yes, Human Cloning should be Permitted

1 Patricia Baird's discussion of human cloning (*Annals RCPSC*, June 2000) challenges the prospect of nuclear-transfer cloning for the purposes of human reproduction. Baird reviews a long list of familiar worries about human cloning, but the most striking feature of her discussion is its frankness in placing the onus of justification on the shoulders of those who would permit human cloning. The reasons for permitting cloning, she argues, are "insufficiently compelling," so cloning should be prohibited. The implication is that any new

---

Reprinted from *The Royal College of Physicians and Surgeons of Canada*, July 17, 2000, by permission of the author.

technology should be forbidden unless and until enough justification can be found for allowing its use.

Baird is to be commended for her frankness. But the onus is misplaced, or at least too severe. One need not be a single-minded defender of liberty to think that, contrary to Baird's implication, we need good reasons to limit the actions of others, particularly when those actions do no clear and specific harm. The fact that a portion of society—even a majority—finds an activity distasteful is insufficient grounds for passing a law forbidding it. For example, it is presumably true that at one point, roughly 90 per cent of the public (the same proportion that Baird says is against human cloning) was opposed to homosexuality. Does (or did) this justify action on the part of government to ban homosexual lifestyles? Surely not.

There may be a flaw in my analogy. Human cloning, according to critics, has harmful effects (or at least risks). Indeed, Baird suggests that the arguments regarding potential physical and psychological harm to clones have been "well delineated." In fact, a convincing case has yet to be made for the claim that the physical and psychological risks to clones are more severe than, or different in kind from, those faced by children produced in more traditional ways. Identical twins live with the psychological "burden" of not being genetically unique. Children born to women over 35 are at an increased risk of genetic illness. Children resulting from in-vitro fertilization or other reproductive technologies live with the knowledge that their origins were unusual. They may even live with the knowledge that their genetic profile has been manipulated (for example, through pre-implantation selection of embryos). Human cloning for reproductive purposes is another novel—and as yet untested—medical technology. As such, it should be approached with caution. Thorough animal trials should be completed before attempts on humans are contemplated. But this is true of any new medical technology.

Baird worries about the shift that human cloning might provoke in the way that we view children. This in turn would change the type of community that we are. The central worry is that human cloning "commodifies" children (i.e. that cloning may make us think of children as a commodity or product to be bought and sold). Why would cloning have this effect? Is it simply because it is likely to be expensive, so that it costs money to have children? Surely this is insufficient to worry us. Raising children already costs money—the statistics show us how many hundreds of thousands of dollars it costs to raise a

140

child through to adulthood. Yet no one has suggested that we see our children as products, or love them any less. (In the mid 1940s—before publicly funded health care—my grandparents sold their car to pay the hospital bill related to my father's birth, so "purchasing" the birth of a child is nothing new!)

5   Baird argues that an "important part of human identity is the sense of arising from a maternal and a paternal line while at the same time being a unique individual." Yet without supporting evidence, this sounds like pop psychology. And we can reply in kind: most people I know do not identify with both their maternal and paternal lineages. One of my friends, who was raised by a single mother, identifies with her maternal eastern European heritage, and not with the French paternal heritage implied by her surname. Another friend identifies with his father's black heritage, rather than with his maternal Chinese lineage, despite his Asian physical features. Such patterns are not unusual. Dual heritage may be normal, but it hardly seems central to our conception of ourselves as humans. And identical twins seem none the worse for the knowledge that they are not genetically unique individuals. Claims about challenges to what makes us "human" may be powerful rhetorical devices, but they must be substantiated if they are to be convincing.

Baird is correct to exhort us to look beyond harms to identifiable individuals, to the social implications that human cloning might have. As a comparison, think of fetal sex selection. Most of us think that sex selection is a bad thing—not because of any purported harm to the child, but because we worry about the social implications of valuing children of one sex over those of another. So Baird rightly reminds us that focusing on potential harms to individuals constitutes a "dangerously incomplete framing" of the problem. Furthermore, cloning (and genetic technology in general) is sufficiently new—and its implications sufficiently poorly understood—to warrant a healthy respect, and even the allowance of a margin of safety. But this does not suggest the need for the ban that Baird (with others) proposes. What these worries suggest is a need for caution, for discussion, and for regulation. For instance, laws limiting the number of clones that might be created from one individual, restricting the combination of cloning with genetic modification, and defining lines of parental obligation, would alleviate many of the concerns associated with human cloning. (Françoise Baylis argues that cloning is so likely to be used in combination with gene transfer that we should think of cloning as an enhancement technology

141

rather than as a reproductive technology, in her article "Human cloning: three mistakes and a solution," which has been accepted for publication in the *Journal of Medicine and Philosophy*.)

What I have said here should not be taken as an absolute defence of human cloning in all circumstances. (Indeed, there may be only a few circumstances in which cloning is appropriate.) Nor have I suggested that public monies should be spent on cloning research. All I have suggested is that a ban on research leading toward human cloning is unwarranted by the arguments raised thus far. Caution and discretion are warranted; a ban is not.

Finally, I worry that Baird's point of view exemplifies the way in which human reproductive cloning is being singled out, among cloning-related techniques, as a bogeyman. Almost in chorus, scientists are pleading with regulators not to place restrictions on cloning experimentation per se. At the same time, most scientists seem to be more than willing to swear off reproductive cloning, and indeed to wring their hands over the moral implications of its use. Yet this has the air of a too-hasty concession. The scientific community seems to be too willing to condemn one unpopular application of cloning technology, on the basis of too little convincing argumentation, to appease those who oppose cloning technology in general. But human cloning for reproductive purposes has legitimate, morally acceptable applications—for example, for infertile couples, and for gay couples. And none of the criticisms have been convincingly made. We should not let reproductive human cloning be abandoned as the moral sacrificial lamb of the cloning debate.

Questions on Meaning

1. Why does Baird consider the reasons for human cloning unpersuasive? What are the primary objections to human cloning, according to Baird?

2. Why does the concept of seventh-generation thinking appeal to Baird with regard to human cloning? How reasonable do you find this approach? Explain your response.

3. Why does MacDonald object to the notion that "any new technology should be forbidden unless and until enough justification can be found for allowing its use"? How would you describe his position regarding new technologies?

4. How does MacDonald address Baird's arguments regarding human identity? Do you find his response persuasive? Why, or why not?

5. Why, in Baird's view, should decisions regarding human cloning be considered a public concern rather than an issue of individual autonomy? How persuasive do you find her position?

6. Why does MacDonald consider human cloning to be "the moral sacrificial lamb" of the cloning debate?

Questions on Rhetorical Strategy and Style

1. How does Baird's extended definition of human cloning contribute to the effectiveness of her argument? How does it function to establish her authority and the parameters of her discussion?

2. An effective argument often involves finding common ground with the opposition. Identify several instances in which MacDonald seeks common ground with Baird, and explain the impact of this technique on his argument.

3. Baird's argument includes claims of fact (establishing that something is true), claims of value (arguing that something is right or wrong), and claims of policy (contending that a particular condition should exist). Identify these claims in the selection and explain how they function in her argument.

4. Anecdotal evidence (the use of individual examples) is not always effective in supporting a position, particularly in scientific arguments. Consider the anecdotal evidence MacDonald offers regarding identification with heritage. Do you find this evidence persuasive? Why, or why not?

Writing Assignments

1. Write an essay analyzing the effectiveness of MacDonald's response to Baird. Evaluate the ways in which he addresses specific features of her argument, and comment on elements of her argument to which he does not respond. In all, do you find his response persuasive?

2. Having considered both Baird's and MacDonald's arguments, write your own response to the controversy. In addition to addressing points made by each writer, offer your own reasons for supporting or opposing human cloning.

3. Interview a number of people representing different groups (e.g., gender, age, educational background, socioeconomic status, religion, ethnicity) on their reasons for supporting or rejecting the idea of human cloning. Write a report on your findings, presenting the positions and the rationales for those positions. If it is possible to relate positions and rationales to age, gender, or other characteristics, do so.

It's a Girl!

Kathleen Fackelmann

Kathleen Fackelmann writes regularly for the weekly magazine Science News *and is a health and behavior reporter for* USA Today. *She investigates groups of related research studies and writes essays on a variety of topics; issues she has reported on include genetics, diet and nutrition, medical discoveries, and disease. In this November 1998 article, Fackelmann reports on recent research that has effectively pre-determined the female sex of babies and discusses the ethics of such research.*

1 Some parents-to-be hope for a girl. Some wish for a boy. The outcome, however, has always been pretty much a matter of chance.

Researchers at the Genetics & IVF Institute in Fairfax, Va., recently announced a technique that helps stack the odds in favor of parents getting what they want. Using a mechanical sperm sorter, the Fairfax team reported that nearly 93 percent of the babies born were of the desired sex.

All the couples in this study wanted girls. However, the technique also can easily help those who desire a boy. Will such technology lead to a United States overpopulated by one sex? Most ethicists don't think that will happen any time soon. Nonetheless, the new technology raises some concerns about the future, they say.

Before getting to the ethical debate about sex selection, consider the research itself. Reproductive biologist Edward F. Fugger and his colleagues at the Genetics & IVF Institute began their study by recruiting 119 couples who wanted a baby girl. In most cases, the

"It's a Girl," by Kathleen Fackelmann published in *Science News*, Volume 154, November 28, 1998.

couples already had a boy or boys, and they wanted a girl for variety—
to balance their family, as the scientists say. In a few cases, couples
faced the risk of giving birth to a child with a genetic disorder that
strikes boys only.

5   The patented sperm sorter used by Fugger and his team helps parents pick out the child's gender before fertilization of the egg. The technology, developed during animal studies by Lawrence A. Johnson of the U.S. Department of Agriculture in Beltsville, Md., exploits the difference in amounts of DNA in X and Y chromosomes. Sperm bearing the X, or female, chromosome have more DNA than sperm carrying the Y, or male, chromosome.

An embryo resulting from the merger of an egg, which always carries an X chromosome, and a sperm carrying an X chromosome will have two Xs and, therefore, develop into a girl. An egg fertilized by a sperm carrying a Y chromosome becomes a boy.

In the September issue of HUMAN REPRODUCTION, Fugger and his colleagues describe their use of the method. Each couple provided a sperm sample, which the researchers treated with a dye that attaches to DNA and glows under laser light. The team then exposed the tagged sperm to a laser beam.

The researchers reasoned that the X-carrying sperm would glow the brightest under the laser light. Sure enough, even though sperm carrying an X chromosome—and 22 other chromosomes—contain only 2.8 percent more DNA than those bearing a Y, the sorter separated the bright sperm from the dim sperm. It then directed most of those bearing X chromosomes to swim down one collection tube, and most of the Y-bearing sperm went down another tube.

When the researchers analyzed the sperm in the X collection tube, they found that 85 percent had the X chromosome, as desired. The researchers thus estimate that samples from the X collection tubes are five to six times as likely to result in a girl baby than in a boy.

10   In 92 cases, the researchers inserted the sorted sperm directly into the woman's uterus, a procedure called intrauterine insemination. In this version of artificial insemination, the sperm must latch onto and fertilize an egg in the woman's body for pregnancy to occur.

Some of the couples required more complex—and expensive—techniques to achieve pregnancy. In 27 cases, the researchers united sperm and egg in a laboratory dish and then transferred the resulting embryos to the woman's uterus.

Out of 119 women, 29 got pregnant using the sorted sperm. In 8 women, the pregnancy ended in miscarriage or surgery, the latter because of a dangerous condition in which the fertilized egg starts to grow in a fallopian tube above the uterus. At the time the Fairfax researchers published their journal article, 12 women had ongoing pregnancies and 9 women had already delivered 11 babies, including two sets of twins. As of mid-November, Fugger and his colleagues had not released updated results.

Of the 14 pregnancies in which the gender of the child had been determined, 13 were girls, the researchers say.

Fugger and his team are also conducting a study with parents who want boys. In such cases, the sperm sorter is less effective at concentrating Y-bearing sperm. Still, the method yields a sperm sample in which 65 percent carry the Y chromosome, Fugger says. The team has not announced any results of that study yet.

15 The researchers identified no safety concerns in the published study. "All of the babies born have been healthy," Fugger says. "That doesn't mean that all of the risk has been excluded," he says. "There's a lot that's not known."

The study raised more concerns than just the usual fear about side effects. For some people, a technology that could pick out the sex of a baby raises the specter of China's overabundance of baby boys.

Many Chinese couples opt for an abortion of a female fetus if they lose the natural-reproduction lottery by not conceiving a boy, notes ethicist R. Alta Charo of the University of Wisconsin-Madison. As a result, China has experienced some significant demographic shifts, Charo notes.

Most people in the United States recoil at the thought of a society so geared toward male offspring that abortion—and even infanticide—is the fate of some baby girls. Indeed, Arthur Caplan of the University of Pennsylvania's Center for Bioethics says most U.S. couples have only a moderate preference for a child of a given sex. If they lose the reproduction lottery for the gender they desire, they rarely opt for an abortion, he says.

Furthermore, Caplan says that only a small subset of the U.S. population would try to ensure their baby's gender with this expensive, difficult technique. Charo agrees, noting that a man must first produce a sperm sample for the doctor. Then, his partner must submit to artificial insemination or other techniques performed in a doctor's office or clinic.

20   Of course, Charo notes, for couples who can have children no other way, the difficulties of such high-tech reproductive methods are a small price to pay for a successful pregnancy. But for couples whose only concern is the gender of their baby, the rigmarole might very well put them off.

Caplan argues that sex selection to balance a family is ethically acceptable but that it won't be popular enough in the United States to change Mother Nature's gender sorting.

He wonders whether the preference for a boy or a girl stems from inherently sexist attitudes. Does a U.S. parent's desire for a boy or a girl mean that one sex is viewed as inferior to the other? "Sex selection doesn't bother us—sexism does," Caplan says.

Sex ratios and sexism aside, some ethicists worry about a culture where parents are driven to pick out any of the traits of their unborn children. "There's a notion now that parenting is a kind of consumer experience," says Barbara Katz Rothman, a sociologist at the City University of New York.

Rothman, for example, worries about parents who choose a sex because they are seeking to fill stereotypical, perhaps unrealistic roles. For example, a woman who hopes for a girl may say she wants to shop for a prom gown or go for manicures with a daughter. "You listen to this woman and think, 'This woman is not prepared for a 300-pound, 6-foot girl who wears denim and boots,'" Rothman says.

25   The trend toward more parental control over a child's characteristics will increase in the future, warns biomedical ethicist Thomas H. Murray, the director of the Center for Biomedical Ethics at Case Western Reserve University in Cleveland. Murray notes that scientists working on the human genome project soon will have methods of identifying disease-causing genes as well as the DNA that produces characteristics such as hair color, height, athletic ability, and perhaps some behaviors.

Most ethicists see no problem with parents trying to avoid a genetic disease in their offspring, but Murray and others say that parents should leave the selection of nondisease traits to fate.

"As consumers, we think, 'The more choice the better,'" he says. But even rudimentary attempts to pick one trait from column A and one from column B might encourage the belief that parents can design the perfect baby, Murray says. Substantially increased parental control over their tyke's personality may change the dynamics of the parent-child relationship, he adds.

Charo says that selecting a child's sex is a far cry from designing a baby. Indeed, while parents can now pay for sorting X- and Y-carrying sperm, the technology hasn't been invented that could guarantee a red-haired cellist with a genius-level IQ.

She adds that sex-selection techniques may be useful to limit the size of all-girl families where the parents might otherwise continue having babies until they get a son or of all-boy families intent on having a girl. "This technology would let couples up the odds that their next kid will be the last kid," Charo says.

30 Caplan and Charo both propose that regulation of the technology is not necessary. "The presumption in the United States is that you let people do what they want unless there is a very god reason to stop them," Charo says. "In the United States today, the harm [of sex selection] is not that great."

Although lawnmakers may never regulate sex-selection methods, Murray contends that genetic counselors should begin developing guidelines to steer couples away from the designer-baby concept. The harm to society from attempts to select human characteristics may be subtle, he says. For example, how will parents who think that they have designed a child act toward that offspring when a wrong trait shows up?

Rothman says that even with all the human reproductive genetic advances, one thing should remain the same: "When you parent, you get what you get."

Questions on Meaning

1. Describe the technical processes involved in choosing a child's sex. What objections might many people have to such a process?
2. What has happened in China since the one-child rule went into effect? Is there danger of similar unethical practices spreading to the United States if a child's sex can be chosen?
3. The essay suggests that parents might be disappointed if they spent money to have a girl and got one who was big and tough and wore denim and boots. What kinds of fantasies do parents live out in their children? What are the results of such behavior?

Questions on Rhetorical Strategy and Style

1. The author analyzes why some people would want to choose the sex of their child. What are some of the possible reasons she identifies?
2. Fackelmann ends the essay by suggesting that couples should be "steered away" from trying to create "designer babies" and quotes a sociologist, Barbara Rothman, as saying that parents should accept that "you get what you get." Does this conclusion strengthen or weaken her argument?
3. Fackelmann notes the possibility of all-girl families that might continue having children until they get a son and suggests that such a practice could be stopped by technological gender choice. What do you see as the moral and ethical issues behind this speculation?

Writing Assignments

1. Why do people in some cultures, including some people in the United States, want to have sons rather than daughters? From what attitudes does this desire arise? Discuss the reasons that people have these attitudes.
2. If scientists could engineer physical characteristics, should they? Who should pay, and who should receive first preference in such a situation if the process was expensive?
3. Imagine what your life would have been if you had been born the opposite sex of your own. Describe that life and discuss your reactions to the possibility.

Evolution as Fact and Theory

Stephen Jay Gould

Stephen Jay Gould (1941–2002) was born in New York City. A graduate of Antioch College (1963) and Columbia University (Ph.D., 1967) Gould joined the faculty of Harvard University in 1973, where he taught geology, biology, and the history of science. An evolutionist who enjoyed explaining complex scientific theories to lay audiences, Gould wrote extensively (often on the theory of evolution), including a monthly column for Natural History, *"This View of Life." Gould's books include* Ontogeny and Phylogeny *(1977),* The Mismeasure of Man *(1981),* Time's Arrow, Time's Cycle *(1987), and* Wonderful Life *(1989). His essay collections include* Ever Since Darwin *(1977),* The Panda's Thumb *(1980),* Hen's Teeth and Horse's Toes *(1983),* The Flamingo's Smile *(1985),* Urchin in the Storm: Essays About Books and Ideas *(1987),* Bully for Brontosaurus *(1991), and* Eight Little Piggies *(1993). Gould received a National Book Award and was named a MacArthur Prize Fellow. This essay, originally published in* Discover *(1981), criticizes creationists, particularly those who would attempt to apply Gould's theories of evolution to substantiate their beliefs.*

1 Kirtley Mather, who died last year at age 89, was a pillar of both science and the Christian religion in America and one of my dearest friends. The difference of half a century in our ages evaporated before our common interests. The most curious thing we shared was a battle we each fought at the same age. For Kirtley had gone to Tennessee with Clarence Darrow to testify for evolution at the

Scopes trial of 1925. When I think that we are enmeshed again in the same struggle for one of the best documented, most compelling and exciting concepts in all of science, I don't know whether to laugh or cry.

According to idealized principles of scientific discourse, the arousal of dormant issues should reflect fresh data that give renewed life to abandoned notions. Those outside the current debate may therefore be excused for suspecting that creationists have come up with something new, or that evolutionists have generated some serious internal trouble. But nothing has changed; the creationists have not a single new fact or argument. Darrow and Bryan were at least more entertaining than we lesser antagonists today. The rise of creationism is politics, pure and simple; it represents one issue (and by no means the major concern) of the resurgent evangelical right. Arguments that seemed kooky just a decade ago have re-entered the mainstream.

Creationism Is Not Science

The basic attack of the creationists falls apart on two general counts before we even reach the supposed factual details of their complaints against evolution. First, they play upon a vernacular misunderstanding of the word "theory" to convey the false impression that we evolutionists are covering up the rotten core of our edifice. Second, they misuse a popular philosophy of science to argue that they are behaving scientifically in attacking evolution. Yet the same philosophy demonstrates that their own belief is not science, and that "scientific creationism" is therefore meaningless and self-contradictory, a superb example of what Orwell called "newspeak."

In the American vernacular, "theory" often means "imperfect fact"—part of a hierarchy of confidence running downhill from fact to theory to hypothesis to guess. Thus the power of the creationist argument: evolution is "only" a theory, and intense debate now rages about many aspects of the theory. If evolution is less than a fact, and scientists can't even make up their minds about the theory, then what confidence can we have in it? Indeed, President Reagan echoed this argument before an evangelical group in Dallas when he said (in what I devoutly hope was campaign rhetoric): "Well, it is a theory. It is a scientific theory only, and it has in recent years been challenged in the world of science—that is, not believed in the scientific community to be as infallible as it once was."

5   Well, evolution *is* a theory. It is also a fact. And facts and theories   5
are different things, not rungs in a hierarchy of increasing certainty.
Facts are the world's data. Theories are structures of ideas that explain
and interpret facts. Facts do not go away when scientists debate rival
theories to explain them. Einstein's theory of gravitation replaced
Newton's, but apples did not suspend themselves in mid-air pending
the outcome. And human beings evolved from apelike ancestors
whether they did so by Darwin's proposed mechanism or by some
other, yet to be discovered.

Moreover, "fact" does not mean "absolute certainty." The final
proofs of logic and mathematics flow deductively from stated premises
and achieve certainty only because they are not about the empirical
world. Evolutionists make no claim for perpetual truth, though creationists often do (and then attack us for a style of argument that they
themselves favor). In science, "fact" can only mean "confirmed to such
a degree that it would be perverse to withhold provisional assent." I
suppose that apples might start to rise tomorrow, but the possibility
does not merit equal time in physics classrooms.

Evolutionists have been clear about this distinction between fact
and theory from the very beginning, if only because we have always
acknowledged how far we are from completely understanding the
mechanisms (theory) by which evolution (fact) occurred. Darwin continually emphasized the difference between his two great and separate
accomplishments: establishing the fact of evolution, and proposing a
theory—natural selection—to explain the mechanism of evolution.
He wrote in *The Descent of Man:* "I had two distinct objects in view;
firstly, to show that species had not been separately created, and
secondly, that natural selection had been the chief agent of
change . . . Hence if I had erred in . . . having exaggerated its [natural
selection's] power . . . I have at least, as I hope, done good service in
aiding to overthrow the dogma of separate creations."

Thus Darwin acknowledged the provisional nature of natural selection while affirming the act of evolution. The fruitful theoretical debate that Darwin initiated has never ceased. From the 1940s through
the 1960s, Darwin's own theory of natural selection did achieve a temporary hegemony that it never enjoyed in his lifetime. But renewed debate characterizes our decade, and, while no biologist questions the
importance of natural selection, many now doubt its ubiquity. In particular, many evolutionists argue that substantial amounts of genetic

change may not be subject to natural selection and may spread through populations at random. Others are challenging Darwin's linking of natural selection with gradual, imperceptible change through all intermediary degrees; they are arguing that most evolutionary events may occur far more rapidly than Darwin envisioned.

Scientists regard debates on fundamental issues of theory as a sign of intellectual health and a source of excitement. Science is—and how else can I say it?—most fun when it plays with interesting ideas, examines their implications, and recognizes that old information may be explained in surprising new ways. Evolutionary theory is now enjoying this uncommon vigor. Yet amidst all this turmoil no biologist has been led to doubt the fact that evolution occurred; we are debating *how* it happened. We are all trying to explain the same thing: the tree of evolutionary descent linking all organisms by ties of genealogy. Creationists pervert and caricature this debate by conveniently neglecting the common conviction that underlies it, and by falsely suggesting that we now doubt the very phenomenon we are struggling to understand.

10   Using another invalid argument, creationists claim that "the   10 dogma of separate creations," as Darwin characterized it a century ago, is a scientific theory meriting equal time with evolution in high school biology curricula. But a prevailing viewpoint among philosophers of science belies this creationist argument. Philosopher Karl Popper has argued for decades that the primary criterion of science is the falsifiability of its theories. We can never prove absolutely, but we can falsify. A set of ideas that cannot, in principle, be falsified is not science.

The entire creationist argument involves little more than a rhetorical attempt to falsify evolution by presenting supposed contradictions among its supporters. Their brand of creationism, they claim, is "scientific" because it follows the Popperian model in trying to demolish evolution. Yet Popper's argument must apply in both directions. One does not become a scientist by the simple act of trying to falsify another scientific system; one has to present an alternative system that also meets Popper's criterion—it too must be falsifiable in principle.

"Scientific creationism" is a self-contradictory, nonsense phrase precisely because it cannot be falsified. I can envision observations and experiments that would disprove any evolutionary theory I know, but I cannot imagine what potential data could lead creationists to abandon their beliefs. Unbeatable systems are dogma, not science. Lest I seem harsh or rhetorical, I quote creationism's leading intellectual, Duane Gish, Ph.D., from his recent (1978) book *Evolution? The Fossils Say No!* "By creation we mean the bringing into being by a supernatural Creator of the basic kinds of plants and animals by the process of sudden, or fiat, creation. We do not know how the Creator created, what processes He used, *for He used processes which are not now operating anywhere in the natural universe* [Gish's italics]. This is why we refer to creation as special creation. We cannot discover by scientific investigations anything about the creative processes used by the Creator." Pray tell, Dr. Gish, in the light of your last sentence, what then is "scientific" creationism?

The Fact of Evolution

Our confidence that evolution occurred centers upon three general arguments. First, we have abundant, direct, observational evidence of evolution in action, from both the field and the laboratory. It ranges from countless experiments on change in nearly everything about fruit flies subjected to artificial selection in the laboratory to the famous British moths that turned black when industrial soot darkened the trees upon which they rest. (The moths gain protection from sharp-sighted bird predators by blending into the background.) Creationists do not deny these observations; how could they? Creationists have tightened their act. They now argue that God only created "basic kinds," and allowed for limited evolutionary meandering within them. Thus toy poodles and Great Danes come from the dog kind and moths can change color, but nature cannot convert a dog to a cat or a monkey to a man.

The second and third arguments for evolution—the case for major changes—do not involve direct observation of evolution in action. They rest upon inference, but are no less secure for that reason. Major evolutionary change requires too much time for direct observation on the scale of recorded human history. All historical sciences rest upon inference, and evolution is no different from geology, cosmology, or human history in this respect. In principle, we cannot observe processes that operated in the past. We must infer them from results that still survive: living and fossil organisms for evolution, documents and artifacts for human history, strata and topography for geology.

15   The second argument—that the imperfection of nature reveals   15
evolution—strikes many people as ironic, for they feel that evolution
should be most elegantly displayed in the nearly perfect adaptation ex-
pressed by some organisms—the chamber of a gull's wing, or butterflies that cannot be seen in ground litter because they mimic leaves so
precisely. But perfection could be imposed by a wise creator or evolved
by natural selection. Perfection covers the tracks of past history. And
past history—the evidence of descent—is our mark of evolution.

Evolution lies exposed in the *imperfections* that record a history of
descent. Why should a rat run, a bat fly, a porpoise swim, and I type
this essay with structures built of the same bones unless we all inherited them from a common ancestor? An engineer, starting from
scratch, could design better limbs in each case. Why should all the
large native mammals of Australia be marsupials, unless they descended from a common ancestor isolated on this island continent?
Marsupials are not "better," or ideally suited for Australia; many have
been wiped out by placental mammals imported by man from other
continents. This principle of imperfection extends to all historical sciences. When we recognize the etymology of September, October, November, and December (seventh, eighth, ninth, and tenth, from the
Latin), we know that two additional items (January and February)
must have been added to an original calendar of ten months.

The third argument is more direct: transitions are often found in
the fossil record. Preserved transitions are not common—and should
not be, according to our understanding of evolution (see next section)—but they are not entirely wanting, as creationists often claim.
The lower jaw of reptiles contains several bones, that of mammals only
one. The non-mammalian jawbones are reduced, step by step, in
mammalian ancestors until they become tiny nubbins located at the
back of the jaw. The "hammer" and "anvil" bones of the mammalian
ear are descendants of these nubbins. How could such a transition be
accomplished? the creationists ask. Surely a bone is either entirely in
the jaw or in the ear. Yet paleontologists have discovered two transitional lineages or therapsids (the so-called mammal-like reptiles) with
a double jaw joint—one composed of the old quadrate and articular
bones (soon to become the hammer and anvil), the other of the
squamosal and dentary bones (as in modern mammals). For that matter, what better transitional form could we desire than the oldest
human, *Australopithecus afarensis,* with its apelike palate, its human

upright stance, and a cranial capacity larger than any ape's of the same body size but a full 1,000 cubic centimeters below ours? If God made each of the half dozen human species discovered in ancient rocks, why did he create in an unbroken temporal sequence of progressively more modern features—increasing cranial capacity, reduced face and teeth, larger body size? Did he create to mimic evolution and test our faith thereby?

An Example of Creationist Argument

Faced with these facts of evolution and the philosophical bankruptcy of their own position, creationists rely upon distortion and innuendo to buttress their rhetorical claim. If I sound sharp or bitter, indeed I am—for I have become a major target of these practices.

I count myself among the evolutionists who argue for a jerky, or episodic, rather than a smoothly gradual, pace of change. In 1972 my colleague Niles Eldredge and I developed the theory of punctuated equilibrium [*Discover,* October]. We argued that two outstanding facts of the fossil record—geologically "sudden" origin of new species and failure to change thereafter (stasis)—reflect the predictions of evolutionary theory, not the imperfections of the fossil record. In most theories, small isolated populations are the source of new species, and the process of speciation takes thousands or tens of thousands of years. This amount of time, so long when measured against our lives, is a geological microsecond. It represents much less than 1 per cent of the average life span for a fossil invertebrate species—more than 10 million years. Large, widespread, and well-established species, on the other hand, are not expected to change very much. We believe that the inertia of large populations explains the stasis of most fossil species over millions of years.

20 We proposed the theory of punctuated equilibrium largely to provide a different explanation for pervasive trends in the fossil record. Trends, we argued, cannot be attributed to gradual transformation within lineages, but must arise from the differential success of certain kinds of species. A trend, we argued, is more like climbing a flight of stairs (punctuations and stasis) than rolling up an inclined plane. 20

Since we proposed punctuated equilibria to explain trends, it is infuriating to be quoted again and again by creationists—whether through design or stupidity, I do not know—as admitting that the

157

fossil record includes no transitional forms. Transitional forms are generally lacking at the species level, but are abundant between larger groups. The evolution from reptiles to mammals, as mentioned earlier, is well documented. Yet a pamphlet entitled "Harvard Scientists Agree Evolution Is a Hoax" states: "The facts of punctuated equilibrium which Gould and Eldredge . . . are forcing Darwinists to swallow fit the picture that Bryan insisted on, and which God has revealed to us in the Bible."

Continuing the distortion, several creationists have equated the theory of punctuated equilibrium with a caricature of the beliefs of Richard Goldschmidt, a great early geneticist. Goldschmidt argued, in a famous book published in 1940, that new groups can arise all at once through major mutations. He referred to these suddenly transformed creatures as "hopeful monsters." (I am attracted to some aspects of the non-caricatured version, but Goldschmidt's theory still has nothing to do with punctuated equilibrium.) Creationist Luther Sunderland talks of the "punctuated equilibrium hopeful monster theory" and tells his hopeful readers that "it amounts to tacit admission that anti-evolutionists are correct in asserting there is no fossil evidence supporting the theory that all life is connected to a common ancestor." Duane Gish writes, "According to Goldschmidt, and now apparently according to Gould, a reptile laid an egg from which the first bird, feathers and all, was produced." Any evolutionist who believed such nonsense would rightly be laughed off the intellectual stage; yet the only theory that could ever envision such a scenario for the evolution of birds is creationism—God acts in the egg.

Conclusion

I am both angry at and amused by the creationists; but mostly I am deeply sad. Sad for many reasons. Sad because so many people who respond to creationist appeals are troubled for the right reason, but venting their anger at the wrong target. It is true that scientists have often been dogmatic and elitist. It is true that we have often allowed the white-coated, advertising image to represent us–"Scientists say that Brand X cures bunions ten times faster than . . . " We have not fought it adequately because we derive benefits from appearing as a new priesthood. It is also true that faceless bureaucratic state power intrudes more and more into our lives and removes choices that should belong to individuals and communities. I can understand that requiring that evolution be taught in the schools might be seen as one more insult on all these grounds. But the culprit is not, and cannot be, evolution or any other fact of the natural world. Identify and fight your legitimate enemies by all means, but we are not among them.

I am sad because the practical result of this brouhaha will not be expanded coverage to include creationism (that would also make me sad), but the reduction or excision of evolution from high school curricula. Evolution is one of the half dozen "great ideas" developed by science. It speaks to the profound issues of genealogy that fascinate all of us—the "roots" phenomenon writ large. Where did we come from? Where did life arise? How did it develop? How are organisms related? It forces us to think, ponder, and wonder. Shall we deprive millions of this knowledge and once again teach biology as a set of dull and unconnected facts, without the thread that weaves diverse material into a supple unity?

25 But most of all I am saddened by a trend I am just beginning to 25 discern among my colleagues. I sense that some now wish to mute the healthy debate about theory that has brought new life to evolutionary biology. It provides grist for creationist mills, they say, even if only by distortion. Perhaps we should lie low and rally round the flag of strict Darwinism, at least for the moment—a kind of old-time religion on our part.

But we should borrow another metaphor and recognize that we too have to tread a straight and narrow path, surrounded by roads to perdition. For if we ever begin to suppress our search to understand nature, to quench our own intellectual excitement in a misguided effort to represent a united front where it does not and should not exist, then we are truly lost.

Questions on Meaning

1. At the end of the first paragraph, Gould writes, "I don't know whether to laugh or cry." What would cause him that amusement—or frustration? (Look up the 1925 Scopes trial if you are unfamiliar with it.)
2. According to Gould, what is the difference between "fact" and "theory"? How do evolutionists apply these definitions?
3. Describe the theory of "punctuated equilibrium" developed by Gould and Niles Eldredge. How have creationists altered this theory so they can claim that Eldredge and Gould *do not* support the theory of evolution?

Questions on Rhetorical Strategy and Style

1. Reread Gould's essay and circle each definition you find. Why are definitions so important to his argument?
2. Find examples of cause and effect in the "Creationism Is Not Science" section that supports this belief. Why would Gould use cause and effect as his rhetorical strategy when discussing the relationship between fact and theory?
3. The organization of Gould's essay into three distinct sections reflects his orderly, methodical, scientific mind. What are the themes and key points of each section? What words does he use in his conclusion to link directly with his introduction?

Writing Assignments

1. Gould wrote this essay in 1981. Research the evolution versus creationism debate today. Compare the arguments of the opposing views with the arguments discussed in this essay. Identify any "fresh data" in the current debate.
2. Scientific debate can be enlightening and stimulating, as Gould would attest. Research a scientific topic currently being debated and present your views, such as nuclear power, human cloning, organic farming, estrogen-replacement therapy, or genetic engineering. Use facts to develop your theories. Explain why you disagree with the opposing views.

Biotech Hope and Hype

Stephen Leahy

The biotechnology industry has made many promises in the past few decades. The study of genetics has been optimistically undertaken to cure a host of incurable diseases, feed the world's hungry, and clean up the environment. But, in reality, how many of these promises have panned out, and who's really reaping the benefits? According to environmental journalist Stephen Leahy, the golden age of biotechnology has yet to materialize. In this article, which appeared in the September 30, 2002 issue of Maclean's *magazine, Leahy reviews the achievements of the biotech business since the early '80s and wonders what the hidden costs might ultimately be to the environment and to our pocketbooks.*

Stephen Leahy is a freelance journalist from Brooklin, Ontario, who covers biotechnology, science, and environmental issues. He is a regular contributor to Wired *and* Maclean's.

Critical Thinking

What do you see as the benefits of biotechnology now and in the future? What are some of the claims that the biotechnology business has promised? Have expectations been met?

[1] Come to Canada. We have lovely scenery, low crime, industry-friendly regulators and low corporate taxes. That, in essence, was the sales pitch Industry Minister Allan Rock gave the 15,565 biotechnonauts from 52 countries attending the world's largest biotechnology industry convention in Toronto this summer. And if that wasn't enticement enough, Rock announced $200 million in new funding for biotech start-ups to go with Ontario's $51 million in new funding initiatives.

Federal and provincial governments have long had a love affair with genetics, pumping billions into the biotech biz since the early 1980s. And who wouldn't love a new technology that promises to feed the hungry, cure intractable diseases, clean up the environment and, thanks to patent rights, usher in the Golden and Profitable Age of Biotechnology?

Reprinted from *Maclean's*, September 30, 2002.

So, 20 years later and how many breakthrough products has biotech produced? Gene therapy may actually have harmed more people than it's helped. Genetically engineered (GE) crops haven't aided hard-pressed farmers, improved the quality of our food or fed the hungry. The few drugs derived from GE such as insulin simply replace existing products while creating new risks. And Canadians remain nervous about the technology.

With good reason. The industry consistently overhypes the benefits and downplays the potential risks of a revolutionary new technology. Genetic engineering is revolutionary because its products incorporate genes from unrelated species. The process of evolution and traditional plant and animal breeding is an incestuous, only-with-close-relatives affair—a vertical gene exchange. The between-species aspect of biotechnology, a horizontal gene exchange, is a whole new ball game.

Only through GE can a gene from a soil bacterium that makes a toxin become part of a corn plant's DNA. Now this exchange is not easily done. First a DNA package has to be built that contains the toxin-producing bacterial gene as well as elements known as promoters and vectors of bacterial viruses, antibiotic-resistance marker genes and other assorted bits of DNA. These packages are "glued" onto thousands of tiny metal pellets and blasted into corn plant cells with a device called a gene gun. A few will hit the right place, and the bacterial virus promoters and vectors will stitch the foreign gene into the corn's DNA. The process will produce many freakish, non-functional plants. The odd corn plant will produce the bacterial toxin in every cell. Known as Bt corn, it kills any moth or butterfly larvae that nibble on it.

One major reason to proceed with caution on bioteck innovation: the pedal-to-the-metal attitude in an industry where even the biggest players concede that many vital questions remain unanswered. "My view of biology is, we don't know shit," the U.S. geneticist Craig Venter told a magazine writer. Yet the company he founded heralded its successful decoding of the human genome (the total DNA package) two years ago as a key step in ushering in the Biotech Age. It discovered—surprise!—that the human genome contains just 35,000 genes instead of the expected 100,000. So, rather than performing single duties, genes appear to multi-task and work in combination with other genes. In other words, pluck a gene from an organism because it performs one desired function, place it in another organism—and who knows what unanticipated business it will get up to. Besides, genes are just a small part of DNA.

Biotech critics like geneticist David Suzuki say it's much too soon to have planted GE crops and used them in food and drugs. "Scientists just don't know enough about the technology right now," argues Suzuki. Not surprisingly, the biotech business says it's high time to move forward. "People don't realize that biotechnology is starting to transform the world," says Janet Lambert, president of the industry trade association, BIOTECanada. "Is it too soon to feed the starving in Africa?"

Canada's first GE crops were planted in 1996. Three patented versions—canola, corn and soy—are now found in 60 to 70 per cent of our food. Yet they don't improve food quality or boost yields appreciably—in fact, critics argue both quality and yield are poorer. The main reason farmers plant something like Monsanto's Round-Up Ready canola is that it offers them the convenience of using a single herbicide—made by Monsanto, natch—to control weeds, rather than a whole bunch. But the jury is still out as to whether GE farmers actually spray less.

The economics are also iffy. Although GE seeds cost more than the seeds they replace, some farmers, mainly those with large operations, make a couple more dollars per acre using them. Others, however, are being badly hurt. First it was the loss of export markets for formerly GE-free crops in GE-shy Europe. Now, because GE plants are living creatures that reproduce, disperse and evolve, there's genetic pollution and contamination. Thanks to winds and insects, engineered genes are travelling long distances in pollen and seeds, turning up in non-GE crops across the Prairies.

10 Given those concerns, it's not surprising there was an uproar in Prairie 10 farm communities last year when Agriculture Canada announced that Monsanto's GE wheat will be submitted to regulators for approval this fall. While the company stands to make as much as $7 billion from that crop, a University of Saskatchewan study showed Canadian farmers would end up losing $185 million a year through lost sales. Monsanto says it is sensitive to the contamination concerns. "We are not going to sell it," says company spokesperson Trish Jordan, "until a segregation system is in place to keep it separate from non-GE wheat."

Meanwhile, hundreds of millions of North Americans are eating foods made from GE crops without any documented ill effects. But then, how could we document any harm without data on who is eating those foods and in what quantities? That would require food labelling and a tracking system for GE crops. But while the vast majority of Canadians want foods with GE ingredients to be labelled, that's not going to happen. The reason: it would spell the end of agricultural biotech. Food processors admit they'd insist on GE-free crops from farmers because if people could easily identify GE foods, some, perhaps many, wouldn't buy them.

As for global hunger, no one can deny it's a major economic and social problem. But the GE crops that the large multinationals have brought to developing countries so far are cotton, corn and soy—all engineered to resist herbicides, and all affordable only by large commercial farmers. If biotechnologists really want to feed the poor, notes Sakiko Fukuda-Parr of the United Nations

Development Program, they need to create virus-resistant, drought-tolerant, nutrient-enhanced versions of such staple crops as millet, sorghum and cassava. "Of course," she adds, "farmers living on less than a dollar a day don't represent much of a market."

Perhaps that's why fewer companies are now involved in "green" (agricultural) biotech and many more in "red" (medical/health) biotech. With one blockbuster health product capable of bringing in billions in revenue, the big drug companies are quickly transmogrifying into biopharmaceutical corporations. Today, something like 100 medical products are derived from genetic engineering. Thousands more are being tested.

The first, and likely the most profitable, GE product is "human- derived" insulin. Approved for use in Canada in 1983, it rapidly replaced the more expensive insulin traditionally made from the pancreas of cows and pigs. It also produced biotech's first human casualties.

15   Hundreds of Canadian diabetics have reported reactions to GE insulin,   15
says Vancouver health policy expert Colleen Fuller, spokesperson for Society for Diabetic Rights. Using access-to-information law, that new group has associated the deaths of eight Canadians with use of synthetic insulin as of January, 2001. Fuller, a diabetic who has reacted badly to GE insulin, has also heard from more than 400 people complaining of bad responses to the medication. Hundreds of deaths and thousands of unwanted side effects have also been noted in the U.S., Britain and elsewhere. Problems clear up quickly when diabetics return to animal insulin, says Fuller. What really makes her angry, she says, is that she and thousands like her have paid a high price so insulin manufacturers could make more money.

The financial successes of GE insulin and another multi-billion dollar product, GE erythropoietin (EPO), an anti-anemia drug made by placing a human gene in the ovarian cells of a Chinese hamster, jump-started the production of "biofactories." The term refers to bacteria, plants and animals engineered to produce human proteins of all kinds. Wisconsin dairy cows produce a blood-clotting agent called fibrinogen in their milk. Sheep, rabbits, goats and even mice make human proteins in their milk. While the mammary gland is the biofactory of choice, TGN Biotech of Quebec City produces complex proteins in pig semen.

Plants are the bargain-basement biofactories with the potential for manufacturing material at just a fraction of the traditional costs. Molecular farmers at Medicago Inc. of Sainte-Foy, Que., have genetically engineered alfalfa to produce human hemoglobin proteins for blood transfusions. Tobacco fields outside London, Ont., produce Interleukin-10, a human immune system modulator, for treating Crohn's disease. In the U.S. there are experimental fields of corn containing anti-sperm and anti-herpes antibodies, an HIV protein for a future vaccine, and an enzyme that may help cystic fibrosis patients digest food.

While none of these products are in general use yet, some are in human trials. Critics worry about the possibility of contamination of other crops or the altered items getting into food. Joe Cummins, a retired University of Western Ontario geneticist, is concerned about the effects human proteins may have on bugs and micro-organisms in the soil and water. There is a danger, he says, that by incorporating a human protein, a common soil virus could become a health threat.

Gene therapy is a more direct route to solving medical problems—introducing engineered genes straight into human cells. While billions of dollars have been invested and some 3,500 clinical trials conducted worldwide since 1990, there have been few claims of cures. But there are substantial risks. In 1999, 18-year-old Jesse Gelsinger died while undergoing gene therapy at the University of Pennsylvania. Researchers have since reported hundreds of adverse reactions among patients in gene therapy trials, 691 in the U.S. alone. In Canada, where more than 30 human trials have been approved, one man, James Dent, died while undergoing gene therapy for a brain tumour. Human trials continue.

20   The heart of the problem with gene therapy and genomic medicine in general is the complexity of the human body. Single-gene diseases, the kind most likely to be treatable by gene therapy, are very rare. And nearly all ailments, including cancer, diabetes and cardiovascular disease, are the result of many factors: lifestyle, diet, exposure to toxins, stress, hygiene and, yes, genes. The current focus and fascination with genes produces a fix-it mentality toward disease and health, rather than a better examination of the conditions that create illness.

Currently 99 per cent of genomic research is about making money, not curing people, says Dr. Nancy Olivieri, head of the thalassemia and sickle cell anemia research programs at Toronto's Hospital for Sick Children. Moreover, Olivieri questions huge investments in biotech research that may never yield results when that money could be put to good use improving conventional treatments or the distribution of existing medicines, particularly in emerging countries.

The current passion for all things genetic has blinded many to biotech's faults and limitations. The hard-hearts of Canadian business continue to pump billions into an industry where only a small number of companies has ever made a profit. Last year, the publicly traded firms netted a collective loss of $784 million. Perhaps, in the end, genetics is a numbers game. Canadian biotechs have 17,000 new products in the pipeline. Undoubtedly some will earn substantial profits and benefit some people. But at what cost, and at what risk to the public and the planet?

Freewriting Assignment

In this article, Stephen Leahy claims that Canadians are "nervous" about biotechnology. What are your feelings about some of the technologies mentioned here, such as genetically modified crops or gene therapy?

Critical Reading

1. What is Leahy's thesis in this article? Does he believe that the biotech industry is good for Canada? Why or why not?
2. Why does the author believe that genetic research should proceed with caution? What are some of the dangers he mentions here?
3. Why are genetically engineered crops not being used to fight global hunger? Who benefits from Canada's production of genetically engineered crops?
4. What does Leahy mean by the "fix-it mentality" produced by the current focus on genes (paragraph 20)? What might be a better focus to combat disease?
5. Why is there no available data on the possible results of eating genetically modified food?

Critical Writing

6. *Research and Analysis*: Stephen Leahy refers to Canadian scientist and environmental activist David Suzuki in this article. Read Suzuki's views on genetic engineering at **www.davidsuzuki.org/files/General/DTSbiotech .pdf**. Summarize his arguments in an essay.
7. *Persuasive Writing*: Compose a letter to a Canadian government official stating why you feel that the labelling, or even the banning altogether, of GE foods is necessary. Alternatively, compose a letter to the same government official urging him or her to invest more into Canada's expanding biotech industry. Use points from Leahy's article or other research to support your argument.
8. *Interview*: Leahy mentions how Canadians are wary about the biotech industry as a whole. Interview several people of varying ages about their knowledge of biotechnology. What are their general ideas, fears, hopes, and beliefs on the subject? How do they feel about specific technologies, such as cloning, genetically modified food, or gene therapy? How do they feel about the government subsidizing such industries? Evaluate the results in a short essay on how Canadians view the biotech business in general.

Group Projects

9. In this article, the author mentions the industry trade association, BIOTE-Canada. Go to their Web site at **www.biotech.ca/EN/biotech.html** and read the material they distribute to teachers as a teaching resource. How does the material deal with many of the questions in this article? Does this change your opinion of some of Leahy's points? With your group, discuss how you would teach a class of elementary schoolchildren about the subjects mentioned on the BIOTECanada Web site.

Be Fruitful or Else: How Having More Babies Can Solve All Our Problems

Peter Shawn Taylor

1   The crisis in health-care funding. Collapsing public pension plans. A looming economic slowdown. What if I told you all these problems could be easily solved but that the solution might offend some people? Would you still want to hear it?

Canada, along with most other developed countries, is in a demographic strait-jacket, and the consequences are dire. Canadians are living longer than ever and, thus, expecting more from public health care, pensions, and welfare systems. At the same time. Statistics Canada forecasts that between 2000 and 2040, the ratio of seniors to members of the working population will double from the current two per ten workers to four per ten. And by 2040, the overall population of Canada will begin to shrink due to a declining birth rate. The strain these twin phenomena—more seniors and fewer young workers to support them—place on Canadian social programs such as medicare and the Canada Pension Plan is plain to see. In more mature countries such as Japan, Germany, and Italy, where the birth rate is even lower, these problems are far more advanced. In his 1999 book Gray Dawn, Peter Peterson argued that an ageing population is a "global hazard" on par with nuclear weapons and super viruses. The United Nations last year declared that only massive international migration on a scale never before seen could keep the ageing trend at bay and economies in rich nations functioning. The future, however, is more flexible than most people seem to think.

All these grim discussions are strangely incomplete. While no one would wish to reverse the many improvements in life expectancies, nearly every demographic jeremiad leaves out the equally important front end of the population equation—the birth rate. The number of children an average Canadian woman bears over her lifetime has fallen to 1.48 from 1.65 twenty years ago. The rate required for a population to maintain itself without immigration is 2.1 per woman (one each to replace the parents and a fraction to cover the possibility that a child might die before procreating). If we were to make a concerted effort to push the birth rate above 2.1, it would create a growing supply of young workers to support ageing pensioners and their health problems. More young workers would keep the economy staffed-up and remove the need for massive tax increases to sustain our imperilled social programs. Despite the views of the United Nations, increased fertility is the only permanent solution to the future work-force shortage since immigrants tend to be adults and are already that much closer to retirement age. Encouraging greater fertility is not an argument against immigration, mind you. Immigrants would still be a necessary part of the equation since it takes eighteen years for a rising birth rate to produce more workers.

Given the simplicity of the prescription, it is puzzling that so few people are willing to seriously discuss the fact that having more babies would be a good thing. In Germany, when conservative politicians promote richer baby bonuses, this argument is dismissed as anti-immigrant rhetoric. And when Bjorn Borg, the Swedish tennis icon, sponsored a full-page ad in a newspaper earlier this year urging his countryfolk to procreate because "there aren't enough babies being born," his concerns rated only a twitter—just another libidinous Swede advocating more nookie. Back home, the only province to make it an explicit objective has been Quebec. Between 1988 and 1997 the province offered a sliding scale of baby bonuses that peaked with an $8,000 payment on the birth of a third child. That system was then replaced with a range of programs aimed at making parents' lives easier, such as five-dollars-a-day universal daycare and a generous parental-leave system. While the baby bonuses did have a positive impact on the birth rate, the results seemed to diminish over time. All other jurisdictions in Canada appear to accept insufficient fertility as part of the landscape.

5   Some might say that this is a good thing, that governments have no business sticking their noses into what is a very private and complex decision. True enough; but Ottawa has not exactly been shy in lecturing us on such delicate matters as smoking, drinking, exercise, and safe sex when it has been deemed to be in the national interest.

And the need for more babies is surely that. Even still, many women will doubtless take the suggestion that they should have more children to be a personal insult and a step backwards for feminism, and oppose it on those grounds. Certainly no one wants to press parenthood onto people who are unwilling to accept the burdens. And the responsibility for the birth dearth should be properly shouldered by males as well as females who have put off or decided against having progeny for careers or other reasons. Thus the goal of any pro-natalist policy must be to convince people of the greater good in having offspring. It will not be an easy task. But consider that in the 1970s, wild predictions of massive global overpopulation spurred governments and international agencies around the world to focus on lowering birth rates through public campaigns as well as direct action such as birth-control distribution and education with obvious, and now regrettable, success. Surely a similar level of urgency and purpose could be mustered to promote the opposite notion.

Whether changing several generations of attitudes on parenthood and family size is best accomplished by a hard sell, as with Quebec's cash payments and universal daycare, or a softer approach that merely promotes fecundity as a virtue, is open for debate. Perhaps the best chance for success comes from a recent high-court ruling in Germany that held that childless adults constitute a greater burden on society and thus should be expected to pay more in taxes to support future social programs. From this perspective, making babies is not only patriotic, productive, and a lot of fun; it is also cheaper than the alternative.

Stories

Dead Men's Path

Chinua Achebe

Named Albert by his missionary parents at his birth in Ogidi, Nigeria, Achebe (1930–) later adopted the traditional name Chinua. He studied at the Church Mission Society School and the Government College and University College (B.A. 1953), where he cultivated his writing. Achebe's first novel, Things Fall Apart, *appeared in 1958. His writing, which draws on African oral traditions, reflects the tumultuous period of civil wars at home in the 1960s. He has published widely in several genres, including the novels* A Man of the People *(1966) and* Home and Exile *(2000); the short story collections* The Sacrificial Egg, and Other Stories *(1962) and* Girls at War *(1972); the essay collections* Morning Yet on Creation Day *(1975) and* The Trouble with Nigeria *(1984); and the poetry collections* Beware, Soul-Brother, and Other Poems *(1971) and* Christmas in Biafra, and Other Poems *(1973). Achebe taught at a number of colleges and universities throughout the world, including the University of Nigeria, the University of Massachusetts-Amherst, the University of California-Los Angeles, Bard College, and Cambridge University. In 1981 he founded the Association of Nigerian Authors and served as its president from 1981 to 1986. During his career Achebe received awards ranging from the Margaret Wrong Memorial Prize (1959) for* Things Fall Apart; *to the Nigerian National Trophy (1961) for* No Longer at Ease; *and the Commonwealth Poetry Prize (1972) for* Beware, Soul-Brother, and Other Poems. *He was nominated for the Booker Prize in 1987 for* Anthills of the Savannah *and for the Nobel Prize in Literature in 2000.*

In 2007, Achebe was awarded the Man Booker International Prize in honor of his literary career. Among institutions that have awarded Achebe honorary degrees are Dartmouth College, the University of Nigeria, the University of Prince Edward Island, the Open University, and Georgetown University. This story, originally published in 1953 and later collected in Girls at War, *features an ambitious and progressive young headmaster of an African mission school who learns a painful lesson about respecting ancient traditions.*

1   Michael Obi's hopes were fulfilled much earlier than he had expected. He was appointed headmaster of Ndume Central School in January 1949. It had always been an unprogressive school, so the Mission authorities decided to send a young and energetic man to run it. Obi accepted this responsibility with enthusiasm. He had many wonderful ideas and this was an opportunity to put them into practice. He had had sound secondary school education which designated him a "pivotal teacher" in the official records and set him apart from the other headmasters in the mission field. He was outspoken in his condemnation of the narrow views of these older and often less-educated ones.

"We shall make a good job of it, shan't we?" he asked his young wife when they first heard the joyful news of his promotion.

"We shall do our best," she replied. "We shall have such beautiful gardens and everything will be just *modern* and delightful. . . ." In their two years of married life she had become completely infected by his passion for "modern methods" and his denigration of "these old and superannuated people in the teaching field who would be better employed as traders in the Onitsha market." She began to see herself already as the admired wife of the young headmaster, the queen of the school.

The wives of the other teachers would envy her position. She would set the fashion in everything. . . . Then, suddenly, it occurred to her that there might not be other wives. Wavering between hope and fear, she asked her husband, looking anxiously at him.

5   "All our colleagues are young and unmarried," he said with enthusiasm which for once she did not share. "Which is a good thing," he continued.

"Why?"

"Why? They will give all their time and energy to the school."

Nancy was downcast. For a few minutes she became skeptical about the new school; but it was only for a few minutes. Her little personal misfortune could not blind her to her husband's happy prospects. She looked at him as he sat folded up in a chair. He was stoop-shouldered and looked frail. But he sometimes surprised people with sudden bursts of physical energy. In his present posture, however, all his bodily strength seemed to have retired behind his deep-set eyes, giving them an extraordinary power of penetration. He was only twenty-six, but looked thirty or more. On the whole, he was not unhandsome.

"A penny for your thoughts, Mike," said Nancy after a while, imitating the woman's magazine she read.

10 "I was thinking what a grand opportunity we've got at last to 10 show these people how a school should be run."

Ndume School was backward in every sense of the word. Mr. Obi put his whole life into the work, and his wife hers too. He had two aims. A high standard of teaching was insisted upon, and the school compound was to be turned into a place of beauty. Nancy's dream-gardens came to life with the coming of the rains, and blossomed. Beautiful hibiscus and allamanda hedges in brilliant red and yellow marked out the carefully tended school compound from the rank neighborhood bushes.

One evening as Obi was admiring his work he was scandalized to see an old woman from the village hobble right across the compound, through a marigold flower-bed and the hedges. On going up there he found faint signs of an almost disused path from the village across the school compound to the bush on the other side.

"It amazes me," said Obi to one of his teachers who had been three years in the school, "that you people allowed the villagers to make use of this footpath. It is simply incredible." He shook his head.

"The path," said the teacher apologetically, "appears to be very important to them. Although it is hardly used, it connects the village shrine with their place of burial."

15 "And what has that got to do with the school?" asked the headmaster. 15

"Well, I don't know," replied the other with a shrug of the shoulders. "But I remember there was a big row some time ago when we attempted to close it."

173

"That was some time ago. But it will not be used now," said Obi as he walked away. "What will the Government Education Officer think of this when he comes to inspect the school next week? The villagers might, for all I know, decide to use the schoolroom for a pagan ritual during the inspection."

Heavy sticks were planted closely across the path at the two places where it entered and left the school premises. These were further strengthened with barbed wire.

Three days later the village priest of *Ani* called on the headmaster. He was an old man and walked with a slight stoop. He carried a stout walking-stick which he usually tapped on the floor, by way of emphasis, each time he made a new point in his argument.

20   "I have heard," he said after the usual exchange of cordialities,   20
"that our ancestral footpath was recently been closed. . . ."

"Yes," replied Mr. Obi. "We cannot allow people to make a highway of our school compound."

"Look here, my son," said the priest bringing down his walking stick, "this path was here before you were born and before your father was born. The whole life of this village depends on it. Our dead relatives depart by it and our ancestors visit us by it. But most important, it is the path of children coming in to be born. . . ."

Mr. Obi listened with a satisfied smile on his face.

"The whole purpose of our school," he said finally, "is to eradicate just such beliefs as that. Dead men do not require footpaths. The whole idea is just fantastic. Our duty is to teach your children to laugh at such ideas."

25   "What you say may be true," replied the priest, "but we follow   25
the practices of our fathers. If you reopen the path we shall have nothing to quarrel about. What I always say is: let the hawk perch and let the eagle perch." He rose to go.

"I am sorry," said the young headmaster. "But the school compound cannot be a thoroughfare. It is against our regulations. I would suggest your constructing another path, skirting our premises. We can even get our boys to help in building it. I don't suppose the ancestors will find the little detour too burdensome."

"I have no more words to say," said the old priest, already outside.

Two days later a young woman in the village died in child bed. A diviner was immediately consulted and he prescribed heavy sacrifices to propitiate ancestors insulted by the fence.

Obi woke up next morning among the ruins of his work. The beautiful hedges were torn up not just near the path but right round the school, the flowers trampled to death and one of the school buildings pulled down. . . . That day, the white Supervisor came to inspect the school and wrote a nasty report on the state of the premises but more seriously about the "tribal-war situation developing between the school and the village, arising in part from the misguided zeal of the new headmaster."

Questions on Meaning

1. How does Achebe characterize Michael Obi? At what point in the story do you become aware of his shortcomings?
2. How does the village priest attempt to persuade Obi to restore the path? How does his approach distinguish him from Obi?
3. After finishing the story, how do you interpret the diviner's prescription of "heavy sacrifices"?

Questions on Rhetorical Strategy and Style

1. Achebe employs limited description in this story. Reread several descriptions of characters or settings and explain their significance to the story. How would the story's impact have been altered had the author used more elaborate description?
2. Although this story is not constructed in a traditional comparison-contrast format, the contrast between progressivism and tradition is implicit throughout. What are the distinguishing features of each? Based on your reading of the story, which does Achebe consider more important?
3. What is the impact of the ironic conclusion to the story?

Writing Assignments

1. Write an essay analyzing this story as a commentary on blind adherence to progress. Focus on character, dialogue, description, and tone.
2. Imagine that you are the supervisor who inspected the school. Compose the report the supervisor might have written, including guidelines for headmasters to follow when dealing with tribal customs and local practices.
3. Write a brief essay explaining the effects of progress on the traditions of your culture. To what extent does progress respect those traditions? To what extent do traditions suffer at the hands of progress? Do you think it is possible to strike a balance between progress and tradition?

The Story of an Hour

Kate Chopin

Kate Chopin (b. Katherine O'Flaherty, 1851–1904) began her life in St. Louis, Missouri. Her father died when she was four years old, so she was reared by three widows: her mother, her grandmother, and her great-grandmother. She was graduated from Sacred Heart convent in 1870 and then married Oscar Chopin, following him to New Orleans and later to his plantation in northern Louisiana. The mother of six children, she was widowed in 1882 and moved back to St. Louis where she began to write stories and publish in stylish literary magazines. Her novels, At Fault (1890) and The Awakening (1899), shocked conservative Victorian society but are praised by modern critics. Her collections of short stories, Bayou Folk (1894) and A Night in Acadie (1897) draw on her years of experience on a Louisiana plantation among Creole people. She died of a brain hemorrhage at only fifty-three. "The Story of an Hour" caused Chopin to be shunned by both her literary club and magazine publishers at the close of the nineteenth century, but it has persevered to become especially appealing to women in the late twentieth century.

1   Knowing that Mrs. Mallard was afflicted with a heart trouble, great care was taken to break to her as gently as possible the news of her husband's death.

It was her sister Josephine who told her, in broken sentences, veiled hints that revealed in half concealing. Her husband's friend Richards was there, too, near her. It was he who had been in the newspaper office when intelligence of the railroad disaster was received, with Brently Mallard's name leading the list of "killed." He had only taken the time to assure himself of its truth by a second telegram, and had hastened to forestall any less careful, less tender friend in bearing the sad message.

The Story of an Hour (1894)

She did not hear the story as many women have heard the same, with a paralyzed inability to accept its significance. She wept at once, with sudden, wild abandonment, in her sister's arms. When the storm of grief had spent itself she went away to her room alone. She would have no one follow her.

There stood, facing the open window, a comfortable, roomy armchair. Into this she sank, pressed down by a physical exhaustion that haunted her body and seemed to reach into her soul.

5 She could see in the open square before her house the tops of trees that were all aquiver with the new spring life. The delicious breath of rain was in the air. In the street below a peddler was crying his wares. The notes of a distant song which someone was singing reached her faintly, and countless sparrows were twittering in the eaves.

There were patches of blue sky showing here and there through the clouds that had met and piled above the other in the west facing her window.

She sat with her head thrown back upon the cushion of the chair, quite motionless, except when a sob came up into her throat and shook her, as a child who has cried itself to sleep continues to sob in its dreams.

She was young, with a fair, calm face, whose lines bespoke repression and even a certain strength. But now there was a dull stare in her eyes, whose gaze was fixed away off yonder on one of those patches of blue sky. It was not a glance of reflection, but rather indicated a suspension of intelligent thought.

There was something coming to her and she was waiting for it, fearfully. What was it? She did not know; it was too subtle and elusive to name. But she felt it, creeping out of the sky, reaching toward her through the sounds, the scents, the color that filled the air.

10 Now her bosom rose and fell tumultuously. She was beginning to recognize this thing that was approaching to possess her, and she was striving to beat it back with her will—as powerless as her two white slender hands would have been.

When she abandoned herself a little whispered word escaped her slightly parted lips. She said it over and over under her breath: "Free, free, free!" The vacant stare and the look of terror that had followed it went from her eyes. They stayed keen and bright. Her pulses beat fast, and the coursing blood warmed and relaxed every inch of her body.

She did not stop to ask if it were or were not a monstrous joy that held her. A clear and exalted perception enabled her to dismiss the suggestion as trivial.

She knew that she would weep again when she saw the kind, tender hands folded in death; the face that had never looked save with love upon her, fixed and gray and dead. But she saw beyond that bitter moment a long procession of years to come that would belong to her absolutely. And she opened and spread her arms out to them in welcome.

There would be no one to live for her during those coming years; she would live for herself. There would be no powerful will bending her in that blind persistence with which men and women believe they have a right to impose a private will upon a fellow-creature. A kind intention or a cruel intention made the act seem no less a crime as she looked upon it in that brief moment of illumination.

15   And yet she had loved him—sometimes. Often she had not. What did it matter! What could love, the unsolved mystery, count for in face of this possession of self-assertion which she suddenly recognized as the strongest impulse of her being!

"Free! Body and soul free!" she kept whispering.

Josephine was kneeling before the closed door with her lips to the keyhole, imploring for admission. "Louise, open the door! I beg; open the door—you will make yourself ill. What are you doing, Louise? For heaven's sake open the door."

"Go away. I am not making myself ill." No; she was drinking in a very elixir of life through that open window.

Her fancy was running riot along those days ahead of her. Spring days, and summer days, and all sorts of days that would be her own. She breathed a quick prayer that life might be long. It was only yesterday she had thought with a shudder that life might be long.

20   She arose at length and opened the door to her sister's importunities. There was a feverish triumph in her eyes, and she carried herself unwittingly like a goddess of Victory. She clasped her sister's waist, and together they descended the stairs. Richards stood waiting for them at the bottom.

Someone was opening the front door with a latchkey. It was Brently Mallard who entered, a little travel-stained, composedly carrying his grip-sack and umbrella. He had been far from the scene of accident, and did not even know there had been one. He stood

179

amazed at Josephine's piercing cry; at Richards' quick motion to screen him from the view of his wife.

But Richards was too late.

When the doctors came they said she had died of heart disease—of joy that kills.

Questions on Meaning

1. The main character dies at the end of the story. What causes her death, and why?
2. The St. Louis literary society refused to accept Chopin into their ranks because her stories shocked their polite sensibilities. What issues of gender and gender conflicts in this story would have caused this reaction?
3. Chopin was the mother of six children in only twelve years of marriage. What picture of family might Chopin have had from such an experience, and what "family" emotions might she be injecting into her story?

Questions on Rhetorical Strategy and Style

1. "The Story of an Hour" limits its narrative time to exactly one hour. How does it stay within that limit and yet capture the reader's close attention?
2. The story illustrates the need for freedom that some people, both men and women feel. How does Chopin describe scenes that convey this desire for freedom?
3. The woman in the story appears to be in shock when she hears of her husband's death but is actually shocked by his being alive. How does this reaction illustrate literary irony (the reader's knowing more about the character than the character knows or appears to know)?

Writing Assignments

1. Write a paper about some common cultural expectation (for example, that all mothers will bond with their children or that all fathers will be happy to share their incomes with their families). How do we respond when a storyteller challenges those expectations?
2. Illustrate an event in your life when your emotions did not appropriately fit the situation (maybe you didn't like your holiday presents or you weren't glad to have a little sister). How did you react emotionally to the contrast between your feelings and your family's expectations?
3. Learning that things are not always as they seem may be the first step in coming of age. Illustrate a time in your life when you suddenly realized that someone you knew was different from the

person you had imagined her or him to be, or describe a time when you found out that a prominent figure was not the person everyone had imagined. Discuss and describe your experience of this discovery.

Cathedral

Raymond Carver

Raymond Carver (1938-1988) was born in Chatskanie, Oregon. He received a B.A. from Humbolt State College (1963) and studied creative writing at the University of Iowa and (with the late novelist John Gardner) at Chico State College. A dedicated writer with a worldwide following, Carver is one of the better-known short story writers of the late twentieth century. His books include the short story collections Will You Be Quiet, Please *(1976) (a National Book Award nominee),* What We Talk About When We Talk About Love *(1981),* Cathedral *(1983), and* Where I'm Calling From *(1988); the miscellaneous collection* Fires: Essays, Poems, Stories *(1983); and the poetry collections* In a Marine Light *(1987) and—posthumously—*A New Path to the Waterfall *(1989). In addition, he published stories in* The Atlantic Monthly, Esquire, *and* The New Yorker. *Carver's stories are often sparse and seldom without the poignancy of the dark side of life—such as depression, unemployment, alcoholism, and divorce. In this story, Carver explores the ironies behind a sighted man learning to see his world through the eyes of a blind man.*

1   This blind man, an old friend of my wife's, he was on his way to spend the night. His wife had died. So he was visiting the dead wife's relatives in Connecticut. He called my wife from his in-laws'. Arrangements were made. He would come by train, a five-hour trip, and my wife would meet him at the station. She hadn't seen him since she worked for him one summer in Seattle ten years ago. But she and the blind man had kept in touch. They made tapes

and mailed them back and forth. I wasn't enthusiastic about his visit. He was no one I knew. And his being blind bothered me. My idea of blindness came from the movies. In the movies, the blind moved slowly and never laughed. Sometimes they were led by seeing-eye dogs. A blind man in my house was not something I looked forward to.

That summer in Seattle she had needed a job. She didn't have any money. The man she was going to marry at the end of the summer was in officers' training school. He didn't have any money, either. But she was in love with the guy, and he was in love with her, etc. She'd seen something in the paper: HELP WANTED—*Reading to Blind Man*, and a telephone number. She phoned and went over, was hired on the spot. She'd worked with this blind man all summer. She read stuff to him, case studies, reports, that sort of thing. She helped him organize his little office in the county social-service department. They'd become good friends, my wife and the blind man. How do I know these things? She told me. And she told me something else. On her last day in the office, the blind man asked if he could touch her face. She agreed to this. She told me he touched his fingers to every part of her face, her nose—even her neck! She never forgot it. She even tried to write a poem about it. She was always trying to write a poem. She wrote a poem or two every year, usually after something really important had happened to her.

When we first started going out together, she showed me the poem. In the poem, she recalled his fingers and the way they had moved around over her face. In the poem, she talked about what she had felt at the time, about what went through her mind when the blind man touched her nose and lips. I can remember I didn't think much of the poem. Of course, I didn't tell her that. Maybe I just don't understand poetry. I admit it's not the first thing I reach for when I pick up something to read.

Anyway, this man who'd first enjoyed her favors, the officer-to-be, he'd been her childhood sweetheart. So okay. I'm saying that at the end of the summer she let the blind man run his hands over her face, said goodbye to him, married her childhood etc., who was now a commissioned officer, and she moved away from Seattle. But they'd kept in touch, she and the blind man. She made the first contact after a year or so. She called him up one night from an Air Force base in Alabama. She wanted to talk. They talked. He asked her to send him a tape and tell him about her life. She did this. She sent the tape. On the tape, she told the blind man about her husband and about their life together in the military. She told the blind man she loved her husband but she didn't like it where they lived and she didn't like it that he was a part of the military-industrial thing. She told the blind man she'd written a poem and he was in it. She told him that she was writing a poem about what it was like to be an Air Force officer's wife. The poem wasn't finished yet. She was still writing it. The blind man made a tape. He sent her the tape. She made a tape. This went on for years. My wife's officer was posted to one base and then another. She sent tapes from Moody AFB, McGuire, McConnell, and finally Travis, near Sacramento, where one night she got to feeling lonely and cut off from people she kept losing in that moving-around life. She got to feeling she couldn't go it another step. She went in and swallowed all the pills and capsules in the medicine chest and washed them down with a bottle of gin. Then she got into a hot bath and passed out.

But instead of dying, she got sick. She threw up. Her officer—why should he have a name? he was the childhood sweetheart, and what more does he want?—came home from somewhere, found her, and called the ambulance. In time, she put it all on a tape and sent the tape to the blind man. Over the years, she put all kinds of stuff on tapes and sent the tapes off lickety-split. Next to writing a poem every year, I think it was her chief means of recreation. On one tape, she told the blind man she'd decided to live away from her officer for a time. On another tape, she told him about her divorce. She and I began going out, and of course she told her blind man about it. She told him everything, or so it seemed to me. Once she asked me if I'd like to hear the latest tape from the blind man. This was a year ago. I was on the tape, she said. So I said okay, I'd listen to it. I got us drinks and we settled down in the living room. We made ready to listen. First she inserted the tape into the player and adjusted a couple of dials. Then she pushed a lever. The tape squeaked and someone began to talk in this loud voice. She lowered the volume. After a few minutes of harmless chitchat, I heard my own name in the mouth of this stranger, this blind man I didn't even know! And then this: "From all you've said about him, I can only conclude—" But we were interrupted, a knock at the door, something, and we didn't ever get back to the tape. Maybe it was just as well. I'd heard all I wanted to.

Now this same blind man was coming to sleep in my house.

"Maybe I could take him bowling," I said to my wife. She was at the draining board doing scalloped potatoes. She put down the knife she was using and turned around.

"If you love me," she said, "you can do this for me. If you don't love me, okay. But if you had a friend, any friend, and the friend came to visit, I'd make him feel comfortable." She wiped her hands with the dish towel.

"I don't have any blind friends," I said.

10 "You don't have *any* friends," she said. "Period. Besides," she said, 10 "goddamn it, his wife's just died! Don't you understand that? The man's lost his wife!"

I didn't answer. She'd told me a little about the blind man's wife. Her name was Beulah, Beulah! That's a name for a colored woman.

"Was his wife a Negro?" I asked.

"Are you crazy?" my wife said. "Have you just flipped or something?" She picked up a potato. I saw it hit the floor, then roll under the stove. "What's wrong with you?" she said. "Are you drunk?"

"I'm just asking," I said.

15 Right then my wife filled me in with more detail than I cared to 15 know. I made a drink and sat at the kitchen table to listen. Pieces of the story began to fall into place.

Beulah had gone to work for the blind man the summer after my wife had stopped working for him. Pretty soon Beulah and the blind man had themselves a church wedding. It was a little wedding—who'd want to go to such a wedding in the first place?—just the two of them, plus the minister and the minister's wife. But it was a church wedding just the same. It was what Beulah had wanted, he'd said. But even then Beulah must have been carrying the cancer in her glands. After they had been inseparable for eight years—my wife's word, *inseparable*—Beulah's health went into a rapid decline. She died in a Seattle hospital room, the blind man sitting beside the bed and holding on to her hand. They'd married, lived and worked together, slept together—had sex, sure and then the blind man had to bury her. All this without his having ever seen what the goddamned woman looked like. It was beyond my understanding. Hearing this, I felt sorry for the blind man for a little bit. And then I found myself thinking what a pitiful life this woman must have led. Imagine a woman who could never see herself as she was seen in the eyes of her loved one. A woman who could go on day after day and never receive the smallest compliment from her beloved. A woman whose husband could never read the expression on her face, be it misery or something better. Someone who could wear makeup or not—what difference to him? She could, if she wanted, wear green eye-shadow around one eye, a straight pin in her nostril, yellow slacks and purple shoes, no matter. And then to slip off into death, the blind man's hand on her hand, his blind eyes streaming tears—I'm imagining now—her last thought maybe this: that he never even knew what she looked like, and she on an express to the grave. Robert was left with a small insurance policy and half of a twenty-peso Mexican coin. The other half of the coin went into the box with her. Pathetic.

So when the time rolled around, my wife went to the depot to pick him up. With nothing to do but wait—sure, I blamed him for that—I was having a drink and watching the TV when I heard the car pull into the drive. I got up from the sofa with my drink and went to the window to have a look.

I saw my wife laughing as she parked the car. I saw her get out of the car and shut the door. She was still wearing a smile. Just amazing. She went around to the other side of the car to where the blind man was already starting to get out. This blind man, feature this, he was wearing a full beard! A beard on a blind man! Too much, I say. The blind man reached into the back seat and dragged out a suitcase. My wife took his arm, shut the car door, and, talking all the way, moved him down the drive and then up the steps to the front porch. I turned off the TV. I finished my drink, rinsed the glass, dried my hands. Then I went to the door.

My wife said, "I want you to meet Robert. Robert, this is my husband. I've told you all about him." She was beaming. She had this blind man by his coat sleeve.

The blind man let go of his suitcase and up came his hand.

I took it. He squeezed hard, held my hand, and then he let it go.

"I feel like we've already met," he boomed.

"Likewise," I said. I didn't know what else to say. Then I said, "Welcome. I've heard a lot about you." We began to move then, a little group, from the porch into the living room, my wife guiding him by the arm. The blind man was carrying his suitcase in his other hand. My wife said things like, "To your left here, Robert. That's right. Now watch it, there's a chair. That's it. Sit down right here. This is the sofa. We just bought this sofa two weeks ago."

187

I started to say something about the old sofa. I'd liked that old sofa. But I didn't say anything. Then I wanted to say something else, small-talk, about the scenic ride along the Hudson. How going to New York, you should sit on the right-hand side of the train, and coming from New York, the left-hand side.

25 "Did you have a good train ride?" I said. "Which side of the train 25 did you sit on, by the way?

"What a question, which side!" my wife said. "What's it matter which side?" she said.

"I just asked," I said.

"Right side," the blind man said. "I hadn't been on a train in nearly forty years. Not since I was a kid. With my folks. That's been a long time. I'd nearly forgotten the sensation. I have winter in my beard now," he said. "So I've been told, anyway. Do I look distinguished, my dear?" the blind man said to my wife.

"You look distinguished, Robert," she said. "Robert," she said. "Robert, it's just so good to see you."

30 My wife finally took her eyes off the blind man and looked at me. 30 I had the feeling she didn't like what she saw. I shrugged.

I've never met, or personally known, anyone who was blind. This blind man was late forties, a heavy-set, balding man with stooped shoulders, as if he carried great weight there. He wore brown slacks, brown shoes, a lightbrown shirt, a tie, a sports coat. Spiffy. He also had this full beard. But he didn't use a cane and he didn't wear dark glasses. I'd always thought dark glasses were a must for the blind. Fact was, I wished he had a pair. At first glance, his eyes looked like anyone else's eyes. But if you looked close, there was something different about them. Too much white in the iris, for one thing, and the pupils seemed to move around in the sockets without his knowing it or being able to stop it. Creepy. As I stared at his face, I saw the left pupil turn in toward his nose while the other made an effort to keep in one place. But it was only an effort, for that eye was on the roam without his knowing it or wanting it to be.

I said, "Let me get you a drink. What's your pleasure? We have a little of everything. It's one of our pastimes."

"Bub, I'm a Scotch man myself," he said fast enough in this big voice.

"Right," I said. Bub! "Sure you are. I knew it."

188

35   He let his fingers touch his suitcase, which was sitting alongside 35
the sofa. He was taking his bearings. I didn't blame him for that.

    "I'll move that up to your room," my wife said.

    "No, that's fine," the blind man said loudly. "It can go up when I
go up.

    "A little water with the Scotch?" I said.

    "Very little," he said.

40   "I knew it," I said. 40

    He said, "Just a tad. The Irish actor, Barry Fitzgerald? I'm like that
fellow. When I drink water, Fitzgerald said, I drink water. When I
drink whiskey, I drink whiskey." My wife laughed. The blind man
brought his hand up under his beard. He lifted his beard slowly and
let it drop.

    I did the drinks, three big glasses of Scotch with a splash of water
in each. Then we made ourselves comfortable and talked about
Robert's travels. First the long flight from the West Coast to Connecticut, we covered that. Then from Connecticut up here by train.
We had another drink concerning that leg of the trip.

    I remembered having read somewhere that the blind didn't smoke
because, as speculation had it, they couldn't see the smoke they ex-
haled. I thought I knew that much and that much only about blind
people. But this blind man smoked his cigarette down to the nubbin
and then lit another one. This blind man filled his ashtray and my wife
emptied it.

    When we sat down at the table for dinner, we had another drink.
My wife heaped Robert's plate with cube steak, scalloped potatoes,
green beans. I buttered him up two slices of bread. I said, "Here's
bread and butter for you." I swallowed some of my drink. "Now let
us pray," I said, and the blind man lowered his head. My wife looked
at me, her mouth agape. "Pray the phone won't ring and the food
doesn't get cold," I said.

45   We dug in. We ate everything there was to eat on the table. We 45
ate like there was no tomorrow. We didn't talk. We ate. We scarfed.
We grazed that table. We were into serious eating. The blind man had
right away located his foods, he knew just where everything was on
his plate. I watched with admiration as he used his knife and fork on
the meat. He'd cut two pieces of meat, fork the meat into his mouth,
and then go all out for the scalloped potatoes, the beans next, and then
he'd tear off a hunk of buttered bread and eat that. He'd follow this

up with a big drink of milk. It didn't seem to bother him to use his fingers once in a while, either.

We finished everything, including half a strawberry pie. For a few moments, we sat as if stunned. Sweat beaded on our faces. Finally, we got up from the table and left the dirty plates. We didn't look back. We took ourselves into the living room and sank into our places again. Robert and my wife sat on the sofa. I took the big chair. We had us two or three more drinks while they talked about the major things that had come to pass for them in the past ten years. For the most part, I just listened. Now and then I joined in. I didn't want him to think I'd left the room, and I didn't want her to think I was feeling left out. They talked of things that had happened to them—to them!—these past ten years. I waited in vain to hear my name on my wife's sweet lips: "And then my dear husband came into my life"—something like that. But I heard nothing of the sort. More talk of Robert. Robert had done a little of everything, it seemed, a regular blind jack-of-all-trades. But most recently he and his wife had had an Amway distributorship, from which, I gathered, they'd earned their living, such as it was. The blind man was also a ham radio operator. He talked in his loud voice about conversations he'd had with fellow operators in Guam, in the Philippines, in Alaska, and even in Tahiti. He said he'd have a lot of friends there if he ever wanted to go visit those places. From time to time, he'd turn his blind face toward me, put his hand under his beard, ask me something. How long had I been in my present position? (Three years.) Did I like my work? (I didn't.) Was I going to stay with it? (What were the options?) Finally, when I thought he was beginning to run down, I got up and turned on the TV.

My wife looked at me with irritation. She was heading toward a boil. Then she looked at the blind man and said, "Robert, do you have a TV?"

The blind man said, "My dear, I have two TVs. I have a color set and a black-and-white thing, an old relic. It's funny, but if I turn the TV on, and I'm always turning it on, I turn on the color set. It's funny, don't you think?"

I didn't know what to say to that. I had absolutely nothing to say to that. No opinion. So I watched the news program and tried to listen to what the announcer was saying.

50 "This is a color TV," the blind man said. "Don't ask me how, but 50 can tell."

190

"We traded up a while ago," I said.

The blind man had another taste of his drink. He lifted his beard, sniffed it, and let it fall. He leaned forward on the sofa. He positioned his ashtray on the coffee table, then put the lighter to his cigarette. He leaned back on the sofa and crossed his legs at the ankles.

My wife covered her mouth, and then she yawned. She stretched. She said, "I think I'll go upstairs and put on my robe. I think I'll change into something else. Robert, you make yourself comfortable," she said.

"I'm comfortable," the blind man said.

55 "I want you to feel comfortable in this house," she said. 55

"I am comfortable," the blind man said.

After she'd left the room, he and I listened to the weather report and then to the sports roundup. By that time, she'd been gone so long I didn't know if she was going to come back. I thought she might have gone to bed. I wished she'd come back downstairs. I didn't want to be left alone with a blind man. I asked him if he wanted another drink, and he said sure. Then I asked if he wanted to smoke some dope with me. I said I'd just rolled a number. I hadn't, but I planned to do so in about two shakes.

"I'll try some with you," he said.

"Damn right," I said. "That's the stuff."

60 I got our drinks and sat down on the sofa with him. Then I rolled 60 us two fat numbers. I lit one and passed it. I brought it to his fingers. He took it and inhaled.

"Hold it as long as you can," I said. I could tell he didn't know the first thing.

My wife came back downstairs wearing her pink robe and her pink slippers.

"What do I smell?" she said.

"We thought we'd have us some cannabis," I said.

65 My wife gave me a savage look. Then she looked at the blind man 65 and said, "Robert, I didn't know you smoked."

He said, "I do now, my dear. There's a first time for everything. But I don't feel anything yet."

"This stuff is pretty mellow," I said. "This stuff is mild. It's dope you can reason with," I said. "It doesn't mess you up."

"Not much it doesn't, bub," he said, and laughed.

191

My wife sat on the sofa between the blind man and me. I passed her the number. She took it and toked and then passed it back to me. "Which way is this going?" she said. Then she said, "I shouldn't be smoking this. I can hardly keep my eyes open as it is. That dinner did me in. I shouldn't have eaten so much."

70 "It was the strawberry pie," the blind man said. "That's what did it," he said, and he laughed his big laugh. Then he shook his head.

"There's more strawberry pie," I said.

"Do you want some more, Robert?" my wife said.

"Maybe in a little while," he said.

We gave our attention to the TV. My wife yawned again. She said, "Your bed is made up when you feel like going to bed, Robert. I know you must have had a long day. When you're ready to go to bed, say so." She pulled his arm. "Robert?"

75 He came to and said, "I've had a real nice time. This beats tapes, doesn't it?"

I said, "Coming at you," and I put the number between his fingers. He inhaled, held the smoke, and then let it go. It was like he'd been doing it since he was nine years old.

"Thanks, bub," he said. "But I think this is all for me. I think I'm beginning to feel it," he said. He held the burning roach out for my wife.

"Same here," she said. "Ditto. Me, too." She took the roach and passed it to me. "I may just sit here for a while between you two guys with my eyes closed. But don't let me bother you, okay? Either one of you. If it bothers you, say so. Otherwise, I may just sit here with my eyes closed until you're ready to go to bed," she said. "Your bed's made up, Robert, when you're ready. It's right next to our room at the top of the stairs. We'll show you up when you're ready. You wake me up now, you guys, if I fall asleep." She said that and then she closed her eyes and went to sleep.

The news program ended. I got up and changed the channel. I sat back down on the sofa. I wished my wife hadn't pooped out. Her head lay across the back of the sofa, her mouth open. She'd turned so that her robe had slipped away from her legs, exposing a juicy thigh. I reached to draw her robe back over her, and it was then that I glanced at the blind man. What the hell! I flipped the robe open again.

80 "You say when you want some strawberry pie," I said.

"I will," he said.

I said, "Are you tired? Do you want me to take you up to your bed? Are you ready to hit the hay?"

"Not yet," he said. "No, I'll stay up with you, bub. If that's all right. I'll stay up until you're ready to turn in. We haven't had a chance to talk. Know what I mean? I feel like me and her monopolized the evening." He lifted his beard and he let it fall. He picked up his cigarettes and his lighter.

"That's all right," I said. Then I said, "I'm glad for the company."

85 And I guess I was. Every night I smoked dope and stayed up as long as I could before I fell asleep. My wife and I hardly ever went to bed at the same time. When I did go to sleep, I had these dreams. Sometimes I'd wake up from one of them, my heart going crazy.

Something about the church and the Middle Ages was on the TV. Not your run-of-the-mill TV fare. I wanted to watch something else. I turned to the other channels. But there was nothing on them, either. So I turned back to the first channel and apologized.

"Bub, it's all right," the blind man said. "It's fine with me. Whatever you want to watch is okay. I'm always learning something. Learning never ends. It won't hurt me to learn something tonight. I got ears," he said.

We didn't say anything for a time. He was leaning forward with his head turned at me, his right ear aimed in the direction of the set. Very disconcerting. Now and then his eyelids drooped and then they snapped open again. Now and then he put his fingers into his beard and tugged, like he was thinking about something he was hearing on the television.

On the screen, a group of men wearing cowls was being set upon and tormented by men dressed in skeleton costumes and men dressed as devils. The men dressed as devils wore devil masks, horns, and long tails. This pageant was part of a procession. The Englishman who was narrating the thing said it took place in Spain once a year. I tried to explain to the blind man what was happening.

90 "Skeletons," he said. "I know about skeletons," he said, and he nodded.

The TV showed this one cathedral. Then there was a long, slow look at another one. Finally, the picture switched to the famous one in Paris, with its flying buttresses and its spires reaching up to the clouds. The camera pulled away to show the whole of the cathedral rising above the skyline.

There were times when the Englishman who was telling the thing would shut up, would simply let the camera move around over the cathedrals. Or else the camera would tour the countryside, men in fields walking behind oxen. I waited as long as I could. Then I felt I had to say something. I said, "They're showing the outside of this cathedral now. Gargoyles. Little statues carved to look like monsters. Now I guess they're in Italy. Yeah, they're in Italy. There's paintings on the walls of this one church."

"Are those fresco paintings, bub?" he asked, and he sipped from his drink.

I reached for my glass. But it was empty. I tried to remember what I could remember. "You're asking me are those frescoes?" I said. "That's a good question. I don't know."

The camera moved to a cathedral outside Lisbon. The differences in the Portuguese cathedral compared with the French and Italian were not that great. But they were there. Mostly the interior stuff. Then something occurred to me, and I said, "Something has occurred to me. Do you have any idea what a cathedral is? What they look like, that is? Do you follow me? If somebody says cathedral to you, do you have any notion what they're talking about? Do you know the difference between that and a Baptist church, say?"

He let the smoke dribble from his mouth. "I know they took hundreds of workers fifty or a hundred years to build," he said. "I just heard the man say that, of course. I know generations of the same families worked on a cathedral. I heard him say that, too. The men who began their life's work on them, they never lived to see the completion of their work. In that wise, bub, they're no different from the rest of us, right?" He laughed. Then his eyelids drooped again. His head nodded. He seemed to be snoozing. Maybe he was imagining himself in Portugal. The TV was showing another cathedral now. This one was in Germany. The Englishman's voice droned on. "Cathedrals," the blind man said. He sat up and rolled his head back and forth. "If you want the truth, bub, that's about all I know. What I just said. What I heard him say. But maybe you could describe one to me? I wish you'd do it. I'd like that. If you want to know, I really don't have a good idea."

I stared hard at the shot of the cathedral on the TV. How could I even begin to describe it? But say my life depended on it. Say my life was being threatened by an insane guy who said I had to do it or else.

I stared some more at the cathedral before the picture flipped off into the countryside. There was no use. I turned to the blind man and said, "To begin with, they're very tall." I was looking around the room for clues. "They reach way up. Up and up. Toward the sky. They're so big, some of them, they have to have these supports. To help hold them up, so to speak. These supports are called buttresses. They remind me of viaducts, for some reason. But maybe you don't know viaducts, either? Sometimes the cathedrals have devils and such carved into the front. Sometimes lords and ladies. Don't ask me why this is," I said.

He was nodding. The whole upper part of his body seemed to be moving back and forth.

"I'm not doing so good, am I?" I said.

100 He stopped nodding and leaned forward on the edge of the sofa. 100 As he listened to me, he was running his fingers through his beard. I wasn't getting through to him, I could see that. But he waited for me to go on just the same. He nodded, like he was trying to encourage me. I tried to think what else to say. "They're really big," I said. "They're massive. They're built of stone. Marble, too, sometimes. In those olden days, when they built cathedrals, men wanted to be close to God. In those olden days, God was an important part of everyone's life. You could tell this from their cathedral-building. I'm sorry," I said, "but it looks like that's the best I can do for you. I'm just no good at it."

"That's all right, bub," the blind man said. "Hey, listen. I hope you don't mind my asking you: Can I ask you something? Let me ask you a simple question, yes or no. I'm just curious and there's no offense. You're my host. But let me ask if you are in any way religious? You don't mind my asking?"

I shook my head. He couldn't see that, though. A wink is the same as a nod to a blind man. "I guess I don't believe in it. In anything. Sometimes it's hard. You know what I'm saying?"

"Sure, I do," he said.

"Right," I said.

105 The Englishman was still holding forth. My wife sighed in her 105 sleep. She drew a long breath and went on with her sleeping.

"You'll have to forgive me," I said. "But I can't tell you what a cathedral looks like. It just isn't in me to do it. I can't do any more than I've done."

The blind man sat very still, his head down, as he listened to me.

I said, "The truth is, cathedrals don't mean anything special to me. Nothing. Cathedrals. They're something to look at on late-night TV. That's all they are."

It was then that the blind man cleared his throat. He brought something up. He took a handkerchief from his back pocket. Then he said, "I get it, bub. It's okay. It happens. Don't worry about it," he said. "Hey, listen to me. Will you do me a favor? I got an idea. Why don't you find us some heavy paper? And a pen. We'll do something. We'll draw one together. Get us a pen and some heavy paper. Go on, bub, get the stuff," he said.

110   So I went upstairs. My legs felt like they didn't have any strength   110 in them. They felt like they did after I'd done some running. In my wife's room, I looked around. I found some ballpoints in a little basket on her table. And then I tried to think where to look for the kind of paper he was talking about.

Downstairs, in the kitchen, I found a shopping bag with onion skins in the bottom of the bag. I emptied the bag and shook it. I brought it into the living room and sat down with it near his legs. I moved some things, smoothed the wrinkles from the bag, spread it out on the coffee table.

The blind man got down from the sofa and sat next to me on the carpet.

He ran his fingers over the paper. He went up and down the sides of the paper. The edges, even the edges. He fingered the corners.

"All right," he said. "All right, let's do her."

115   He found my hand, the hand with the pen. He closed his hand   115 over my hand. "Go ahead, bub, draw," he said. "Draw. You'll see. I'll follow along with you. It'll be okay. Just begin now like I'm telling you. You'll see. Draw," the blind man said.

So I began. First I drew a box that looked like a house. It could have been the house I lived in. Then I put a roof on it. At either end of the roof, I drew spires. Crazy.

"Swell," he said. "Terrific. You're doing fine," he said. "Never thought anything like this could happen in your lifetime, did you, bub? Well, it's a strange life, we all know that. Go on now. Keep it up."

I put in windows with arches. I drew flying buttresses. I hung great doors. I couldn't stop. The TV station went off the air. I put down the pen and closed and opened my fingers. The blind man felt around over the paper. He moved the tips of his fingers over the paper, all over what I had drawn, and he nodded.

"Doing fine," the blind man said.

120 I took up the pen again, and he found my hand. I kept at it. I'm no artist. But I kept drawing just the same.

My wife opened up her eyes and gazed at us. She sat up on the sofa, her robe hanging open. She said, "What are you doing? Tell me, I want to know."

I didn't answer her.

The blind man said, "We're drawing a cathedral. Me and him are working on it. Press hard," he said to me. "That's right. That's good," he said. "Sure. You got it, bub. I can tell. You didn't think you could. But you can, can't you? You're cooking with gas now. You know what I'm saying? We're going to really have us something here in a minute. How's the old arm?" he said. "Put some people in there now. What's a cathedral without people?"

My wife said "What's going on? Robert, what are you doing? What's going on?"

125 "It's all right," he said to her. "Close your eyes now," the blind man said to me.

I did it. I closed them just like he said.

"Are they closed?" he said. "Don't fudge."

"They're closed," I said.

"Keep them that way," he said. He said, "Don't stop now. Draw."

130 So we kept on with it. His fingers rode my fingers as my hand went over the paper. It was like nothing else in my life up to now.

Then he said, "I think that's it. I think you got it," he said. "Take a look. What do you think?"

But I had my eyes closed. I thought I'd keep them that way for a little longer. I thought it was something I ought to do.

"Well?" he said. "Are you looking?"

My eyes were still closed. I was in my house. I knew that. But I didn't feel like I was inside anything.

135 "It's really something," I said.

Questions on Meaning

1. What expectations does the narrator harbor about the blind man? What sources provide him with images of blind people? How do Robert's appearance and demeanor contradict these images?
2. How would you characterize the narrator? What is his attitude toward his wife? toward his job? toward his life in general?
3. When the narrator draws the cathedral with Robert's hand on top of his, Robert gains a sense of what a cathedral is. What does the narrator gain? Why does this physical act, rather than simply describing the cathedral, change him?

Questions on Rhetorical Strategy and Style

1. Effective narration depends upon careful use of detail. Choose several passages in which the narrator describes people, rooms, or objects, and explain how the details enhance the narrative.
2. The contrast between Robert and the narrator is evident throughout the story. Outline the two characters, pointing out contrasts in their attitudes toward life, their relationships with the narrator's wife, their relationships with others, and anything else you find significant.
3. What is the immediate cause of the narrator's transformation? Throughout the story, what incidents and observations lead to the climax, contributing to the transformation?

Writing Assignments

1. Although the narrator claims that he is not religious, it is the act of drawing a cathedral that prompts his transformation. Analyze the significance of the cathedral to this story, considering both its religious and historical implications.
2. Compose (in writing) a tape for the narrator to send to Robert after the blind man returns home. Comment on the importance of the visit, the significance of drawing the cathedral, and the changes that the narrator has undergone.

I'm a Banana and Proud of It

Wayson Choy

Wayson Choy (1939–) was born in Vancouver and now lives in Toronto, where he teaches at Humber College. His first novel, The Jade Peony *(1995), was awarded the Trillium Award for best book of 1996, an award he shared with Margaret Atwood. He has also published* Paper Shadows: A Chinatown Childhood *(2001), a book about growing up in Vancouver's Chinatown, and is currently at work on* The Ten Thousand Things, *a sequel to* The Jade Peony. *In the following essay, which first appeared in* The Globe and Mail, *Choy considers the significance of nicknames and their ability to appropriately reflect those who have them assigned to them.*

1 Because both my parents came from China, I took Chinese. But I cannot read or write Chinese and barely speak it. I love my North American citizenship. I don't mind being called a "banana," yellow on the outside and white inside. I'm proud I'm a banana.

After all, in Canada and the United States, native Indians are "apples" (red outside, white inside); blacks are "Oreo cookies" (black and white); and Chinese are "bananas." These metaphors assume, both rightly and wrongly, that the culture here has been primarily anglo-white. Cultural history made me a banana.

History: My father and mother arrived separately to the B.C. coast in the early part of the century. They came as unwanted "aliens." Better to be an alien here than to be dead of starvation in China. But after the Chinese Exclusion laws were passed in North America (late 1800s, early 1900s), no Chinese immigrants were granted citizenship in either Canada or the United States.

Like those Old China village men from *Toi San* who, in the 1850s, laid down cliff-edge train tracks through the Rockies and the Sierras, or like those first women who came as mail-order wives or concubines and who as bond-slaves were turned into cheaper labourers or even prostitutes—like many of those men and women, my father and mother survived ugly, unjust times. In 1917, two hours after he got off the boat from Hong Kong, my father was called "chink" and told to go back to China. "Chink" is a hateful racist term, stereotyping the shape of Asian eyes: "a chink in the armour," an undesirable slit. For the Elders, the past was humiliating. Eventually, the Second World War changed hostile attitudes toward the Chinese.

5   During the war, Chinese men volunteered and lost their lives as members of the American and Canadian military. When hostilities ended, many more were proudly in uniform waiting to go overseas. Record Chinatown dollars were raised to buy War Bonds. After 1945, challenged by such money and ultimate sacrifices, the Exclusion laws in both Canada and the United States were revoked. Chinatown residents claimed their citizenship and sent for their families.

By 1949, after the Communists took over China, those of us who arrived here as young children, or were born here, stayed. No longer "aliens," we became legal citizens of North America. Many of us also became "bananas."

Historically, "banana" is not a racist term. Although it clumsily stereotypes many of the children and grandchildren of the Old Chinatowns, the term actually follows the old Chinese tendency to assign endearing nicknames to replace formal names, semicomic names to keep one humble. Thus, "banana" describes the generations who assimilated so well into North American life.

In fact, our families encouraged members of my generation in the 1950s and sixties to "get ahead," to get an English education, to get a job with good pay and prestige. "Don't work like me," Chinatown parents said. "Work in an office!" The *lao wahkiu* (the Chinatown old-timers) also warned, "Never forget—you still be Chinese!"

None of us ever forgot. The mirror never lied.

10   Many Chinatown teen-agers felt we didn't quite belong in any one world. We looked Chinese, but thought and behaved North American.

Impatient Chinatown parents wanted the best of both worlds for us, but they bluntly labelled their children and grandchildren "*juk-sing*" or even "*mo no*." Not that we were totally "shallow bamboo butt-ends" or entirely "no brain," but we had less and less understanding of Old China traditions, and less and less interest in their village histories. Father used to say we lacked Taoist ritual, Taoist manners. We were, he said, "*mo li*."

This was true. Chinatown's younger brains, like everyone else's of whatever race, were being colonized by "white bread" U.S. family television programs. We began to feel Chinese home life was inferior. We co-operated with English-language magazines that showed us how to act and what to buy. Seductive Hollywood movies made some of us secretly weep that we did not have moviestar faces. American music made Chinese music sound like noise.

By the 1970s and eighties, many of us had consciously or unconsciously distanced ourselves from our Chinatown histories. We became bananas.

Finally, for me, in my 40s or 50s, with the death first of my mother, then my father, I realized I did not belong anywhere unless I could understand the past. I needed to find the foundation of my Chinese-ness. I needed roots.

I spent my college holidays researching the past. I read Chinatown oral histories, located documents, searched out early articles. Those early citizens came back to life for me. Their long toil and blood sacrifices, the proud record of their patient, legal challenges, gave us all our present rights as citizens. Canadian and American Chinatowns set aside their family tongue differences and encouraged each other to fight injustice. There were no borders. "After all," they affirmed, "*Daaih ga tohng yahn* . . . We are all Chinese!"

15   In my book, *The Jade Peony,* I tried to recreate this past, to explore   15
the beginnings of the conflicts trapped within myself, the struggle between being Chinese and being North American. I discovered a truth: these "between world" struggles are universal.

In every human being, there is "the Other"—something that makes each of us feel how different we are to everyone else, even to family members. Yet, ironically, we are all the same, wanting the same security and happiness. I know this now.

I think the early Chinese pioneers actually started "going bananas" from the moment they first settled upon the West Coast. They had no choice. They adapted. They initiated assimilation. If they had not, they and their family would have starved to death. I might even suggest that all surviving Chinatown citizens eventually became bananas. Only some, of course, were more ripe than others.

That's why I'm proudly a banana: I accept the paradox of being both Chinese and not Chinese.

Now at last, whenever I look in the mirror or hear ghost voices shouting, "You still Chinese!," I smile.

20   I know another truth: In immigrant North America, we are all   20 Chinese.

Questions on Meaning

1. Choy distinguishes between nicknames and racist terms. Why does Choy consider "banana" not racist? Why might someone find the term offensive? How would you explain the difference between these two categories?

2. Many immigrants have written about the challenges of maintaining one's cultural heritage while simultaneously seeking assimilation. Why is this situation, in Choy's word, paradoxical?

3. What are some of the other ways in which different social groups characterize themselves in an effort to maintain their ethnic and racial identities?

Questions on Strategy and Style

1. How would you characterize Choy's voice in this essay? Is it appealing to you? If so, why? What kind of person do you take him to be?

2. In his essay Choy often uses the term "banana." What effect does the term take on as it is repeated throughout? Do you think the author had a specific reason for using the term as often as he did?

3. Why did Choy write this essay? Who are his intended readers and what is he trying to accomplish with them? Why might the essay be important to his primary readers?

Writing Assignments

1. The use of nicknames, particularly during childhood, is common in our society. Write a memory piece in which you recall different people from your past and the names people gave them, or they gave themselves. Describe how those people received those names or came to use them. Discuss how those names reflected or characterized them. What function do you imagine the names had for these people?

2. The Choy essay is about cultural or ethnic heritage. As we know, most people in North America have a heritage that began in another country. Genealogy has become a popular hobby. Perhaps the trend reflects developments in our society. There are numerous genealogical sites on the Internet. Go to one of them and produce your own family history. Write it up as a narrative.

"The Sun is Your Enemy" from *Generation X*

Douglas Coupland

Douglas Coupland was born in Germany in 1961, lived on a Canadian military base there as a child and grew up in West Vancouver. He attended McGill University in Montreal, the Emily Carr Institute of Art and Design in Vancouver, the Hokkaido College of Art and Design in Japan, and the Instituto Europeo di Design in Milan, Italy. He graduated from the Japan-America Institute of Management Science in 1986. He has been a culture writer for Vancouver Magazine *and* Western Living Magazine *and writes a blog called "Time Capsules" for* The New York Times. *Coupland has written many books of fiction, such as* The Gum Thief *(2007),* jPod *(2006),* Eleanor Rigby *(2004) and* Hey Nostradamus! *(2003). His non-fiction works include* Terry *(2005),* Souvenir of Canada 2 *(2004),* School Spirit *(2002), and* Lara's Book: Lara Croft and the Tomb Raider Phenomenon *(1998). The following selection is taken from Coupland's first novel,* Generation X: Tales for an Accelerated Culture *(1991) and deals with friends who attempt to escape the commercialized world by living in the desert.*

1 You know, Dag and Claire smile a lot, as do many people I know. But I have always wondered if there is something either mechanical or malignant to their smiles, for the way they keep their outer lips propped up seems a bit, not false, but *protective*. A minor realization hits me as I sit with the two of them. It is the realization that the smiles that they wear in their daily lives are the same

Reprinted from *Generation X: Tales for an Accelerated Culture* (2003), by permission of Bedford/St. Martin's Press.

as the smiles worn by people who have been good-naturedly fleeced, but fleeced nonetheless, in public and on a New York sidewalk by card sharks, and who are unable because of social convention to show their anger, who don't want to look like poor sports. The thought is fleeting.

The first chink of sun rises over the lavender mountain of Joshua, but the three of us are just a bit too cool for our own good; we can't just let the moment happen. Dag must greet this flare with a question for us, a gloomy aubade: "What do you think of when you see the sun? Quick. Before you think about it too much and kill your response. Be honest. Be gruesome. Claire, you go first."

Claire understand the drift: "Well, Dag. I see a farmer in Russia, and he's driving a tractor in a wheat field, but the sunlight's gone bad on him—like the fadedness of a black-and-white picture in an old *Life* magazine. And another strange phenomenon has happened, too: rather than sunbeams, the sun has begun to project the odor of old *Life* magazines instead, and the odor is killing his crops. The wheat is thinning as we speak. He's slumped over the wheel of his tractor and he's crying. His wheat is dying of history poisoning."

"Good, Claire. Very weird. And Andy? How about you?"

5 "Let me think a second."

"Okay, I'll go instead. When I think of the sun, I think of an Australian surf bunny, eighteen years old, maybe, somewhere on Bondi Beach, and discovering her first keratosis lesion on her shin. She's screaming inside her brain and already plotting how she's going to steal Valiums from her mother. Now *you* tell *me*, Andy, what do you think of when you see the sun?"

I refuse to participate in this awfulness. I refuse to put people in my vision. "I think of this place in Antarctica called Lake Vanda, where the rain hasn't fallen in more than two million years."

"Fair enough. That's all?"

"Yes, that's all."

10 There is a pause. And what I *don't* say is this: that this is also the same sun that makes me think of regal tangerines and dimwitted butterflies and lazy carp. And the ecstatic drops of pomegranate blood seeping from skin fissures of fruits rotting on the tree branch next door—drops that hang like rubies from their old brown leather source, alluding to the intense ovarian fertility inside.

The carapace of coolness is too much for Claire, also. She breaks the silence by saying that it's not healthy to live life as a succession of isolated little cool moments. "Either our lives become stories, or there's just no way to get through them."

I agree. Dag agrees. We know that this is why the three of us left our lives behind us and came to the desert—to tell stories and to make our own lives worthwhile tales in the process.

Questions on Meaning

1. What realization does the narrator come to about Dag and Claire? Why is this insight significant for understanding the meaning of the sketch? Why is this thought by the narrator "fleeting"?

2. What is your opinion of Dag? Why does he ask the question about the sun? An aubade is generally considered a type of compliment. What makes this one gloomy? How do you interpret Claire's and Andy's relationship to Dag?

3. What is Claire's reaction to the narrator's answer to the question? What does she mean by "Either our lives become stories, or there's just no way to get through them"? How does that statement connect to the reasons why they came to the desert?

Questions on Rhetorical Strategy and Style

1. Coupland is often referred to as a postmodern writer. Postmodern literature is often characterized by a certain structural fragmentation. Explain how this selection exemplifies this characteristic.

2. Postmodern literature breaks with modernism on questions of meaning. That is, postmodernism questions the possibility of meaning and therefore parodies that quest. In what ways does this selection strike you as a parody? How does the title signal this?

3. What kind of narrator tells the story? What is the narrator's relationship to the plot and the other characters?

Writing Assignments

1. What is the definition of Generation X? Write a report on the use of this social term. What distinguishes members of that generation from others in terms of cultural tastes, attitudes, and experiences in the world?

2. Recall a time with a group of friends when you had a conversation about life's deeper meanings and write an account of it. What did you talk about? What made the conversation meaningful? What understandings did you come away with?

3. Write your own answer to the question "What do you think about when you see the sun?" Try to write your response as spontaneously as you can. Compare your response to those of a few of your classmates. Discuss what the differences tell about each of you.

Appendix A

SUMMARIES OF NONFICTION BOOKS AND ARTICLES

Summarizing a nonfiction book or an article from a newspaper, magazine, or scholarly journal means briefly explaining the work's content, not analyzing its meaning. Self-contained summaries appear in annotated bibliographies, abstracts accompanying research papers, formal reports, and proposals. You will most likely integrate your summary into a review, position paper, or research paper. Follow the steps below when summarizing nonfiction works.

Steps for Summarizing Nonfiction Works

1. Write down complete bibliographical information for the article, chapter, or book, using the appropriate format (MLA, APA, or other) for your audience.

2. Identify the thesis, which is most likely in the introduction or conclusion, and restate it in your own words. If no thesis is stated, formulate one in your own words.

3. Identify the main sections. Look for guideposts: Does the thesis outline the structure of the piece? Do topic sentences or transitions indicate stages in development? Do headings or other typographical devices suggest the main divisions?

4. State the main idea of each section in your own words.

5. Locate and record subpoints and examples for the main idea of each section. Using point form will remind you not to merely paraphrase every sentence. Include brief quotations when the author's own words seem particularly important. Put quotation marks around any three or more consecutive words and include the page reference.

6. Define all important key terms in your own words and include them in your summary. Pay special attention to words in italics or boldface. Look up unfamiliar words.

Writing the Summary

1. Give complete bibliographical information (author, title, place of publication, publisher, date), either as a heading or in the first sentence of your summary.

2. First, state your summing up and the writer's thesis in a sentence or two. Then, in a few paragraphs, explain the main idea of each section, using enough subpoints and examples to clarify it. Show how these points are connected by emphasizing the writer's purpose or method of development, such as comparison or classification.

3. Keep the material in the same order and proportion as in the original. Do not exaggerate the importance of an interesting point or ignore a confusing one.

4. Use denotative (emotionally neutral) language, and focus on the article or chapter itself rather than your responses to it. Mention the writer frequently to make it clear that you are presenting his or her opinions on the subject, not your own. Remember to use quotation marks and to give page references for all quotations.

5. If you have been asked to include an evaluation of either the content or the style of the original, put your evaluation, clearly indicated as such, in a separate paragraph.

SAMPLE SUMMARY OF EXPOSITORY ESSAY

John Intini's article "Look at Us: Suddenly We're All Celebrities," published in *Maclean's* magazine in November 2006, uses causal analysis and examples to support its thesis: that the "Me Media" generation, which is both a product of technology and an instigator of technological innovations, is both narcissistic and solipsistic.

Intini begins his article with a typical example of what Allison Hearn terms the "Barney generation" (¶3): Michael Tyas, who creates a blog of his daily existence. In subsequent paragraphs, Intini explains how technology allows people to immortalize themselves or transform into celebrities. He mentions a company that makes personal home movies (eDv), websites allowing "users to create their own soap operas by posting messages, pictures and video from their own lives" (¶5), and a video camera that places gamers in the game. Even your genetic code, Intini says, can be transformed into a unique piece of art.

Intini blames technology and media trends for causing and perpetuating this narcissism. Firstly, the digital camera made it easy to take pictures and post them on the web. Secondly, the media, first through reality TV and now through YouTube, has glorified the hyperpersonalized and elevated the ordinary.

In the end, Intini points out the effects, some ironic, of people expressing their individuality. Because people are modelling their behaviour after celebrity culture and other bloggers, they end up being more similar than unique. Also, according to cultural studies professor Marc Ouellette, openly sharing actually creates an adolescent solipsism for a whole culture continually preoccupied with "What's in it for me?" (¶11).

LOOK AT US. SUDDENLY WE'RE ALL CELEBRITIES
John Intini

1   Michael Tyas's Hollywood experiment lasted eight long months. "I was an intern on a reality TV show in L.A., and was hating it with a passion because it wasn't reality," says Tyas, who prefers not to reveal the name of the show. "I logged all of the original footage—about 500 hours—so I saw the real story, and then I saw the fantasy story they made out of it." So the 23-year-old free-lance photographer, now back in his parents' Shelburne, Ont., home, did what thousands from his generation have done: he turned the camera on himself.

Tyas began a vlog—an online video diary of his life. "I always thought it would be cool to get my face in front of hundreds of people." He's unapologetic about building a site around his remarkably ordinary existence—his first post was a six-minute tour of his filthy L.A. apartment; more recently he's included a clip of his trip to the Ontario Science Centre, and another just hanging out at a friend's apartment. "I make narcissism look good," says Tyas, who has made $8.49 in ad sales on his site since April 2005. "It's a very positive thing to like your-self and think you're marketable enough to put your face out there."

His confidence, cultural observers point out, is not an anomaly. "This is the Barney Generation," says Alison Hearn, an assistant professor of information and media studies at the University of Western Ontario. "These kids have grown up in a world in which they've constantly been told they're special." This age of narcissism has spawned an industry that's all about you and me. And now, a few years into the Me Media revolution, an array of professional-grade vanity products and services have cropped up to meet the new narcissists' needs. "They're all ways of defining yourself," says Hearn. "Creating an image of yourself and then falling in love with it."

Anyone interested in a bit of immortality? No problem. For a fee rang-ing from $15,000 to $80,000, London, Eng.-based eDv, which bills itself as the "personal motion picture company," gets professional filmmakers to sort through your old home videos, conduct and tape interviews with your family, and edit together a high quality biography. If that seems too com-mercial or too much work, try buying your way into the pages of a book by a favourite author. This is often done through charity auctions. Last September, John Grisham, Dave Eggers and Stephen King put the names of upcoming characters on the block (a Florida woman paid US$25,100 for the right to put her brother's name to a character in King's new book).

5   There are many other ways of making yourself a star. One website, based in the Netherlands, allows users to create their own soap opera by posting messages, pictures and video from their own lives. While it

doesn't much resemble your typical mid-afternoon guilty pleasure, that hasn't stopped people from posting and visitors from checking in and voting for their favourites. The highest ranking "stars" can win prizes, including a celebrity magazine feature (the site is run by a magazine publisher). Then there's Playstation 2's EyeToy—a digital camera that literally places gamers within a video game. In *Kung Fu,* users can show off their martial arts skills by taking on the bad guys with their very own digitized hands and feet.

Technology is in part to blame. It's helped us meet these needs—and create them. The affordability of digital cameras, for instance, has sparked a surge in the popularity of self-portraits. Most young people are perfectly comfortable taking their own pictures—a key part of their Internet egos on MySpace and the like. Some change their photo almost every day. "It's an image economy," says Hearn. "It's all about branding yourself."

Some, like Erica Morgan, have devoted entire websites to self-portraiture— a form in which one can be a star on *both* sides of the camera. Since February 2003, Morgan, who was born in South Carolina and now lives in Sydney, Australia, takes a photo of herself every day and posts it on her site (1,111 at last count). "At first I was a little concerned about obsessive strangers," says the 27-year-old photographer. "And a little self-conscious about pulling out my camera and turning it in my direction." Apparently, she got over it.

These days—again thanks to technology—you can pretty much get your likeness plastered on anything. This business niche hearkens back to those booths at shopping malls that would print your picture on a coffee mug or a T-shirt. By contemporary standards, that old personalized fare appears like cave art. Today, fond parents can get a replica doll made of their children for US$139. To create a 23-inch Mini Me, parents can go on *mytwinn.com* and build the doll themselves, or send in a photo of junior and have the toy specialists do the legwork. The doll is an exact likeness; freckles and birthmarks are hand-painted at no additional cost. A couple of years ago, a California-based firm started selling personalized confetti— your digital images were turned into tiny paper scraps. Before they shut down, the company had sold 30,000 bags—starting at US$17 each—to people who wanted to be the life of the party.

Our look-at-me industry has even found its way into the art world. Send about $400 and a saliva sample to Ottawa-based DNA 11, and you'll receive an 18 x 24-inch portrait (available in one of eight colours) of your very own personal genetic code. "Before we started, we thought that everyone with a big ego would want one of these hanging in their offices— and we have lots of CEOs, power-brokers, investment brokers and venture capitalists that own our artwork," says co-founder Adrian Salamunovic, whose company has shipped art to 30 countries and sold more than 1,000 prints since last July. "But moms and grandmas have done it too. For most, ego doesn't play a factor." In celebration of its one-year anniversary, the company is unveiling this week a new twist on the original: fingerprint portraits. "What we do is not in-your-face narcissistic—like say an oil painting of my face over the fireplace," says Salamunovic, 30. "This is highly personal art—it's one of one. And you're a collaborator."

The proliferation of personalized services may just be a logical next step for a society in which everything—from weddings to funerals—is hyper-personalized. For several years now, thanks in large part to the reality TV craze, we've been told that we can be stars. Now we're starting to act like it. At the extreme end of the spectrum, people, desperate for the rock-star treatment, can hire an entourage—complete with a bodyguard, faux-friends and paparazzi photographers to greet them climbing out of a limo at the hottest club.

An effect of all this is the elevation of the completely ordinary. The clearest model may be YouTube, the video-sharing website with the narcissistic "Broadcast Yourself" tag line, which is getting 70 million video views a day. YouTube has hundreds of thousands of clips from rock concerts and old TV shows, but the very random—and sometimes humorous—videos of regular people doing boring stuff has also played an integral role in the site's success. We're not just finding ways to share our very mundane lives, we're also tuning in to watch other people's. One recent trend involved users posting videos of themselves watching other youtubers watching YouTube.

Or consider the six-month-old vlog of Dan O'Rourke, a provincial government policy worker in Halifax, who says that making himself the star is simply a product of necessity. "I'm the only actor I can afford," says the 26-year-old, who spends as many as 10 hours a week working on his vlog. "I just do things that I think will turn out interesting without a target audience in mind." Road trips, he says, usually make for the best posts, but, much to his own surprise, his most popular clip so far—which has attracted more than 1,000 views—was a 30-second spot during which he pours out a container of spoiled chocolate milk.

People seem to be going to greater heights in the pursuit of real reality—and they aren't exactly succeeding. "Authenticity is a very hazy construct," says Marc Ouellette, who teaches English and cultural studies at McMaster University. "In the race for distinction, everyone ends up ultimately looking the same." And often, he suggests, we end up using the modes of mainstream and celebrity culture, even when we think we're being original.

Look at Us. Suddenly We're All Celebrities

213

"I'd like to think that it's totally their voice, but I don't," he says. "There are so many forces. It's not purely narcissistic since it's almost always attached to some pre-existing cultural and celebrity icon."

In fact, more than narcissism, Ouellette believes many of us today suffer from solipsism—the inability to recognize the existence of another viewpoint. "Solipsism is supposed to end by mid-adolescence, but I don't think it's disappearing at the same stage in the cognitive process that it used to," he says. "Most people get to a point in their lives when they recognize that others have a viewpoint that is just as valid as their own. With adolescence starting earlier and ending later, some never get to that stage. It ultimately comes down to always thinking, 'what's in it for me?'"

Appendix B